D0380256

"These are research-based strategies that, when implemented properly, can transform all school districts—large and small. I recommend it for all educators working in the present age of school accountability to ensure that we leave no school behind."　　　　　**—Patricia Davenport,**
Former District Director of Curriculum and Instruction,
Brazosport School District (Texas); and co-author
(with Gerald Anderson) of *Closing the Achievement Gap: No Excuses*

"Simmons and his colleagues capture the essence of reform and reformers of large urban school systems. A must-read for all concerned about the future of urban public education."　　　　　**—Paul Goren,**
Vice President, The Spencer Foundation

"Many good ideas and examples in this book should help district and school leaders examine data from their own schools and design more effective programs for student success."

—Joyce Epstein,
Director of the Center on School, Family, and Community Partnerships,
Johns Hopkins University

"What a tremendous resource this book will be in helping transform urban school districts! Strict adherence and dedication to principles is key to changing the structures and systems, but it's the belief in the people that will effectively change culture."　　　　　**—Dr. Stephen R. Covey,**
Author, *The 7 Habits of Highly Effective People*
and *The 8th Habit: From Effectiveness to Greatness*

"The nuggets of wisdom imparted throughout this book have been field-tested under combat conditions. Reformers not having the time for this book will have plenty of time to wish they had—too late."

—Michael A. Strembitsky,
Former Superintendent,
Edmonton Public Schools (Alberta, Canada)

"This book hits all the right notes: It calls for an honest, hard look at the incoherence and dysfunction of "a system designed to fail." With courage and clarity, Simmons and his colleagues are calling for an unprecedented, long-overdue emphasis on what we've wandered so far from: a top-to-bottom focus on instructional improvement—and the most powerful, proven (but still overlooked) means of achieving it."

—Mike Schmoker,
Author, *Results: The Key to Continuous School Improvement*

BREAKING THROUGH

Transforming Urban School Districts

JOHN SIMMONS

with

Judy Codding	Judy Karasik
Charlotte Danielson	Carolyn Kelley
Linda Darling-Hammond	Valerie E. Lee
W. Patrick Dolan	Allan Odden
Richard F. Elmore	Kent D. Peterson
Michael Fullan	Marc Tucker
Gail Goldberger	Adam Urbanski
Kate Jamentz	Margery Wallen
Susan Moore Johnson	

Foreword by Deborah Meier

TEACHERS COLLEGE PRESS

Teachers College, Columbia University
New York and London

Published by Teachers College Press, 1234 Amsterdam Avenue, New York, NY 10027

Library of Congress Cataloging-in-Publication Data

Simmons, John.
    Breaking through : transforming urban school districts / John Simmons, with Judy Codding . . . [et al.] ; foreword by Deborah Meier.
        p. cm.
    Includes bibliographical references and index.
    ISBN 0-8077-4658-4 (cloth : alk. paper) — ISBN 0-8077-4657-6 (pbk. : alk. paper)
        1. Urban schools—United States—Case studies. 2. School improvement programs—United States—Case studies.
    3. Educational change—United States—Case studies. I. Codding, Judy B., 1944– II. Title.
    LC5131.S56   2006
    371.00973′2—dc22   2005052996

ISBN-13:   ISBN-10:
978-0-8077-4657-8 (paper)   0-8077-4657-6 (paper)
978-0-8077-4658-5 (cloth)   0-8077-4658-4 (cloth)

Printed on acid-free paper
Manufactured in the United States of America

13 12 11 10 09 08 07 06   8 7 6 5 4 3 2 1

Contents

Foreword

As we read what John Simmons has written, and the words of the other amazing contributors to this volume, we need to have an argumentative mind-set. These are people and places that have made changes—folks who know how to connect their ideas to get impressive results—the means and ends. They have changed the shape and mind-set of various institutions in important and substantial ways. They include school districts and corporations using similar principles and strategies from Brazosport, Texas, Palatine, Illinois, and Edmonton, Canada to Southwest Airlines, the Ford Motor Company, and W.L. Gore and Associates.

Every one of these sections is an invitation to a dialogue. They point the way toward improving the odds or impeding them—those needed to sustain and nourish the always fragile roots of democratic life, and the cultural, economic, and social conditions that democracy depends on—or those that will (even unwittingly) undermine those habits.

In addition to seeing what these districts did, we need to examine both the means and ends—and we need to examine both what they have done and what they have not yet done. If we view change too simplistically, if we fail to analyze fully, although we may honor the change-makers, we may not get to the point where we are able to understand how such approaches can—or cannot—be translated to our unique situations. Without that analysis, we're likely either to dismiss them as inappropriate to our situation or to shoe-horn them in.

So stop often and see how these ideas fit together. Where are the tensions? Are there incompatible recommendations that need to be taken apart and reconstructed? The sweep of the authors is wide and eclectic, but the challenge they take on naturally produces some common threads.

The authors would all probably agree on a wise set of axioms—such as the importance of giving those who must implement any changes a voice in their design. But equally interesting are the many differences that emerge when they turn these principles into practice. What are the trade-offs between the different avenues to deep organizational reform that are presented here? (And what reforms aren't mentioned? What would happen, for instance, if there were no districts at all, as is true in our independent schools? Or if we changed the locus of power—who makes the bottom line decisions?)

If you are a classroom teacher or parent, think about how these would affect you. And in what ways are schools in a unique position to deal with the complexities of deciding what it means to be successful, including the long-term nature of the payoff in this and future generations. (Corporations, too, need to keep their eye on more than the immediate bottom line; when they don't, both they and we pay a price.)

Changing school districts can release energy—and time—inside each school and classroom. Each day that we ignore those changes, some teacher or some kid somewhere is frustrated, someone wastes endless days getting "around" the system rather than turning to it with the assumption that it will be helpful. We're stuck being "creative compliers"—using our smarts to outwit the system in ways that won't be caught.

If we are to produce schools that can seriously tackle the task of producing a citizenry—not just some citizens—with the habits, skills, and knowledge needed by a strong democracy, we have to make changes at every level. Each reform step, at every level, not just the classroom level, must be in keeping with such democratic goals. Equity serves a purpose—to ensure that all our voices are heard and all our voices are powerful. Not just some. Literacy matters. An illiterate people cannot learn from as wide a range of sources to help them judge the merits of what others propose, nor can they make their own wonderful ideas heard. Without literacy, they are citizens waiting to be conned. Only thoughtful adults can help pass on thoughtfulness; only adults accustomed to view themselves as responsible citizens of their own schools can help young people grasp what such a concept might mean.

As I considered the issues of systemic, district-level change—the scaling-up issue—at the heart of all these essays, I asked myself this question: How will these ideas promote a system that rests on what we know it takes to have a good school, rather than build our schools around what is easiest to do systemically? As schools become more human-sized, how can we increase the degree to which their choices and activities are regulated by what happens within them rather than by dictates from above? How can we increase the chance that school people—those closest to the action— will focus on their students, families, and the work taking place before their eyes, rather than on the complex systems invented by those farther away? The task isn't easy, and the answers are open to abuse—different abuses depending on how we skew the balance between decisions made in schools and those made at the district, state, or federal level.

We know that having a strong say in one's work—for teachers and students—is an effective way to improve our learning curves. We know that doing work that seems important, significant, and valued—not only to us individually but also to the larger community—produces higher-quality work. Instead of teachers driving themselves to exhaustion trying to "motivate" kids, and principals doing the same with teachers, and districts to principals—when we have these three relationships in place, motivation more or less answers itself. But building a system that supports these three is too often like fitting a square peg into a round hole—too often we squeeze the authentic life out of the school to make them fit together.

Similarly, too often we start with large issues of external accountability when the questions of internal accountability—"Are we what we claim to be?" and "Are we what we ought to be?"—should be tackled first.

It's intriguing to see a book full of ideas that hopes to redesign, or scale up, our schools so as to create a revolution in, as John Simmons says, a mere seven years. But impatient revolutionaries may have their timing off, even if their ideas are right on. While I found these essays a delight, I imagined them unfolding in far more than seven years. Change will take longer, and it will take a political will we clearly do not yet have. It will also require similar will in other quarters to tackle the inequities increasingly confronting the children in our urban communities—over matters of income disparities, health disparities, and housing inequities.

Since every step we take brings us closer or farther away, we have to take incremental change with exactly as much enthusiastic fervor and enormous willpower as if we were making a revolution. Children's lives and hopes are at stake, and what we do will shift the odds in children's favor or against them.

This book is an important contribution to taking the right steps. Read its contents as provocations for leaders—whether superintendents, principals, teachers, parents, or students—who have the courage to mold these ideas into their own solutions.

—Deborah Meier

Preface

Every day large urban school systems in America founder in their missions, fall short of their goals, and lose the opportunity to provide all students with the basic skills they need to avoid a lifetime of poverty-wage jobs. This notwithstanding the fact that some of the most far-reaching developments of the latter half of the 20th century have been in deepening our understanding about how to improve large, complex systems. School systems, although they have grown in size and complexity, have not kept pace with the application of best practice about the design, operation, and improvement of large systems.

This book pulls together lessons about improving large organizations—and large school systems in particular. The book offers a practical framework that superintendents and their teams can use to simplify and accelerate the transformation of their big-city school systems into true learning organizations that continually improve results.

Simply put, our thesis is this: To transform the daily workings of the urban classroom, the leaders of big-city systems need to focus on scaling-up, bringing the best practices already being used in *some* classrooms to *all* classrooms and schools and doing it quickly—in less than seven years. How can this result, which has been so elusive, be achieved? It will require a revolution in the way the leaders of urban districts think and operate, from the classroom to the boardroom.

Leaders need to deepen their understanding of how schools and school systems can most effectively achieve change, including their expectations of what students, teachers, and organizations can accomplish. Then they need to apply these lessons of educational and organizational change to mobilize people across the system to design and implement the best ways to accelerate student learning at each of their schools. The leadership of the central office staff needs to determine how to better support the work in all schools, not mandate it. Fifty years of research and experience show that the results are better when people participate in deciding what is best for them, not when they have to be forced to comply.

The framework we present here includes practical principles, strategies, and processes for creating large-scale transformation. To achieve the work of deep and sustained improvement, superintendents, union leaders, principals, teams of teachers, community members, and parents need to work together to help educate one another and then school boards, mayors, and the public about what best practice looks like and how to create conditions that lead to improved classrooms and districts. These strategies will also help people hold each other accountable during the continuous process of improving teaching and learning.

This book's genesis was a report of the Chicago Community Trust, *School Reform in Chicago: Lessons and Opportunities*. That report helped the Trust design its Education Initiative, a five-year, $50 million effort to support Chicago school reform. The two-volume report was the work of Strategic Learning Initiatives and written by the author and 44 others. Donald Stewart, the Trust's past President, encouraged the author to develop a book, and his strong support for both of these projects is greatly appreciated. Terry Mazany, the President of the Trust who has almost 20 years of experience working with K–12 urban school systems, provided essential guidance and comments at each stage in the development of the book.

The authors of the essays have made important revisions in their original papers. Many others have made very helpful comments on the manuscript or sections of it. They include Jo Anderson, Richard and Emily Axelrod, Ed Bales, Charlotte Blackman, Alan Bersin, Kathy Berry, Anthony Bryk, Andrew Bundy, Mary Canchola, Charlotte Danielson, Linda Darling-Hammond, Patricia Davenport, John Easton, Richard Elmore, Michael Fullan, Howard Gardner, Herb Gintis, Peter Goldman, Paul Goren, Ellen Guiney, Sandra Guthman, Anne Hallett, Bahareh Harandi, Mike Klonsky, Carlene Lutz, Mike Strembitsky, Deborah Meier, Samuel Meisels, Don Moore, Karen Morris, Concepcion Oñate, Tom Payzant, Teresa Perez, Kent Peterson, Elaine Ratajczak, Larry Rosenstock, Robert Schwartz, Ian Simmons, Dennis Sparks, Marla Ucelli, Tom Vander Ark, and Cris Whitehead.

The manuscript benefited from the excellent editing assistance of Pat George, Amy Rosenberg, and Lynn Schnaiberg. Judy Karasik helped craft a clear message. Carole Saltz, Catherine Chandler, Catherine Bernard, and Karl Nyberg of Teachers College Press shaped the results with skill and patience while Leyli Shayegan guided us in promotion. Two anonymous readers for the Press provided important insight. Bahareh Harandi, Dorothea Duenow, Eileen Hollinger, Tom Lohrentz, and Mike Stiehl provided superb and unflagging support in the research and preparation of the manuscript. My effort has been well nurtured by Adele and our family.

We hope these ideas will prove useful for those who have dedicated themselves to the daunting task of teaching children and improving schools in our nation's urban districts. This book is for those who strive to achieve that elusive, but achievable, goal: creating systems of schools in which *all* students actually attain high standards of achievement.

John Simmons, Chicago
June 2005

The Challenge of Changing a Complex System

"As we try to improve public education systems, we must recognize that we are dealing with a mountain of past practice that is exceedingly difficult to change."
—Alan Bersin, former Superintendent,
San Diego Public Schools

In the last half of the 20th century, generations of students in America's large urban school systems have been lost. No urban district has yet been able to scale-up and sustain a set of policies and leaders to improve classroom results in *all* schools. This book aims to help districts make that goal a reality. We emphasize the practical solutions that already exist and the urgency of the need.

Dramatically better schools, we believe, are not possible without transformation of the school systems themselves. Without it, improvements will be incremental and piecemeal, confined only to a group of classrooms or a group of schools, not systemwide. The changes will not be sustained. Large-district transformation, although it has not been achieved yet, is possible. Smaller school districts are already applying the lessons and practices that have successfully transformed large corporate organizations in the past century—and, more recently, several small school districts. This book provides powerful examples of those processes and suggests how these could be applied to large school districts.

In Part One, we set out three organizing principles and four strategies for rethinking how to transform the mediocre results that most districts are getting. The four strategies, which come from the authors' years of working in, studying, and consulting to large organizations and school systems are the following:

1. Create more effective leaders at every level of the district and improve schools' capacity for leading change through better delegation, training, and communication.

2. Transform the structure and culture of the district office and its schools to accelerate both adult and student learning while improving system coherence and alignment.
3. Focus on improving the quality of instruction.
4. Build effective support for improvement by both engaging parents and providing more adequate and equitable funding.

Our primary example in Part One is Chicago, with its mixed results from a decade and a half of school reform and the strategies for scaling-up that have emerged from that effort.

Chicago is our lead example because (1) the School Reform Law of 1988 offered a paradigm shift in leadership authority, and (2) the progress achieved in the past 16 years may be the best in the nation for urban districts.

Sometimes it takes nothing more than a phrase to spur change in a large, failing organization. In 1987, then-Secretary of Education William Bennett demonstrated this when he used the words "worst in the nation" to describe the Chicago public school system. With leadership by Chicago Mayor Harold Washington, within a year, parents, teachers, school reform advocates, and community groups had convinced Illinois state legislators to pass the Chicago School Reform Act, sending the city's schools on a remarkable journey of transformation that continues today (Staff of the *Chicago Tribune*, 1988).

Some 17 years and four superintendents later, reform in Chicago, which is based on decentralized control by Local School Councils and principals, has resulted in strong improvements for *one-half of the schools in the system.*

While Chicago educators have made extraordinary improvements in situations that many believed were hopeless, the district leadership has not succeeded in applying those improvements effectively across the system. The Iowa Reading Test results reveal a widening gap among students in low-income neighborhoods. The ability to improve does not correspond simply to income, race, or neighborhood. Schools that continue to fail are in some cases down the street from schools where students thrive.

We will explore why some Chicago schools are succeeding while others are failing. We will attempt to understand how districts can identify and scale-up those practices that are working and infuse them throughout the entire system.

We also explore experiences and strategies for scaling-up that have emerged in Boston, San Diego, Edmonton, Canada, Palatine, Illinois, and Brazosport, Texas, as well as in other districts (albeit smaller ones) that have succeeded at improving their systems. Although Houston began as a positive example when the research was starting, it has ended by demonstrating bad leadership and a dishonesty in reporting its results that others should avoid. At the same time Houston has management reforms at the district office, such as decentralizing budget authority to the schools, that are important.

In Part Two, we offer analyses from a notable range of experts. Their essays flesh out the four core strategies and highlight specific tools and steps that should be put into place if real reform is to occur and be sustained.

These essays were originally written for *School Reform in Chicago: Lessons & Opportunities,* funded by the Chicago Community Trust, the nation's second-oldest community foundation, serving the charitable needs of metropolitan Chicago, and compiled by Strategic Learning Initiatives, a Chicago-based not-for-profit organization that carries out policy research and works with networks of neighborhood schools and their districts to help them accelerate their daily performance. That two-volume report brought together for the first time the research and experiences of more than 100 scholars and practitioners who have been working in the trenches of reform in Chicago and across the country. The perspectives and experiences of these experts are invaluable, and we are pleased to be able to include their voices.

Finally, in Part Three, we explore a process for redesigning systems that has worked successfully in high-performing corporate organizations—and now, in several small school districts. We tell the story of how this model—the Z Process—has been implemented with significant success in the school district of Brazosport, Texas, improving classroom results.

When the core strategies for high performance are implemented through the system redesign model of the Z Process, supported by partnerships between district management and union leaders, and sustained by external support for change, it is possible to close the gap in student performance and educate all of our students. Figure I.1 represents those key efforts, which can create more effective ways of administering, teaching, and learning—from procurement to phonics to performance review. It should improve how everyone does his or her job; change what each person expects from each other person and from him- or herself; and make those changes a habit of excellence, just like regular exercise is for good health.

To begin removing the barriers to urban school reform, people need to work smarter, not harder. We don't need more pilot projects or more research to understand why neither the educational nor organizational research is being implemented. (Some of the early research on factors affecting the scaling-up of best practice in any organization—or, as it was then called, adoption of innovations—was done in the 1930s with the introduc-

FIGURE I.1. To Close the Gap in Student Performance

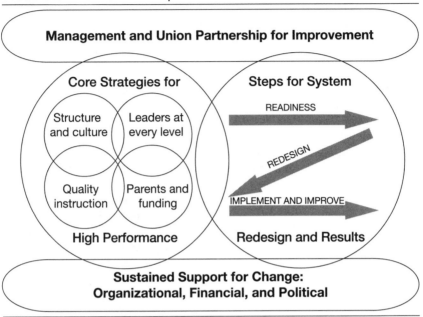

tion of hybrid corn (Cole, 1989; Light, 1998; Rogers, 1995). Instead, superintendents need to put in place a sound process for the people across their school district to learn from both the best practice in their own classrooms and from the experiments, pilot projects, and initiatives that *already* have proven successful in their own classrooms and for a growing number of large organizations. This is working smarter. These are processes that are beginning to be used in urban districts such as Chicago, Houston, San Diego, Boston, and others.

These ideas and frameworks, we hope, will add to a practical understanding of how to plan and execute large-scale improvement in the complex systems that are large urban school districts.

REFERENCES

Cole, R. E. (1989). *Strategies for learning: Small group activities in American, Japanese and Swedish industry.* Berkeley: University of California Press.

Light, P. C. (1998). *Sustaining innovation: Creating nonprofits and government organizations that innovate naturally.* San Francisco: Jossey-Bass.

Rogers, E. (1995). *Diffusion of innovations* (4th ed.). New York: Free Press.

Staff of the *Chicago Tribune.* (1988). *Chicago schools: "Worst in America": An examination of schools that fail Chicago.* Chicago: *Chicago Tribune.*

Part One

NO EXCUSES: TRANSFORMING URBAN SCHOOL DISTRICTS

"You need to stop making excuses and find a way to teach these children."
—Joe Bowman, Brazosport School Board (1991)

Many problems facing urban school systems nationwide derive from the fact that traditional district leadership has lacked the vision, the understanding, and the political support necessary to solve the complex problems inherent in transforming large organizations. The barriers to success fall into two categories: a lack of vision for what a high-performance school district should look like and the lack of a strategic framework for understanding the steps needed to close the gap in student performance.

Richard Elmore at Harvard University writes that "large school systems are incompetent and incapable of learning from success in one place and moving it to another" (See his essay in Chapter 6). Large-system change, however, although difficult, is not impossible. In the American auto and steel industries in the 1970s, it often took the threat of losing their jobs to get executives and union leaders to fundamentally rethink what they were doing, including the way their organizations functioned. Many companies did change, however, often thanks to a CEO or union executive who had a vision of the kind of world-class organization he or she wanted. For example, Procter & Gamble, General Foods, Hermon Miller, Quad/Graphics, and W. L. Gore Associates made real change in the 1970s, redefining work and organizations in the process. Ford Motor and Southwest Airlines did the same in the 1980s. They achieved these results by identifying and exceeding the needs of their customers, working smarter through doing the work in teams, improving the quality of life at work for all employees, decentralizing problem solving and decision making to the lowest levels in the organizations, providing the coaching and training needed, and continuously improving the work processes that improved the quality of the services and products. In Part Three, we discuss lessons learned from business in more detail.

In this section, after grounding the discussion in an analysis of the recent history in Chicago, we describe the building blocks—three organizing principles and four strategies—that district leaders can use to learn from success and replicate it citywide.

THE THREE ORGANIZING PRINCIPLES

The three organizing principles, themes that run throughout all of the essays in Part Two of this book, help reformers look at the system in new ways, helping to shift thinking from the level that created the problems to a different level, where new solutions become possible.

- *Consistency: One vision in the classroom and the central office.* Create consistent patterns of communication, culture, and leadership throughout the system. Ensure that what goes on in each classroom to improve instruction is in line with what goes on in the principal's office and central office to improve the overall system—and vice versa.
- *Simultaneity: Work everywhere at once.* Transform system elements simultaneously. Don't start in one place; start everyplace. Improvements in the classroom and improvements in the central office and in principals' offices need to be underway at the same time.
- *Quality: Learn from the best.* Integrate and communicate knowledge about high-performance organizations into your efforts. Your ambitious project can be helped by lessons already learned by others, especially in large businesses and in some small school districts that have turned themselves around.

THE FOUR STRATEGIES

Following these principles, we suggest four central, research-based strategies to focus on. The essays in Part Two are grouped according to these four strategies, and districts that focus their resources around them are likely to set better objectives and be better able to identify cost-effective policies and practices to accelerate student learning.

- *Create leaders at every level.* Leaders who believe in shared leadership and creating high-performing teams need to be recruited, trained, and supported in a time of increasing accountability.
- *Transform the structure and culture of the system.* Each district must face the immense challenge of getting an entire urban school system, often involving tens of thousands of adults, to think differently about their daily work and improve their results to accelerate adult and student learning.
- *Improve instruction.* Teachers need to apply more effective strategies and tools to meet the diverse needs of their students, and they need to work together better to do this.
- *Involve parents and make funding adequate and equitable.* The district will not succeed in closing the achievement gap without a partnership with its parents, and it will not succeed unless funding is adequate and equitable.

These four strategies need to be applied at the same time to create the synergy that is essential to accelerate a district's results. The process for designing and implementing the strategies successfully is described in Part Three.

In Chapters 2 and 3, we examine each of these principles and strategies in greater depth, illustrating them often with the experience over the past 16 years in Chicago.

In the next section, we begin with an overview of Chicago's history and a summary of what worked and what didn't. This history demonstrates the success a system can have when it draws from some of the best practices of high-performance organizations—and also demonstrates some of the pitfalls when the model for improvement is inadequate.

Chapter One

School Reform in Chicago, 1988–2005

Chicago's experience from 1988 through 2005 demonstrates that large urban district school reform is not only possible—it's powerful. In Chicago, reform has been based on a model that combines strong neighborhood and teacher involvement with school-based, decentralized authority at the local level.

Success in reform efforts has come primarily from activity at the local level and through the implementation of practices developed in the past 50 years by high-performing organizations. The district's central office, while it has provided some positive support with union and financial issues, academic standards, training, coaching, and accountability, thus far has been unable to find a way to truly support all schools.

Improvements have been dramatic, but have taken hold in only about half of the low-scoring elementary schools. Close examination of the schools that have made steady and impressive progress on the one hand, and those that have not on the other, reveals clear lessons about what has worked and what has not worked in reform.

About half of the low-scoring public elementary schools in Chicago— 181 schools—have made extraordinary gains and have sustained the process of continuous improvement. Three hundred and sixty of Chicago's elementary schools, 82% of the total number of elementary schools, had very low results on the 1990 Iowa Test of Basic Skills (ITBS) in reading. Nearly all the schools were in low-income neighborhoods. As Figure 1.1 shows, in 1990 half of these started scoring at 20% and they now have 49% of their students at or above the national average on the norm-referenced ITBS—scoring nearly as well as a representative national sample of urban, suburban, and rural schools. (Norm-referenced tests are designed so that 50% of the students must fall below the national average.) The gains in math in the high gain schools were even better than in reading.

These impressive results may be better than those of any other large urban district between 1990 and 2005 (Barton, 2001; Haycock, Jerald, & Huang, 2001).

FIGURE 1.1. Half of Chicago's Elementary Schools Almost Reach the National Average in Reading (Iowa Reading Test Grades 3–8 Combined Percent of Students at or Above National Norms)

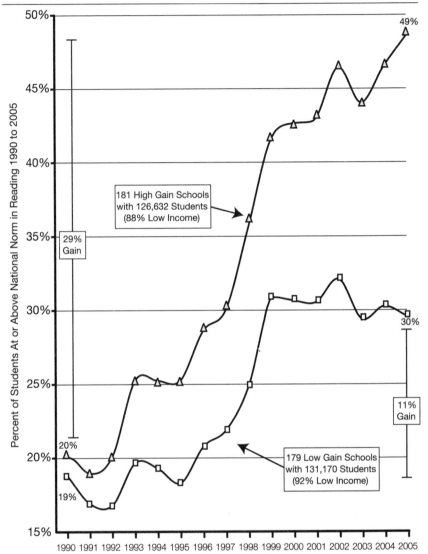

Source: Analysis by Strategic Learning Initiatives 2005 of data provided by Chicago Public Schools (2005) and Designs for Change (2005).

Note: This Diagram uses the 1988 national norm for 1990 to 1998, and the 2000 national norm for 1999 to 2004. The renorming raised the scores about 3% for the average CPS school in 1999, thus lengthening the lines between 1998 and 1999. All demographic data is from 2004 and the data for 2005 is preliminary.

Figure 1.1 shows that the 181 high-gain schools have raised scores almost three times faster than the low-gain schools in the other half: a gain of 28 percentage points versus just 11 points. Why the split? Numbers of low-income students were higher in the low-gain schools, but only slightly—92% as opposed to 88%. The high-gain group started only one percentage point higher than the low-gain group (20% versus 19%). Neighborhood does not determine success or failure—high-gain schools are in every neighborhood in the city and, in some cases, a high-gain school is literally down the street from a low-gain school.

While the gap in achievement has widened between the high- and low-gain schools, the gap has also narrowed between the high-gain schools and the 68 highest scoring elementary schools, which already had high scores in 1990.

We need to say a few more words about the data in Figure 1.1 to clarify what it represents.

In 1990, Chicago had 429 regular elementary schools (special education schools excluded) that remained open through 2005. Of these schools, 360 were low-achieving in 1990; those are the schools represented in Figure 1.1. The average score in these 360 schools was 19.5% in 1990. Fewer than 40% of the students scored at or above the national average in reading, and are included in this analysis. These schools averaged 91% low-income families in 2001.

The 68 elementary schools not included in Figure 1.1 had average Iowa reading results in 1990 that were three times higher than the students in the other 360 schools. In these 68 schools, results averaged 58% on the 1990 test. These schools were about 54% low-income families in 2005. In 2005, 69% of these schools' students scored at or above the national average, a gain of 11 percentage points.

HISTORY

Some basic history of the three phases to date of Chicago reform and an analysis of what worked and what didn't clarifies what made the difference.

Chicago's reform happened in three stages.

Phase One: 1988–1995

In 1988, the Illinois State Legislature, at the request of parents, neighborhood groups, foundations, and Mayor Harold Washington, passed a law that did the following:

- Replaced the Chicago Board of Education
- Ended principal tenure and teacher seniority rules
- Created Local School Councils (LSCs) composed of parents, teachers, and community members elected by each school, each with the power to hire and fire the principal and to approve the budget for state and federal funds
- Gave principals, in turn, the power to move teachers out of their schools

The aim was to empower the people closest to the situation to define the problem, make decisions, and be accountable. The principals were accountable to the Local School Council; if the principal and the Local School Council couldn't turn around a failing school, the central office could intervene and remove the principal and council or shut down the school. The positive results achieved by this partly decentralized model are well-documented (Bryk, Sebring, Kerbow, Rollow, & Easton, 1998; Designs for Change, 2005; Russo, 2004; Simmons, 2001).

Because it was not until 1990 that all almost all the Councils had selected their first principal, improvement in the scores didn't start happening until after 1992.

In the spring of 1993, reform started to deliver results: after 20 years of little progress, the Iowa reading scores rose dramatically—five percentiles for the average high-gain school and three percentiles for low-gain.

Studies attribute this to professional development of teachers through external partners, increased parental involvement, principals using their authority to move out ineffective teachers, and deepening trust among teachers, parents, and administrators (Bryk et al., 1998; Bryk & Schneider, 2002; Designs for Change, 2005; Simmons, 1995). These findings are corroborated with case studies: stories of principals who moved to build trust with the teachers and parents, who painted over graffiti on the walls, who talked with the gang leaders, who met with parents in their home and church meetings, and who counseled out teachers that didn't show up for work, screamed at their students, or read newspapers at their desks.

Between 1993 and 1995, Figure 1.1 reveals a small but clear dip in scores in those low-gain schools while the high-gain schools held steady.

Principals and Local School Councils of what were to become the low-gain schools got off to a slower start. Some of them were not scheduled as part of the transition plan to select their principals for a year. Others had difficulty deciding whether or not to change their existing principal, and gave them a 4-year contract. Generally, there were two kinds of failing schools: one where the principal was unable to learn and apply what was needed to turn around his or her school, and another where the principal was capable of learning from others, but lacked the support to do so. The problem, then, could be ineffective leadership from either the principals or the LSCs.

Phase Two: 1995–2001

In 1995, believing that improvements were not happening fast enough, the state legislature gave the mayor, who by then was Richard M. Daley, the right to appoint the board of education and the CEO. Paul Vallas, the mayor's budget director, became CEO. Daley's priority mandate to Vallas was to improve performance in the high schools in order to encourage the middle class with children to stay in the city rather than move to the suburbs.

In addition, new laws partially recentralized the Chicago system under the control of the mayor and his appointed board of education. Paul Vallas improved the district budget's ability to finance new school construction, reduced corruption (bringing an end to the days when, for example, the newspapers could run stories supplied by the Chicago Public Schools of employees stealing and reselling supplies), and negotiated a 4-year teacher contract. [In a telling detail, however, demonstrating that the principals still had real authority, the 1995 Reform Act finally allowed principals to carry keys to their own school buildings (Richards, 2001).]

Other Vallas initiatives were not so successful. Starting in October 1996, Vallas put 147 elementary schools on probation. These schools made up 80% of the low-gain schools in Figure 1.1. Vallas instituted high-stakes testing, and scores rose for just 3 years, until 2000, when they plateaued, in half of the elementary schools. (This may be due to the "test prep effect"—teachers can improve scores by teaching test-taking techniques. Research shows, however, that after 3 or 4 years the impact of "test prep effect" declines. Also, the data below by the Consortium on Chicago School Research suggests that the improvement may also have been due more to the central office reducing the percentage of low-performing students who were counted than to "test prep.")

Other unsuccessful initiatives included "retention," holding back children from passing to the next grade who did not reach a set level on the Iowa Reading Test. Some students were held back as many as 3 years, discouraging them and their parents; few of these held-back students ever caught up with their peers and many dropped out of school. Researchers from the Consortium concluded that "retaining low achieving students . . . is simply not working" (Nagaoka & Roderick, 2004, p. 18).

Vallas' team also failed to implement a redesign plan in 1996 for most of the high schools. During his tenure, high school student achievement scores rose, but only to the same level as the level of scores brought in by new classes of entering students who had achieved those scores in previous years at elementary and middle schools. In other words, the high schools had added no value (Designs for Change, 2003; Hess, 2001; Lee, 2001; Roderick, Tepper Jacob, & Stone, 2003; Simmons, 2001). The percentage of middle-class children going to Chicago high schools did not increase. Most high schools ranked very low in employing the practices elementary schools had used to substantially improve their achievement (Designs for Change, 1998).

Finally, a power struggle broke out between some Local School Councils (which included principals) and the central office over recentralization of some authority, reawakening an antipathy that had been beneath the surface since the 1988 law took effect. Many in the central office had not liked the new law and the way in which it gave independence to principals, removing them from central office control.

Phase Three: 2001–

In 2001, Daley removed Vallas for failing to get the results he wanted. The board of education appointed Arne Duncan as CEO.

In his first 4 years, Duncan's policies emphasized professional development for teachers, especially in reading and math, increased funding for early childhood education, and reduced class size in grades 1–3. He attracted nationally recognized individuals to his senior team from business and education.

Duncan placed about 40% of the schools on probation and mandated what those schools can do with all of their federal and state funds. In July 2004 he launched Renaissance 2010, a program to close or reconstitute about 60 failing schools and to create 100 new ones—mainly charter schools and contract schools, which would not be required to have union teachers or Local School Councils. A $52 million reading initiative begun in 2001 features literacy coaches in 365 schools. Early results are not encouraging: Only 45 of the 109 schools that have participated posted gains higher than the city-wide average. Scores at another 44 schools are declining (Russo, 2004).

On the other hand, in June 2005, Duncan launched a new initiative to provide 85 of the better-operated schools with substantial autonomy from CPS requirements. The aim, according to David Vitale, the district's Chief Administrative Officer, is to turn the central office "into a support center, rather than a command and control center. Ideally we'd like to have all 600 schools doing this" (Dell'Angela, 2005). This strategy builds on the 30 years of experience of high performance, including the Edmonton School District and private firms. It also reinforces the autonomy established by the 1988 school reform law and the excellent results that the majority of Local School Councils have gotten with their elementary schools.

So far, under Duncan, the gap in student achievement has continued to narrow between the 68 schools that were already doing well and the 181 high-gain elementary schools. The elementary schools already doing well in 1990 improved their Iowa reading results at 0.7% per year over the 15 years, and the 181 high-gain schools improved at the rate of 1.3%, an 86% higher annual rate of improvement, and thereby closing the achievement gap for half of the schools.

At the same time, the gap has continued to widen between high-gain and low-gain elementary schools (See Figure 1.1). High-gain school scores have risen; low-gain schools have tended to plateau and decline.

WHAT WORKED IN THE HIGH-GAIN SCHOOLS?

The Local School Councils in what were to become the high-gain schools selected and supported principals who then started to implement best practices. For the first time in the history of the Chicago public schools, principals were freed from the authority of incompetent and corrupt central office staff whose jobs depended on a system of political patronage and who have gone to jail for their deeds. Principals used their freedom to create their own annual School Improvement Plan, as well as to use the state and federal funds that they controlled to invest in the priorities identified by the people closest to the problems. They focused on Essential Supports for Learning—including professional development for teachers, parent engagement in student learning, and shared leadership (Consortium for Chicago School Research, 2005; Strategic Learning Initiatives, 2005). Here are the specifics.

Freedom from Central Office Mismanagement and Corruption

The 1988 reform law minimized the negative consequences of central office mismanagement and corruption compared with the prereform years. Most egregiously, in those days people often applied to the local alderman and even paid to become a teacher or principal in the Chicago Public Schools.

Autonomous Principals Built Strong Teaching Staffs

The principals in the high-gain schools removed 50% or more of their teachers. Those teachers either found jobs in the 179 low-gain schools or retired. The principals at the high-gain schools made better hires, too, and better decisions about the internal assignments that they now controlled, regardless of seniority. Many of the new teachers at the high-gain schools had previously been the better teachers at the schools that would become low-gain schools.

Ineffective Principals Left

During the first 6 years of reform, about 80% of the principals left. Some retired as part of an incentive plan. Others from the schools that were to become high-gain schools found jobs in the low-gain schools.

At High-Gain Schools, LSCs Effectively Assessed and Directed Principals and Budgets

Local School Councils hired, fired, and evaluated principals, and approved the schools' annual budgets. High-gain schools had higher-quality leadership.

People Trusted Each Other and Enjoyed Working Together

A school culture of trust—where people worked effectively together toward improvement of instruction and the systems supporting teachers and students—permeated the high-gain schools (Bryk & Schneider, 2002). At the high-gain schools, leaders usually sought outside help, emphasized professional development for teachers and principals, engaged parents, and shared leadership (Bryk et al., 1998; Moore, 1998; Simmons, 2001).

Teachers Gained More Authority and Grew as Leaders

Teachers achieved authority for improving school quality through membership on the LSC, and principals more frequently shared leadership, empowering school staff to achieve their best.

Parent Involvement Increased and Improved

As parents gained the power to improve school quality—parents form a majority on the LSCs—they became more welcome in the schools by teachers and staff. Not only did they become engaged as leaders on LSCs, they took advantage of opportunities to be trained in the skills they needed to take active roles in helping their children become better learners.

Training and Professional Development Raised Quality of Performance for Teachers and Principals

High-quality and sustained professional development of principals and teachers made a difference at high-gain schools, especially through the Chicago Principals and Administrators Association and training programs from not-for-profit organizations—including universities—financed by local foundations, each school's LSC, and the central office. As a result, the high-gain schools adopted teaching practices that focused on more rigorous academic work and that integrated powerful new strategies and tools that developed higher-order thinking skills, including cooperative learning and teacher-designed classroom assessments (Simmons, 2001). Washington Irving Elementary, led by Madeline Maraldi, exemplified these new practices and was one of the first to show significant progress (Simmons, 1995).

Fifteen years of sustained improvement for the 181 high-gain schools demonstrate that basic changes took place in student learning and classroom practice. This is not the "test prep effect." The studies of the Consortium for Chicago School Research

> demonstrate the importance of school leadership, parent and community partnerships, a student centered learning climate, professional capacity and the quality of the instructional program. These domains are frequently referred to as the Essential Supports for student learning. Consortium studies show that schools that are strong in these supports are more likely to improve academically. Studies also show that the schools that are weak are more likely to be stagnant. . . . The Essential Supports are most likely to develop in schools where relationship trust suffuses working relationships across the school community. (2005)

With the reading test results of May 1996, it was also becoming clear that the group of 179 low-gain elementary schools were making significant improvement. This continued at the same rate as the high-gain group for 3 more years. Chicago's model for site-based management was beginning to work for almost all the 360 elementary schools that had started out in 1990 with very low scores.

WHAT DID NOT WORK?

What did not work was the top-down approach used by the central office to transform schools that were either barely making progress or declining. This was a management strategy that had been discredited by high-performance organizations for over 50 years. As mentioned before, there are two kinds of failing schools: one where the principal is unable to learn and apply what is needed to turn around his or her school, and another where the principal is capable but lacks support. The Chicago data in Figure 1.1 and the analysis clearly show that the quality of school leadership is the root cause of high performance or low performance. The specifics follow.

Central Office Remained a Problem

Even in 2005, principals report that central office practices and staff are still less supportive and more vexing on a daily basis than they would expect from the training, funded by the central office, that principals have had on how to run a high-performance school. Many improvements in Chicago's high-gain schools have been achieved as a result of actions independent of, or in opposition to, the central office's policies. For years, principals from exemplary schools have told us that they made progress in spite of the central office—by ignoring the mandates to attend meetings and the often contradictory directives that arrived, sometimes daily, via their fax machines.

Low-Gain Schools Rose and Then Plateaued

Everything that worked at the high-gain schools was part of an overall system of improvement that eventually began to work against the low-gain schools. Low-gain schools got the principals that capable LSCs had fired and the teachers that high-gain principals had removed. Low-gain LSCs didn't fire their principals because they lacked the training and support that they needed make effective decisions. They didn't get training initially by the central office because the superintendent eliminated the training budget in 1990. Overall, low-gain schools did not get adequate assistance from either the central office or the outside partners that it mandated (Finnegan & O'Day, 2003).

Probation Did Not Help

The central office's $29 million probation program, which began in October 1996, provided substantial extra funding and "external partners," usually faculty from local universities. To get off probation, schools had to raise their Iowa reading score above 20%. When probation started, however, the low-gain schools had *already* begun to reverse their decline, as demonstrated by their three-point jump in Iowa reading scores in May 1996. As the level scores for low-gain schools from 1999 to 2002 in Figure 1.1 suggest, the probation program had no sustained positive impact on achievement at most probation schools (Gwynne & Easton, 2001; O'Day, 2002). (It is even possible that these schools might have continued to improve at a rate closer to the high-gain schools if they hadn't lost their authority to the central office. We would expect this positive result from the experience of high-performance organizations. Their scores had already turned around in May 1996 before the probation program began.)

The Chicago Public Schools probation officer and school partner took control of the schools and made many decisions that disempowered the principal and the LSC with little effort made to build capacity through coaching or training them. As a result, morale plummeted and the better principals and teachers left, with many families following suit (Finnegan & O'Day, 2003). Although the CEO had the authority to remove failing principals and close down failing schools, Paul Vallas did not use that authority.

Since reading scores had already turned around before probation began, it is possible that the intended effect of probation on schools was weak at best for 3 years (1997–1999). Since the low-gain schools plateaued and then declined for the next 6 years (2000–2005), widening the gap in student achievement between the two groups, probation may have hurt most of the schools it was intended to help.

Anthony Bryk's analysis of these two phases of school reform concludes that while some students and schools benefited, "Little evidence exists of a major overall improvement in the academic productivity of the Chicago Public Schools during Phase II" under Paul Vallas (Bryk, 2003, pp. 260–261). Grouping all elementary schools together, Bryk and others found that ending social promotion, increasing summer school attendance, or placing schools on probation had little sustained effect on student learning. (Bryk, 2003).

The reasons included the CPS changing the rules in 1997 and 1999 for the "reporting of test scores for students in bilingual programs," and excluding a growing number of Special Education students. "In 1992, 83% of the students were tested, but only 74% were tested in 2001" (Bryk, 2003, p. 247).

When the elementary schools are divided into high- and low-gain schools, as shown in Figure 1.1, the results suggest that the high-gain schools were having a very different experience than the low-gain schools, and for the reasons discussed above. These data for the low-gain schools reinforce the negative effects of Phase Two policies described by Bryk and his colleagues.

Chicago has made tremendous progress since 1990, when 90% of the schools were making no progress. Now only 44% of the schools in the system appear to be stalled. The stalled group includes 179 elementary schools and about 75 high schools, or 254 schools out of a total of 600.

Initiatives to transform high school results that were launched in 1996 failed to achieve any measurable results. While new efforts started in 2001 are underway with the strong support of the CPS leadership and several foundations, it is too early to forecast what the results will be.

The experience discussed above indicates that the Central Office leadership does not have a good track record for implementing system-wide programs. Many of Chicago's schoolchildren are depending on the Central Office to learn from the lessons of the past, apply the practices of high-performing organizations, and close the widening gap between schools that succeed and schools that continue to fail.

REFERENCES

Barton, P. E. (2001). *Raising achievement and reducing gaps.* Washington, DC: National Education Goals Panel.

Bryk, A. S. (2003). No child left behind, Chicago style. In P. E. Peterson & M. Bryk (eds.), *The politics and practice of school accountability* (pp. 242–268). Washington, DC: Brookings Institution.

Bryk, A. S., & Schneider, B. (2002). *Trust in schools: A core resource for improvement.* New York: Russell Sage Foundation.

Bryk, A. S., Sebring, P. B., Kerbow, D., Rollow, S., & Easton, J. Q. (1998). *Chicago school reform: Democratic localism as a lever for change.* Boulder, CO: Westview Press.

Consortium for Chicago School Research. (2005). Model of essential supports for student learning. Retrieved May 2005 from www.consortium-chicago.org/research/ria02.html.

Dell'Angela, T. (2005, June 6). 85 schools get reward of freedom, *Chicago Tribune*, p. 1.

Designs for Change. (1998). *What makes these schools stand out: Chicago elementary schools with a seven-year trend of improved student achievement.* Chicago: Author.

Designs for Change. (2003). *Major gains in reading in 186 Chicago schools.* Unpublished manuscript.

Designs for Change. (2005). *The Big Picture: Chicago K–8 elementary schools reading score trends (1990–2003).* Retrieved June 1, 2005 from www.designsforchange.org

Finnegan, K., & O'Day, J. (2003). *External support to schools on probation: Getting a leg up?* Philadelphia: Philadelphia Consortium on Policy Research in Education.

Gwynne, J., & Easton, J. (2001, April). *Probation, organizational capacity and student achievement in Chicago elementary schools.* Paper presented at annual meeting of American Educational Research Association, Seattle.

Haycock, K., Jerald, C., & Huang, S. (2001). *Closing the gap: Done in a decade.* Washington, DC: Education Trust.

Hess, G. A. (2001). The effort to redesign Chicago high schools. In J. Simmons et al., *School reform in Chicago: Lessons and opportunities* (pp. 43–48). Chicago: Chicago Community Trust.

Lee, V. (2001). High school reform in Chicago: Within the national context. In J. Simmons et al., *School reform in Chicago: Lessons and opportunities* (pp. 487–493). Chicago: Chicago Community Trust.

Moore, D. (1998). *Ending social promotion: Results from the first two years.* Chicago: Chicago School Research.

Nagaoka, J., & Roderick, M. (2004). Ending social promotion: The effects of retention. Chicago: Consortium on Chicago School Research.

O'Day, J. (2002). Complexity, accountability and school improvement. *Harvard Educational Review, 72*(3), 1–31.

Richards, C. (2001). Learning from Chicago's results: Thirteen years of reform. In J. Simmons et al., *School reform in Chicago: Lessons and opportunities* (pp. 1–16). Chicago: Chicago Community Trust.

Roderick, M., Tepper Jacob, R., & Stone, S. (2003). *Ending social promotion: The response of teachers and students.* Chicago: Consortium on Chicago School Research.

Russo, A. (2004). *School reform in Chicago: lessons in policy and practice.* Cambridge, MA: Harvard Education Press.

Simmons, J. (1995). *The Washington Irving experience.* Chicago: Strategic Learning Initiatives, Unpublished.

Simmons, J. (2001). Looking at the data: The results of research on Chicago school reform. In J. Simmons et al., *School reform in Chicago: Lessons and opportunities.* (pp. 17–42). Chicago: Chicago Community Trust. Available at www.strategiclearninginitiatives.org

Strategic Learning Initiatives. (2005). Scaling up best practice: A strategic improvement model. Retrieved April 2005 from www.strategiclearninginitiatives.org

Chapter Two

Drawing the New Map: The Three Organizing Principles

As Albert Einstein once pointed out, we cannot solve our problems with the level of thinking that got us the problems in the first place. We need a paradigm shift. Paul Hill (2001) expresses this higher level of problem solving when he writes:

> Virtually all major efforts to improve big city school systems, including mayoral and state takeovers, have been doomed by the same two factors that sank the school systems in the first place. The first factor is lack of a complete strategy; no city has thought through all the changes that must take place before a chronically low-performing school system can operate at a consistently high standard. The second factor is in implementation; no city has organized the political and financial support necessary to sustain a long-term reform strategy. (p. 293)

These three principles can help district superintendents, union presidents, school board members, principals, teachers, and other educators to shift their paradigm in order to design and accelerate systemic improvement:

1. Consistency: One vision in the classroom and central office
2. Simultaneity: Work everywhere at once
3. Quality: Learn from the best

1. CONSISTENCY: ONE VISION IN THE CLASSROOM AND THE CENTRAL OFFICE

Consistent patterns of communication, culture, leadership, and action mean simply this: What goes on in each classroom to improve instruction is philosophically in line with what goes on in the central office and in the principals' offices. This powerful uniformity of culture works to improve the overall system.

Many find it useful to think about redesigning large systems in terms of patterns of self-similar forms, fractals. They recur within a single system on many levels, from the system's smallest aspects to its overarching architecture (Bries, 1992).

One example is what happened in Brazosport, Texas.

CASE STUDY—SUPERINTENDENT JERRY ANDERSON, BRAZOSPORT, TEXAS

The Brazosport school district, where more than 41% of students come from low-income families, was in 1998 the first in Texas to get all children reading at better than 90% on the Texas Assessment of Academic Skills (TAAS), closing the student achievement gap between poor minority and middle-class White children (See Figure 2.1.).

In 1998, the Brazosport district won the Texas Quality Award, previously given only to businesses. And in 1999 Brazosport became the first school district in the country to be a finalist for the national Malcolm Baldrige Award for Quality. Equally important, the Brazosport results are still strong despite the fact that Texas introduced a new, more difficult test in 2003, reaching 88 in reading in 2005. Although a small gap has returned among the different groups, the strong results on the new test demonstrate the strength of their district strategy and culture. At least 10 other districts have used the model to get good results (APQC, 2004). Two other larger districts, Aldine, Texas and Fontana, California have almost closed the gap using Brazosport's strategy. In 2004, Aldine was a runner-up for the National Broad Award for Outstanding School District.

Brazosport's revolution began at a school board meeting on a hot summer evening in 1991. Jerry Anderson, the new district superintendent, was asked why students on the district's south side (made up of predominantly low-income families) weren't doing as well as the students on the north side (the wealthier side of town). Since Texas School Board procedure did not require an answer, he said, "Next item on the agenda."

After the meeting, Joe Bowman, a school board member and an executive from Dow Chemical, the area's largest employer, told Anderson: "Jerry, if we made the excuses in our business like you guys make in your business, we'd be flat broke and closing up shop in a year. You need to stop making excuses and find a way to teach these children." He then shared with Anderson some ideas that had transformed the way his refinery operated, ideas that even

FIGURE 2.1. Reading Test Scores—Brazosport, TX

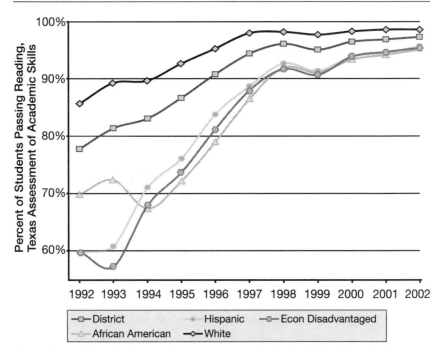

Source: Texas Education Agency (*www.tea.state.tx.us*), Academic Excellence Indicator
System, August, 2005; Davenport and Anderson (2002, p. 111).

"caught the company's management by surprise" (Davenport & Anderson, 2002,
pp. 9, 19).

Intrigued, first Anderson, and then his leadership team, attended a week-
long workshop on transforming organizations that Dow had provided its own
employees. As a result, Anderson and his team developed a shared understanding of the strategy that Dow and thousands of firms around the world have used
to succeed—a strategy that includes W. Edwards Deming's 14 points for effective leadership and redesign. (See Chapter 8.)

After learning the importance of measuring quality and looking at data,
Anderson's team began to look at their data on the quality of teaching and found
teachers from both sides of the city whose students did very well on the TAAS.
When they looked more closely at the teachers in the south side schools, they
found one who stood out: Mary Barksdale, a teacher at the lowest-performing

school in the district. While "94 percent of her third grade students at Velasco Elementary were considered 'at risk,' virtually all of them mastered each section of the TAAS" (Davenport & Anderson, 2002, p. 45).

When Ms. Barksdale was asked what she was doing differently from her colleagues, she replied that she was "simply teaching." Further investigation, revealed that her commonsense approach was in reality a sophisticated, "dynamic process of continuous assessment and re-teaching for those students not up to mastery [which] enabled all of her students to excel" (Davenport & Anderson, 2002, p. 45).

When Anderson's team quietly compared Barksdale's process to that of other teachers who were successful with similar children, they found many common features. They began to make changes. The principal at Velasco started by encouraging all her teachers to share their teaching strategies and lesson plans that worked in staff and grade-level meetings. This way Barksdale was not put on a pedestal by the principal, to be knocked off by her peers. Teachers in her building began—voluntarily—to visit Barksdale's classroom and use her strategy. The first year student achievement improved significantly.

Anderson and Patricia Davenport, District Director of Curriculum and Instruction, then created a similar opportunity for principals, at monthly meetings, to learn and share best practice just as the Velasco principal had done with her teachers, without putting the Velasco principal on a pedestal. As more teachers and principals heard about the results, they visited Barksdale's classroom, and the process spread in less than 2 years to all the other schools.

When the new, more difficult Texas Assessment of Knowledge and Skills was introduced in 2003, the leadership of Rudy Okruhlik, who became Superintendent in 2000, improved scores with the same methods that had been previously successful. District leadership and principals, working as teams, used quality improvement tools to analyze data "to see what it would tell us." Then principals went back to their schools and took all the teachers through a similar process. Based on that analysis, teachers developed and implemented action plans, including particular goals for some individual children as well as larger classroom goals. They drew on the Eight-Step Process for reteaching and data analysis learned in the 4-day induction process, standard for all teachers new to the district. (Veteran teachers, who had to go through the training along with everyone else if they were new to the district, described it as "the best training they have ever had.") And, to reduce isolation and promote communication and cooperation between levels—as well as among teachers—team-building was a part of all meetings (Okruhlik, personal communication).

Here is the key to success in Brazosport: Decisions driving the improvement of classroom instruction were made in a coordinated way at both the top and the bottom that respected and empowered the teachers and principals. While the superintendent and his team actively supported the strategy for scaling-up best practice, the teachers decided for themselves whether to use Mary Barksdale's Eight-Step Process. The leadership of the school system at every level valued and relied on a fractal-like model to scale-up best practice, avoiding the mixed messages from the central office and resistance from principals, teachers, and parents that in other places had undermined purely top-down efforts at reform. (More than 30 years previously, the leadership of the Chicago Public School system had tried and failed to introduce a similar approach called Mastery Learning, developed by University of Chicago professor Benjamin Bloom. It was mandated from the top down.)

The value of effective leadership is apparent from the Brazosport example. To begin with, Anderson and his team focused their attention on high-quality teaching, and they knew that the place to look for that was in the district's own classrooms. Next, they used data to identify superior practice; then they created a powerful process to help teachers and principals discover for themselves how to scale-up a significant best practice: the Eight-Step Process.

In Chicago, since 1994, school partners providing professional development have repeatedly recommended this method of showcasing powerful results, only to have it either ignored or implemented ineffectively. Instead, since 1996, Chicago has used probation, a low-quality policy for school improvement that so far has not significantly altered classroom results. The process of scaling up best practice broke down (Finnegan & O'Day, 2003).

2. SIMULTANEITY: WORK EVERYWHERE AT ONCE

Keeping the different parts of the system aligned and improving is the biggest challenge for a superintendent. Using authority, and broad participation in decision making to create the necessary shared vision, ownership, and responsibility in a large, complex system requires effective leadership by the senior executive team.

To get deep, sustained improvement, separate but interdependent categories of reform must move forward at the same time. The two most basic categories are these:

- A shift in overall organizational behavior—a new way of working together, led by superintendents, union leaders, central office staff, and principals to deepen trust, define and solve problems together at all levels, and accelerate results

- Improved instructional practice—a reform led by principals and teachers and supported by central office and union policy and the daily behavior of the central office staff

District leaders must implement instruction-focused empowerment supported by professional development to build capacity, while they also align systems and priorities. To transform the system elements, the district leadership team, headed by the superintendent, needs to have a shared vision of a high-performance district and the steps needed to get there.

Every district approaches this problem in a different way. Not surprisingly, the better urban superintendents include both traditional educators and émigrés from business, the military, or law. Real-world experience and research by academic experts such as Harvard's Susan Moore Johnson suggest, however, that for all their differences of background and style, the more effective urban district leaders share several key attributes, which mirror their own key personal beliefs and attributes (Johnson, 1996).

- A clear focus on improving classroom learning and student achievement
- A big-picture, systemic view of the district and its many elements
- A willingness to delegate, train, and empower staff effectively
- A capacity to maintain reform priorities in the face of competing demands
- A strong ability to communicate new ideas and popularize reform programs
- An ability to develop strong alliances with community leaders and reform advocates (see Chapter 5 for Johnson's essay.)

Boston's superintendent, Tom Payzant, hasn't achieved every one of Susan Moore Johnson's goals, but he's a good example of someone who's come close, someone who has worked different parts of the system simultaneously.

CASE STUDY—SUPERINTENDENT TOM PAYZANT, BOSTON, MASSACHUSETTS

An anomaly among urban school chiefs, Tom Payzant has been at the helm since 1995 against a backdrop of relative political peace and stability. Payzant has the support of Boston's mayor and the mayorally appointed school board. He also enjoys generally good relations with the teachers union.

"I think that realistically you have to think in terms of 4- to 5-year chunks. Because we are talking about results here. And you have to have a year or two to put things in place, and then 2 to 3 years to get things you put in place to take hold. I think you can see some real progress if you're really focused and driving it over 3 to 5 years," Payzant says. "This assumes not constantly changing directions, changing strategies—you learn from what you are doing, refine and modify, but you're not all over the map. You don't change a whole system in a 3- to 5-year period." For Payzant, a longer-term strategy, paradoxically, is the only thing that can speed up the rate of change: going slow to go fast later.

Payzant says when he first took over the Boston school district in 1995 "there was no coherence of any kind with respect to expectations for learning, curriculum, and teaching. My first challenge was to address what we wanted students to learn, to establish standards in each of the major curriculum areas and align them with what was then emerging as the new Massachusetts curriculum frameworks. The first task was to get some coherence around expectations, first in literacy, math, science, and social studies, then, in the second year, in the arts, world languages, physical education, and so forth.

"I understood, from previous experience, that the real work of teaching and learning has to occur school by school, and that you can't use a single cookie-cutter model in every school to shape the design for improvement. But you have to provide a framework for schools to work within, or lots of time will be spent trying to figure out how to improve student achievement without the necessary knowledge and support for doing so."

Boston tackled assessment, adopting standardized multiple-choice and open-response tests, and designed a framework for whole-school change.

In Boston, whole-school reform relies on the Focus on Children plan and six principles—"Essentials"—to guide schools' reform work. Like San Diego, the city schools emphasize a strong literacy program and use peer coaches to boost teacher capacity. The Boston Plan for Excellence, a nonprofit group backed by prominent business, union, community, and political leaders, has been instrumental in setting and shaping the reform agenda (some call it a shadow cabinet).

While a lot more hiring is done now at the school level rather than centrally, with a personnel subcommittee at each school working with the principal, Payzant ultimately has control over principal selection. A site panel made up of parents, teachers, and administrators, chaired by a principal/cluster leader who works as a peer coach and support person for 12 to 15 schools, come up with principal candidates for Payzant to consider. Although he can also reject the slate and appoint an acting person, he has rarely done it.

"As long as we have a system of schools and I am going to be ultimately accountable as superintendent, then I am not willing to cede total responsibility to a site council to make that critical leadership decision. But I do believe, as I said earlier, very strongly in getting that site panel very much engaged. I think that that is a good middle ground."

In Boston, Effective Practice schools get more autonomy from central office policy and practice because of their student achievement results. Payzant views that exchange of results for autonomy as appropriate. "The real work of teaching and learning obviously occurs at the school, and everything we do ought to be focused on trying to provide support for improvement of that teaching and learning. The bigger question is what is the balance between district direction and the top-down, bottom-up dilemma? My general view is that the relationship between the amount of central direction and site-based autonomy is based on results. So the better the results at a school, the greater autonomy the school should have in decision making. And conversely, more intervention and direction from central will occur when school results are unacceptable."

In contrast, Chicago's 1988 reform law used a different approach. Because central office policies and practices were seen as a major reason why schools could not improve, all Local School Councils were given full autonomy to pick their principals and oversee their poverty funds. At that time 90% of the schools were failing. The results in Figure 1.1 show that granting all schools autonomy made a dramatic difference to almost half of the failing schools in the city. Without autonomy, they would not have had the chance to show what they could do.

3. QUALITY: LEARN FROM THE BEST

The majority of work on school improvement has been guided by educationally based paradigms of curriculum and instruction, with short shrift given to the fact that the work of education occurs within the context of an organization. Despite arguments that schools and school districts are not corporations and should not be run as such, educators still operate within organizations similar to those of a business: managing operations, shaping cultures, responding to politics and government regulatory policy, and meeting the needs of their "customers"—parents, students, and employers of their graduates.

The pace of change can accelerate if more urban school district leaders would study the strategies that have turned around major corporations and smaller districts. To succeed, all district personnel need to have an understanding of these tools and how they have been successfully applied to the transformation of high-performance organizations. The experience of Brazosport, Texas, Palatine, Illinois, and other smaller school districts is important.

We set out the basics of many of these practical approaches in Part Two.

REFERENCES

American Productivity and Quality Center (APQC). (2004). *Education: Examining strategic improvement efforts.* Houston: Author.

Bries, J. (1992). *Fractals: The patterns of chaos.* New York: Simon & Schuster.

Davenport, P., & Anderson, G. (2002). *Closing the achievement gap: No excuses.* Houston: American Productivity and Quality Center.

Finnegan, K., & O'Day, J. (2003). *External support to schools on probation: Getting a leg up?* Philadelphia: Philadelphia Consortium on Policy Research in Education.

Hill, P. (2001). Strategy and philanthropy for urban education reform. In J. Simmons et al., *School reform in Chicago: Lessons and opportunities* (pp. 293–304). Chicago: Chicago Community Trust.

Johnson, S. M. (1996). *Leading to change: The challenge of the new superintendency.* San Francisco: Jossey-Bass.

Chapter Three

Focus Here: Four Necessary Strategies

As child psychologist David Elkind writes:

> While it is true that children are exposed to more information and a greater variety of experiences than were children of the past, it does not follow that they automatically become more sophisticated. We always know much more than we understand, and with the torrent of information to which young people are exposed, the gap between knowing and understanding, between experience and learning, has become even greater than it was in the past. (1987, p. 24).

There is nothing in Elkind's words to suggest that he had urban school reform in mind when he wrote of this gap between experience and learning. Nevertheless, his statement applies: Urban educators have more information than ever before about systemic problems—including incompetent leadership, low-performing schools, dropout rates, ineffective professional development for teachers and administrators, and lack of parental engagement—and what is needed to overcome these problems. But even with all of this information, can large-scale reform efforts be described—to borrow Elkind's words—as significantly "more sophisticated" than they were 20 years ago?

The chronic inadequacy of such efforts—for example, the growing gap in Chicago's student achievement—suggests that more experience and more information have not necessarily led to greater learning or, perhaps, greater application of learning. While differences among states can be significant, the national trends based on data from the National Assessment of Educational Progress indicate little improvement in closing the achievement gap between White and minority students in the 1990s, and we have a widening gap between the high and low achievers (Barton, 2001; Haycock, Jerald, & Huang, 2001).

While data-based decision making is an important objective, reform efforts can be overwhelmed by the sheer volume of information at hand.

How do we turn the data into results? The lessons culled from 17 years of research and experience with Chicago school reform and the experience in other cities suggest four major strategies that require simultaneous implementation for successful systemic reform. These four strategies provide the divisions for Part Two of this book, where essays by a range of scholars and practitioners shed light on understanding and application:

1. Create leaders at every level.
2. Transform the structure and culture.
3. Improve instruction.
4. Involve parents and make funding adequate and equitable.

1. CREATE LEADERS AT EVERY LEVEL

Leaders have to thrive at every level of the district—individuals who have the ability to improve schools' capacity for leading change through better training, communication, teamwork, and stakeholder involvement in problem solving.

Lessons on Leadership from High-Performing Organizations

High-performing organizations follow these principles when creating leadership:

- The CEO, and his or her team, create a vision, shared by key stakeholders, of what their organization can become, identifying the human values like trust, honesty, and teamwork that are essential for building a strong culture and defining the mission that the organization will pursue.
- The CEO's team believes that authority and responsibility for solving problems and making decisions needs to be given to the people closest to the customers, whether the customers are inside the organization or outside. Authority is a function of knowledge and skill, not position.
- Another major CEO responsibility is creating and sustaining an organizational culture that emphasizes continuous learning for all employees (often done in teams). Leaders at all levels are held accountable for "growing" their people.
- The organization has a small number of layers and includes managers whose main role is to function as coach and resource to teams

of employees who operate in self-managing teams. Each team has goals and measurable objectives, and is accountable for them.

* Unions and their leaders are seen as full partners in designing and implementing the transformation process. Through a process of mutual-gains bargaining, contracts are rewritten and simplified to reflect the experience of other high-performance partnerships (Simmons & Mares, 1982). We have superintendents who have transformed their districts and their student results: John Champlin in Johnson City, New York; Jerry Anderson in Brazosport, Texas; Michael Strembitsky in Edmonton; and John Conyers in Palatine, Illinois. Starting over 40 years ago at long-established firms, CEOs like Bob Galvin at Motorola and Howard J. Morgens at Procter & Gamble initiated high-performance concepts. Others followed, including Don Petersen at Ford Motor, Malcolm Stamper at Boeing, David Kearns at Xerox, and Chauncey Cook at General Foods. At start-up firms, the CEOs used the experience at established firms to create new, and initially small, firms that have grown to become multibillion-dollar firms. This includes CEOs like Herb Kelleher at Southwest Airlines; Bill Gore, the inventor of GoreTex, at W.L. Gore and Associates; and thousands of other CEOs of private firms around the world.

Building Local Leadership: Local School Councils

The American auto industry waged a losing battle with the Japanese until it abandoned its top-down management approach, began to listen more carefully to customers, and gave employees closest to the problems the power and skills to make decisions about improving quality and performance. Likewise, when Chicago established Local School Councils (LSCs) in 1988, responsibility for quality was removed from the old patronage system and put squarely in the hands of those most directly in contact with students: teachers, parents, and principals.

In addition, before the LSCs, the appeals of one principal to the school board were often insufficient to receive funding or attention. As principal Myrtle Burton-Sahara of Locke Elementary School said, "[Without a council] I think the [Chicago Public Schools] Board would have looked at it as 'Oh, here's another principal jumping up and down and screaming about what they don't have.' . . . It has some meaning when you say, 'My Local School Council feels this way'" (Pick, 1998, p. 8).

The better the leadership in the LSCs, the better the school. The 181 Chicago schools that substantially improved their reading scores on the Iowa Test of Basic Skills (ITBS) since 1991 were found to have significantly more effective LSCs than the schools without sustained improvement (Ryan et al., 1997).

Effective LSCs had (because they hired and supported) "principals who were instructional leaders and who closely supervised the change process, and teachers who were more involved in decision making" (Moore, 2001, p. 51). The principals in these empowered, decentralized school environments had the authority to hire effective teachers and remove ineffective teachers, they engaged parents and teachers, built a local leadership team, and instituted new training programs. Instruction improved, and site-based management spread through the district (Richards, 2001).

In 1997, the Consortium on Chicago School Research studied the city's LSCs to determine what factors made a council an effective entity in the school improvement effort. Some LSCs were far more effective than others. Searching for the reasons why, researchers compared the backgrounds of the 30 most productive LSCs with those of the 30 least productive oness. They found the following:

- The members of the least effective councils received less training: Fewer than one-third of their members said they went through extensive training, while more than one-half of the members of the most productive groups said that they had. About one-quarter of the members of the least effective LSCs reported having had no training at all, and nearly two-thirds said a lack of training kept them from doing their jobs well.
- Members of the least productive councils were more likely to report lower levels of meeting skills (a result of the lack of training), less commitment among council members, and weaker principals and chairperson leadership.
- The less productive LSCs were more likely to be located in the city's poorest neighborhoods and in predominantly African American schools. Interestingly, however, the converse was not true with regard to the most productive councils. They were not necessarily in the city's richest neighborhoods, but instead were scattered across the city in virtually every neighborhood, located sometimes literally just down the street from the least effective councils (Ryan et al., 1997).

The researchers concluded that the quality of the leadership and cooperative adult relationships in each school community and the level of training LSC members received directly affected the group's efficacy. This finding was confirmed in discussions with council members. The most effective training for LSCs, according to participants in a 2001 focus group, comes from independent school reform groups such as Parents United for Responsible Education, Designs for Change, the Chicago School Leadership Cooperative, the Lawyers' School Reform Advisory Project, Cross City Campaign for School Reform, and the Chicago Panel for School Reform, not from the central office trainers (Simmons, 2001a, 2001b).

A 2001 focus group of council members said LSCs benefited from training in the following:

- *Principal evaluation and selection.* Learning how to evaluate a principal fairly; strategies for reaching out to a wider candidate pool.
- *Budgeting.* Understanding line items and learning where to allocate money. When the LSC is not adequately trained in budget complexities, participants said, they are forced to fully trust that the principal is acting appropriately.
- *Advocacy.* How to get things done for schools when dealing with the central administration.
- *Obtaining and interpreting school data.* Getting needed information to make decisions and use information correctly.
- *Networking with other schools.* Creating relationships with other schools and accelerating the sharing of the lessons that they are learning.
- In addition, training is most helpful when the subject matter is specific, the trainers are familiar with the school, and the training happens in time to deal with the pressing issue at hand.

Building Central Office Leadership

As Susan Moore Johnson discusses in her Chapter 5 essay, the polarized options of top-down leadership versus the exercise of local autonomy do not present an adequate model for understanding the decision-making dynamics required to build a system of successful schools. Top-down decision making lacks essential, context-specific information required for high-quality decisions. And because decisions are removed from those who must implement them, the fidelity of implementation is eroded, if not outright undermined. On the other hand, the exercise of local autonomy is subject to biases, lack of judgment, and the constraints or temptations of local relationships—biases that degrade the decisions' quality relative to the organizational goals.

The correlation between ineffective leadership and low test scores, low morale, high student dropout rates, and a host of other problems associated with urban education is one of the most important lessons learned in Chicago so far.

Under a high-performance model, it is the responsibility of district-level leadership to give schools the authority to get quality results, including the training and support the councils need for finding the best principals. If local leadership is unsuccessful, the first response of the central office should not be to strip away autonomy (and certainly not to mandate classroom practices that it cannot enforce), but rather to provide more effective support for the principals and councils, to more effectively monitor the quality of plans and resource allocation, and to publicly recognize the school's successes. If leadership can't do the job, then change the leaders. Taking over only makes matters worse, as it did during the Vallas probation program by moving responsibility from the local leaders who were closest to the problems into the hands of a distant central office.

Building Principals

Principals are key leaders. See Chapter 5 for Judy Codding and Marc Tucker's, and Kent D. Peterson and Carolyn Kelley's essays for thoughts challenging districts and the systems that create career ladders for principals.

In Boston, Tom Payzant stays close to and develops his principals.

CASE STUDY—SUPERINTENDENT TOM PAYZANT, BOSTON, MASSACHUSETTS

Without question, Tom Payzant says, principals are in "the key leverage position in the whole system." And he has built leaders at that level, giving them the skills and support they need—and terms that are long enough to enable them to systematically build their schools. Under Payzant, the better principals enjoy virtually full autonomy. "Whereas earlier in my career I thought you had to move principals around the system every 3 or 4 years at least, to leverage school improvement, now I want to find the best people I can and provide continuity of leadership at the school level as well as at the district level. It takes time, relentless focus, and continuous support to improve student achievement." One tool Boston created was an Internet portal where principals, teachers, parents, and students can access a wide array of statistics and information. Payzant says that "principals can get all kinds of data on kids and share it with staff to help inform decisions about instruction," in the process arming more people to become leaders.

Payzant says that when he first joined the district, "I did something that organizational specialists would say is ridiculous. I knew there was real alienation between principals and the central office. The principals felt isolated from the superintendent. I wiped out the middle level of administration (assistant superintendents for elementary, middle, and high schools) and said all principals will now report directly to me. And then I brought in one deputy, and she and I during the first 2 years worked directly with the principals—and with 130, we had to use a triage approach." They learned as much as they could about the problems and improved two-way communication.

In fact, today most organizational scientists would applaud Payzant's decision to cut out entire layers of management.

That structure has now evolved into a "more sensible structure that better provides principals with the support they need using a more comprehensive performance evaluation system." Three deputies are now charged with overseeing specific clusters of Boston's 125 schools, being out in the schools on a virtually full-time basis.

Payzant himself works directly with four or five schools, supervising the principals. "Part of my theory of leadership change is you've got to model the behavior and not ask other people to do what you are not willing to do yourself. We make the final decisions together on who gets hired—I'm the ultimate decision maker, but it's a real team effort. And it sends the message that the people who are providing the central office support on the operations side and the teaching and learning side and the three deputies working directly with the schools and the superintendent are all connected to the work of the school."

Principals are also part of the leadership team that meets twice monthly. Payzant acknowledges that the team is "too big on the one hand, but I am not willing to forgo the involvement of those nine principals and headmasters because it makes a critical difference in the conversation" in terms of responsiveness to principals' needs. To accelerate the rate of improvement in their buildings, Payzant expects them to bring him solutions to their problems and to work among themselves to find and share solutions. The principals who have already figured out a solution to the problem can share it. With this organizational structure, including the twice-monthly meetings with his leadership team, Payzant can focus on removing the central office policies and practices that principals find are barriers for improving the quality of their work.

2. TRANSFORM THE STRUCTURE AND CULTURE

Successful transformation of the structure and culture of the district and its schools is key to accelerating both adult and student learning. This happens best through the leadership of the district and the individual schools taking steps to develop a shared vision of the desired future and then to create measurable objectives and action plans. They need to redesign the central office to better support the schools while they implement action plans, continuously improving the system. These basic steps shape the "Z

Process," which has been used successfully for over 40 years with large organizations and which is discussed in Part Three.

Lessons on Culture and Structure from High-Performing Organizations

The culture shapes how people treat each other and how they work together.

First, the culture of an organization drives high performance in schools and district offices. Culture is composed of the accumulated values, beliefs, and behaviors that shape how people treat each other and how they work together—the mental and philosophical habits that predominate in each classroom, among every team of teachers, throughout schools, across the school board, and within the central office of the district. The organization determines its shared vision and mission through a clear process involving the stakeholders, which checks them at key steps in the sequence and returns to them often.

Cultures of high-performance organizations are dominated by people who have high expectations of themselves and others and who work with people based on the powerful values of trust, excellence, respect, fairness, integrity, honesty, and cooperation—which shape the quality of the results. People in low-performing teams and organizations tend to operate from the opposite of these characteristics. Leaders of high-performance organizations practice these values, beliefs, and behaviors and expect them from all employees. The data show that Chicago schools that have such a culture outperform those which do not (Bryk & Schneider, 2002; Fullan, 2001).

Second, the structure of the organization helps shape this culture. High-performance organizations delegate authority for problem solving and decision making to the employees who are closest to the daily needs and problems of the students, parents, and teachers. Principals who ask teams of grade-level teachers to identify and solve problems and assure that they have the skills needed for effective teamwork accelerate student learning faster than those who don't (Schmoker, 1999). Superintendents like Mike Strembitsky and Angus McBeath in Edmonton and Tom Payzant in Boston get better results when they give principals control over most of their budget, thereby delegating the authority of the central office to the people who need to be held accountable for the results, and streamlining decision-making. (See John Simmons and Judy Karasik's essay in Chapter 6; Wohlstetter & Briggs, 2001).

Third, a high-performance culture and structure are essential for establishing and sustaining the coherent actions needed to accelerate improvement of the quality of classroom instruction—the key service that a school system delivers to its stakeholders. In successful Chicago schools the actions that enhance coherence include the following:

- A shared vision and mission for the school that includes shared leadership with the teachers and parents
- Standards for instructional quality
- Spending on professional development that is integrated into a research-based strategy for improving instruction
- A common instructional framework that integrates curriculum, teaching methods, and professional development. (Miles, Hornbeck, & Fermanich, 2002, p. 3.)

Organizations that are underperforming have dysfunctional structures and cultures. They are schools where principals aren't honest with teachers, parents, and students; where teachers don't want to help one another; and parents aren't welcome in the building. They include schools where the principal doesn't use a leadership team wherein teachers are selected by their peers to be members, schools where teachers have little time to share, plan, or reflect together in grade-level meetings or retreats. These schools need to be transformed; fine-tuning does not do the job (Cuban & Tyack, 1995; Sarason, 1999). Their leaders have neither a clear vision of what a high-performance organization looks like nor an understanding of the process needed to transform and sustain the redesign. (See Part Three for how leaders do this.)

Local School Councils: How Structure Shapes Culture

One systemwide change that is a root cause of transformation in Chicago is the presence of Local School Councils (LSCs). This is a good example of how structure shapes culture, how it enables high-performance cultures to thrive. The Reform Act of 1988 drastically reduced the powers of the school board to control daily life in the schools. It created for each school an LSC comprised of six elected parents, two elected community members, two elected teachers, the principal, and, in high schools, one student. LSCs were assigned the power to hire and fire the principal, approve the spending of poverty funds in the school budget, and approve or reject a school improvement plan. Because principals are accountable to the LSCs (which hire and fire them) and are able to hire, remove but not fire, and assign teachers, leadership has been able to accelerate student learning; improve the quality of instruction; engage parents in their children's learning; share leadership decision making; and deepen trust among teachers, parents, and the principals (Bryk & Schneider, 2002; Simmons, 2001). Chicago's LSCs, which have decision-making authority, cannot be confused with the "advisory" councils many cities have. (See the essay by John Simmons and Judy Karasik in Chapter 6 for a description of how one system has put 92% of the district dollars in the hands of the schools, which "buy" services from the central office and elsewhere.)

Breaking Down the District into Smaller Areas

Superintendent Arne Duncan has tried to create another structural difference. In 2002 he broke the district into 24 "areas" of about 25 schools each (as opposed to the previous organization of 100 schools in a single "region") and assigned an Area Instructional Officer (AIO) who is usually a former principal, to each area. The AIOs' original job was to provide coaching and support to help schools to focus on improving the quality of instruction. With the new probation policy of March 2004, however, they acquired authority over the probation schools in the city, changing the relationship from coach to boss. (About 40% of the schools went on probation after the tests in the spring, up from about 20% the year before.)

Networks

In Chicago, voluntarily formed networks are a structural mechanism that have enabled schools to share ideas, relying on social interaction among individual components of whole school systems (Elmore, 2001). When the parts are connected, the result is a more coherent whole. Viewing the organization this way makes it easier to envision and communicate key principles of the scaling-up process. Networks of neighborhood schools, started by Strategic Learning Initiatives (SLI)—a not-for-profit that supports schools and district improvement efforts—use one main criterion for a school's readiness for a long-term network partnership. This is the presence of a principal who has the respect of his or her LSC and teachers and who has shown that he or she could bring some improvements in classroom teaching that were captured by the Iowa Test of Basic Skills in the past 5 years. The major results of the SLI networks of neighborhood schools are improvement in the quality of assistance, reduction of the cost of assistance per school, and accelerated improvement in the results of the Iowa and Illinois tests when compared to schools from similar income groups (Strategic Learning Initiatives, 2004).

The Chicago Annenberg Challenge, an initiative of the Annenberg Foundation implemented from 1995 through 2001, funded 45 networks of schools, with about 250 schools participating, to increase the sharing of resources and interschool communication (and to use the Challenge as a research study that would add to the general body of knowledge). The larger goal was to "improve the ability of schools to improve themselves"—getting entire school systems to learn. According to the report by Ken Rolling, who directed the Annenberg Challenge, now

> teachers are receiving more and better support and collaborating with one another, and school leadership had improved dramatically; thousands of parents across the city have become engaged in school improvement efforts; the community of external providers has increased to involve over fifty providers and the percentage of Annenberg students scoring above national averages in reading has risen by 41 percent. (2001, p. 59)

Based on the Chicago experience, district leaders need to be careful to strike a balance between spreading innovation and holding back on scaling-up until a school or network of schools have the principals needed to do the job. The need for such a balance has become evident in Chicago over the decade and a half of reform. Innovations in leadership, teamwork, instruction, professional development, and parent engagement fail to spread in many schools. At the same time, stakeholders have seen that district leadership tends to make changes too quickly, before the infrastructure is in place to support systemwide change.

How Structural Changes Improve Instruction

Structural changes obviously can improve what happens in the classroom. Valerie E. Lee's essay in Chapter 6 describes several strategies where structure has enhanced instruction: "interdisciplinary teaching teams, mixed-ability classes, schools-within-schools, common planning time for teachers, flexible time for classes, and students keeping the same homeroom throughout high school." These changes improve the culture by encouraging cooperation and communication, including the sharing of ideas and lesson plans. The research shows clearly that smaller schools can create the opportunity to accelerate student learning and graduation rates (Fine, 2001; Meier, 1995).

Small schools, now a nationwide movement that is accelerating student learning and graduation rates, is an excellent example of restructuring (Fine, 2001). The philosophy and results of Central Park East, located in one of New York City's poorest neighborhoods, with over 90% of the students from low-income families, has done more to improve urban education than any other school in the country (Meier, 1995, 2002). It was established in 1974 by Deborah Meier and her colleagues; 95% of the students of the first six graduating classes graduated from high school, and almost 66% enrolled in college (Bensman, 2000). By 2005 there were more than 500 small schools in the country, with New York City and Chicago each having about 100.

Leaders need to be aware of how to use structure to support a common instructional framework that drives virtually all decisions in a given school—from curriculum, teaching methods, and professional development to staff working conditions. (A common framework, however, is *not* a scripted curriculum. See the essays in Chapter 7 by Charlotte Danielson and Linda Darling-Hammond.)

When Cultural Change Is Missing: Chicago's Central Office

In Chicago, the major cultural changes have been at the school level; little has changed at the central office since either the 1988 or the 1995 laws took effect. Although the new leadership selected by the mayor in 2001 is saying the right thing—the central office's role is to support schools—the staff has not been trained and led in such a way as to end the old behavior, historically defined by lack of respect for school-based personnel and a failure to respond with the kind of support and autonomy that is needed to help schools with their daily problems. As Richard Elmore (2001) has written, and as is true in Chicago, "The existing organizational structure and culture of schools and school systems works against large-scale improvement because it embodies the incoherent and unstable residue of earlier reforms" (p. 159). (For an explanation of some typical major barriers—and ways to cut through them—found in large school systems, see Chapter 6 for Elmore's "Large-Scale Improvement in Urban Public School Systems: The Next Generation of Reform" and W. Patrick Dolan's "The Silence of the System: Why Organizations Can't Learn.")

In San Diego, large structural changes have met resistance. Former Superintendent Alan Bersin, now Secretary of Education in California, and who had been a U.S. Attorney for the Southern District of California for the 5 years before his 1998 appointment, describes how he has attempted to manage the human element.

CASE STUDY—DECENTRALIZATION, AUTONOMY, AND ACCOUNTABILITY IN CHICAGO, SAN DIEGO, BOSTON, AND HOUSTON

One of the largest structural questions in a district is the degree of autonomy given to its schools. Chicago used site-based management, where state law gave school leadership major authority and responsibility. The strategy, based on research, trusted the principals selected by the LSCs and gave them autonomy (Mohrman, Wohlstetter, & Associates, 1994; Wohlstetter & Briggs, 2001). The strategy included providing extra support to those who failed to improve and removing those who still hadn't improved. Other systems like Boston and San Diego give more autonomy to principals as they earn it.

"Because of the obvious ineffectiveness of central office mechanisms, and as a political reaction to those failures, quite understandably, site-based management became the ideology of school reform," says Alan Bersin, but in San Diego they are working toward building schools' capacity to successfully handle greater autonomy. Fostering decentralization without providing support is a strategy likely to fail, he says, "a prescription for chaos," rendering site-based management a hollow political exercise without positive impact on student achievement and school improvement.

Bersin describes the concept of reciprocal accountability: Schools get flexibility and freedom because they are accountable for the results of what they do with that flexibility and freedom; the central office is accountable for making sure schools have the tools to do their job well. And school decentralization, Bersin says, is an evolutionary process: Schools should receive more autonomy once they gain capacity and can demonstrate that they can use their autonomy effectively on behalf of student achievement. "Managing the two elements of autonomy and accountability into satisfactory balance . . . strikes me as a major challenge of urban school reform."

Bersin says that probably the most dramatic change his administration has made is "restoring an appropriate role for the principal in the California public education system, a position which had been weakened beyond recognition in the previous 30 years." He explains that the goal is to find "the right balance between ensuring central office expertise and overall system coherence on the one hand, and building capable effective leadership at the school site in the persons of its principal and its lead teachers, on the other. The central office clearly has a definite role to play in this balance: On the instructional side it is to ensure professional development and K–12 curricular coherence, while on the business side it is to enable principals to be instructional leaders rather than plant managers through providing quality support to schools and to their administrators."

In Boston, Effective Practice schools get more autonomy because they are held up as models for the rest of the system, based on their student achievement results. Tom Payzant views that exchange of results for autonomy as appropriate. "The real work of teaching and learning obviously occurs at the school, and everything we do ought to be focused on trying to provide support for improvement of that teaching and learning. The bigger question is what is the balance between district direction and the top-down, bottom-up dilemma? My general view is that the better results at a school, the greater autonomy the school should have in decision making. And conversely, more intervention and direction from central will occur when school results are unacceptable."

In Houston, Kaye Stripling sees school-based budgeting as the cornerstone of the district's decentralization moves. The goal has been to funnel 80% of all district funds to the school sites; currently, the figure is around 66%. "My vision of a central office is that it be as lean as it can possibly be and yet remain effective and creative. At the same time [we need] to be supportive and be good listeners so that we can support what the field is doing and what they need."

The Chicago experience sheds light on the dynamic interaction between centralization and decentralization. Since 1988 the pendulum has swung between advocacy for empowerment/decentralization and advocacy for top-down direction/centralization. Unfortunately, the politically motivated polarization of these approaches forced observers to assess their value from an unproductive either/or perspective. The research on high-performance organizations shows clearly that some decisions need to be retained by the central office, but most should be made by the people closest to the problem (Lawler, 1996; Lawler, Mohrman & Ledford, 1995; Letts, Ryan & Grossman, 1999; Passmore, 1988).

Joseph Viteritti (2001), a former school superintendent and past co-director of the Wagner School's Center for Management at New York University, conducted a study of big-city school governance and sees positive effects in the Chicago model when he writes:

> While seemingly contradictory, the Chicago plan that balances local control at the school level with tough accountability to a central authority may actually serve as a broad outline to the governance arrangement that meets the needs of the next century of big city schooling. (p. 181)

Viteritti's recommendation is also strongly supported by 20 years of research on the success of school-based management and its impact on improving student learning, (Wohlstetter & Briggs, 2001).

Achieving such a balance is the goal of the CEO of any high-performance organization. These organizations have seen that the more decisions that can be made by the people closest to the problems, the better and faster the results will be and the lower the cost in terms of dollars, management time, and dissatisfied customers.

Now the challenge for the leaders of urban districts is to move beyond the tug-of-war between centralization and decentralization, recognize the role that both need to play, and rethink the integration of these approaches in a comprehensive strategy for school improvement—one that features instructionally focused empowerment supported by professional development and aligned systems. The ideas that have emerged can be used to lead urban systems toward a new stage of reform that closes the gap among schools and allows all schools to be high performing.

3. IMPROVE INSTRUCTION

For continued improvement, schools must make bettering the quality of instruction a high priority.

Lessons on Improving Instruction from High-Performing Organizations

School districts cannot become high-performing organizations without continuously improving the skills and information of all employees, starting at the top of the organization.

Most organizations provide training and information to their employees, but high-performance organizations focus on continuously improving the *quality* of the training and information people get (this includes delivering training when it is needed). For example, a high-performing school will improve classroom instruction by ensuring the following:

- The content of the training is carefully aligned with the mission, objectives, and annual plan of the school.
- The teachers and principals are involved in the design, implementation, and evaluation of the training.
- The standards for training and recruiting are benchmarked against best practice.
- The school has a system in place to recognize the improved results teachers get with their students.

Achieving Quality Instruction

Instruction can become a personal issue when it shouldn't. Richard Elmore's (2001) research has revealed that during early site-based management experiments in schools, "school teams would do virtually anything to avoid confronting instructional issues, because teaching practice is regarded as a matter of individual teachers' taste and preference rather than a matter for serious inquiry and discussion and common expectations" (p. 163). To improve instruction, however, teacher leaders and administrators must encourage and model openness to new ideas and objective data-based decision making about how to teach better.

In his study of the effects of elementary school reform, Don Moore (2001) found that Chicago teachers who worked in schools that experienced a substantial improvement in student reading scores between 1990 and 1997 reported a significantly higher staff priority on student learning.

What works? Interactive instruction, less didactic instruction, and less time on review. The research in Chicago elementary schools by Smith, Lee, and Newmann (2001) shows that high levels of interactive instruction added 5% to the average 1-year gain on the Iowa Test of Basic Skills reading and math tests. High levels of didactic instruction reduced those scores by 4%. Didactic instruction includes teachers lecturing students or demonstrating to them, posing questions that ask for single short answers, and assessing students on the correctness of answers. Extensive review of material already covered reduced scores by another 4%. Smith and colleagues (2001) conclude that "while these one-year changes may seem small, the effect can accumulate over many grades: When looked at over the eight years of elementary school, the total impact on learning can be substantial" (2001, p. 24).

Quality assessment goes hand in hand with quality instruction. We can't accurately measure progress through test score results if those results themselves are suspect, and we can't expect teachers to use innovative new teaching methods if they constantly feel pressured to teach to the test. Because teachers often lead students in drill-and-review exercises that are mere gestures at test preparation, rather than engaging them in interactive activities that are challenging and authentically intellectual, Hanson (2001) says, standardized tests not only provide inaccurate measurement but also encourage poor instruction. He recommends that districts such as Chicago put into place multiple local measures to assess school and student progress and use standardized tests as only one part of a multimethod assessment system.

In Chicago, the investments needed to improve teachers—and therefore improve instruction—are not being made, according to Melissa Roderick, University of Chicago professor. She also points out that "high-stakes accountability, without substantial investments in improving instructional capacity, could not have changed how teachers engaged students in learning. . . . The most significant instructional trend in the third grade was a substantial increase in the numbers of teachers preparing students to take standardized tests" (Roderick, Tepper Jacob, & Stone, 2003, p. 138).

Researcher Karen Hawley Miles in a 2002 study found that Chicago's instructional approach suffered from a distinct lack of coherence:

- "Chicago public schools lack standards for instructional quality, which hinders efforts to target support, measure progress, and create accountability."
- "Spending on professional development for schools is not integrated into a comprehensive strategy for improving instruction."
- "CPS functions without line accountability for implementing coherent school improvement programs and improving the quality of instruction." (Miles, Hornbeck, & Fermanich, 2002, p. 3).

Teacher Professional Development

In the teacher focus group conducted by the University of Illinois at Chicago, participants said innovative professional development is one key to improving skills. (See Simmons, 2001c, plus Linda Darling-Hammond's and Charlotte Danielson's essays in Chapter 7.)

A Consortium on Chicago School Research report found that high-quality professional development results in improved student learning (Smylie, Allensworth, Grenberg, Harris, & Luppescu, 2001). The Consortium also, however, found that 75% of the training in Chicago was ineffective:

- Only about 25% of teachers experience high-quality professional development that, among other things, is experiential; engages teachers in instruction, assessment, and observation; is grounded in teachers' own questions and experimentation; is collaborative; is connected to teachers' actual classroom activities with relevance to subject matter and teaching methods; and is sustained and supported by follow-up activities.
- About 50% of teachers experience moderate-quality professional training that includes some effective elements but also may lack essential elements such as adequate follow-up or time for teachers to apply what they learn in their own classrooms.
- About 25% of teachers report low-quality professional development experiences.

The study recommended that Chicago do the following:

- Improve both the quality and content of professional development programs. Simply boosting teacher participation is insufficient.
- Pay attention to who provides professional development and how. Combinations of activities that are school-based and that involve teacher networks with external professional groups provide particularly high-quality professional development.
- Impose mandatory professional development, if necessary, to "jump-start" classroom improvement, but use caution to ensure that mandatory participation doesn't prompt teacher resistance.
- Develop school-level supports for professional development, such as adequate time and principal instructional leadership.
- Provide adequate financial and political resources, inject a sense of urgency, and link training to school-level, systemwide goals for improvement (Smylie et al., 2001).

- Follow clear standards for high-quality professional development that have been developed over the past decade and carry them out districtwide (Miles et al., 2002).

The recommendation above to "impose mandatory professional development" may not be a best practice. One needs to remember that you can "lead a horse to water but you can't make it drink." Also, one teacher in a workshop who does not want to be there can negatively affect the experience for everyone else.

4. INVOLVE PARENTS AND MAKE FUNDING ADEQUATE AND EQUITABLE

Parents and money make a big difference in closing the achievement gap. Parents are the most wasted resource in most schools. For decades the research has been consistent: Parents account for up to 50% of a student's achievement, as measured by standardized tests.

To do their best, students need textbooks, well-trained and experienced teachers and principals, libraries, science labs, and much more that only adequate funding can buy. Only adequate and equitable funding across and within schools can assure this result.

Lessons on Parental Support and Adequate and Equitable Funding from High-Performing Organizations

The experience of high-performing organizations suggests several principles for building effective ways for parents to support learning and to assure that schools get the adequate and equitable financial support they need.

To ensure parental support, remember the following:

- All employees need to understand that parents are customers of the school system. Their tax dollars help to pay teachers' salaries.
- Parents need to be treated as customers are treated by the finest companies in the country.
- The leadership of the school district and the individual schools need to regularly assess the needs of the parents to support their children's learning and determine how well their needs are being met.
- Parents are also partners with the teachers in establishing the best conditions for their children to learn. They need to be treated as full partners.

To ensure adequate and equitable funding support, consider these principles:

- Schools within a district and across districts in a state must have equal access to funds.
- To have a good chance of all schools reaching high performance, the children in that district need as much funding as children in other districts.
- When people are treated unfairly, their motivation to succeed often suffers.

Parent Engagement

Despite the fact that, for decades, research and common sense have shown how important parents are in improving student performance in school (what parents do at home accounts for half of the score on the typical standardized test) (Darling-Hammond, 1997; Ferguson, 1991), in city after city, little is done to tap the single most underutilized asset for school improvement that the school district has: its parents. Teachers and principals in some Chicago schools have little respect for parents, often view them as the problem, and rarely are trained to work with urban parents.

In the average Chicago elementary school, only 7% of families participate in school activities. But when networks of neighborhood schools offer families—even in the city's poorest neighborhoods—the chance to learn how to help their children to read and do math, or help to select their children's friends, as many as 40% of those families have gotten involved and the results improve (Pilsen Education Network, 2004).

Because they hold a majority on their LSCs, parents have an added incentive to help other parents get information and training so as to be better informed about schools and learning. Unfortunately, some central office staff are not sure they want parents better informed or trained because then they learn to stand up for themselves and become a threat to the status quo. And little has been done to identify and scale-up best practice regarding parent engagement programs, let alone continually benchmarking them against the best in the country. (For more details, see Gail Goldberger's essay "Improving Parent Engagement" in Chapter 8.)

More Adequate and Equitable Funding

More adequate and equitable funding is central to assisting schools in Chicago and across the nation to close the achievement gap. Schools in wealthy

Chicago suburbs like Lake Forest and Winnetka spend up to $3 for every $1 the Chicago school system spends, buying better teachers, building newer schools, and purchasing more books—and winding up with better scores on the same tests that Chicago students take.

Before the school reform laws, we couldn't have said that equitable funding was a good idea for Chicago, because there was little assurance that significant new funding would have been wisely spent. Now most LSCs and principals, plus the Chicago Public Schools leadership, have a better idea of how to maximize the use of new resources. For specific strategies to equalize school funding, see Allan Odden's essay "Education Reform and School Finance" in Chapter 8.

Superintendents are cutting costs by devising new ways to manage resources as well. More money is controlled by the schools themselves. Outdated ways of doing business are being replaced by new methods.

REFERENCES

Barton, P. E. (2001). *Raising achievement and reducing gaps.* Washington, DC: National Education Goals Panel.

Bensman, D. (2000). *Central Park East and its graduates: "Learning by heart."* New York: Teachers College Press.

Bryk, A. S., & Schneider, B. (2002). *Trust in schools: A core resource for improvement.* New York: Russell Sage Foundation.

Cuban, L., & Tyack, D. (1995). *Tinkering toward utopia: A century of public school reform.* Cambridge, MA: Harvard University Press.

Darling-Hammond, L. (1997). *Doing what matters most: Investing in quality teaching.* New York: National Commission on Teaching and America's Future, Teachers College, Columbia University.

Elkind, D. (1987). *Miseducation: Preschoolers at risk.* New York: Knopf.

Elmore, R. (2001). Large-scale improvement in urban public school systems. In J. Simmons et al., *School reform in Chicago: Lessons and opportunities* (pp. 159–168). Chicago: Chicago Community Trust.

Ferguson, R. F. (1991). Paying for pursuing education. *Harvard Journal on Legislation, 28,* 465–498.

Fine, M. (2001). Small schools: Going to scale or going to jail? In J. Simmons et al., *School reform in Chicago: Lessons and opportunities* (pp. 245–260). Chicago: Chicago Community Trust.

Fullan, M. (2001). Whole school reform: Problems and promises. In J. Simmons et al., *School reform in Chicago: Lessons and opportunities* (pp. 261–270). Chicago: Chicago Community Trust.

Hanson, M. R. (2001). High-stakes testing. In J. Simmons et al., *School reform in Chicago: Lessons and opportunities* (pp. 55–58). Chicago: Chicago Community Trust.

Haycock, K., Jerald, C., & Huang, S. (2001). *Closing the gap: Done in a decade.* Washington, DC: Education Trust.

Lawler, E. E. (1996). *From the ground up: Six principles for building the new logic corporation.* San Francisco: Jossey-Bass.

Lawler, E. E., Mohrman, S. A., & Benson, G. (2001). *Organizing for high performance: The CEO report,* San Francisco: Jossey-Bass.

Lawler, E. E., Mohrman, S. A., & Ledford, G. E. (1995). *Creating high performance organizations: Employee involvement and total quality management.* San Francisco: Jossey-Bass.

Letts, C. W., Ryan, W. P., & Grossman, A. (1999). *High performance nonprofit organizations.* New York: Wiley.

Meier, D. (1995). *The power of their ideas: Lessons for America from a small school in Harlem.* Boston: Beacon Press.

Meier, D. (2002). *In schools we trust: Creating communities of learning in an era of testing and standardization.* Boston: Beacon.

Miles, K. H., Hornbeck, M., & Fermanich, M. (2002). *Chicago Public Schools Professional Development Project.* Chicago: Chicago Public Education Fund.

Mohrman, S. A., Wohlstetter, P., & Associates. (1994). *School-based management: Organizing for high performance.* San Francisco: Jossey-Bass.

Moore, D. (2001). Effects of elementary school reform. In J. Simmons et al., *School reform in Chicago: Lessons and opportunities* (pp. 49–54). Chicago: Chicago Community Trust.

Passmore, W. (1988). *Designing effective organizations.* New York: Wiley.

Pick, G. (1998, April). Student retention: Trying to succeed where others failed. *Catalyst, 9*(7), 1, 4–8.

Pilsen Education Network. (2004). *Annual report, 2003–2004.* Chicago: Strategic Learning Initiatives.

Richards, C. (2001). Learning from Chicago's results: Thirteen years of reform. In J. Simmons and Others, *School reform in Chicago: Lessons and opportunities* (pp. 1–16). Chicago: Chicago Community Trust.

Roderick, M., Tepper Jacob, R., & Stone, S. (2003). *Ending social promotion: The response of teachers and students.* Chicago: Consortium on Chicago School Research.

Rolling, K. (2001). The Chicago Annenberg challenge. In J. Simmons et al., *School reform in Chicago: Lessons and opportunities* (pp. 59–63). Chicago: Chicago Community Trust.

Ryan, S., Bryk, A. S., Lopez, G., Williams, K. P., Hall, K., & Luppescu, S. (1997). *Charting reform: LSCs—Local leadership at work.* Chicago: Consortium on Chicago School Research.

Sarason, S. B. (1999). *The predictable failure of educational reform: Can we change course before it's too late?* San Francisco: Jossey-Bass.

Schmoker, M. (1999). *Results: The key to continuous improvement* (2nd ed.). Alexandria, VA: Association for Supervision and Curriculum Development.

Simmons, J. (2001a). Voices of Chicago Local School Council members—Designs for change. In J. Simmons et al., *School reform in Chicago: Lessons and opportunities* (pp. 147–158). Chicago: Chicago Community Trust.

Simmons, J. (2001b). Voices of Chicago parents—Parents United for Responsible Education. In J. Simmons et al., *School reform in Chicago: Lessons and opportunities* (pp. 495–500). Chicago: Chicago Community Trust.

Simmons, J. (2001c). Voices of Chicago teachers—College of Education, University of Illinois. In J. Simmons et al., *School reform in Chicago: Lessons and opportunities* (pp. 381–386). Chicago: Chicago Community Trust.

Simmons, J., & Mares, W. (1982). *Working together: Employee participation in action.* New York: Knopf.

Simmons, J., et al. (2001). *School reform in Chicago: Lessons and opportunities.* Chicago: Chicago Community Trust. Available at www.strategiclearninginitiatives.org

Smith, J., Lee, V. E., & Newmann, F. M. (2001). *Instruction and achievement in Chicago elementary schools. A report of the Chicago Annenberg research project.* Chicago: Consortium on Chicago School Research.

Smylie, M. A., Allensworth, E., Grenberg, R. C., Harris, R., & Luppescu, S. (2001). *Teacher professional development in Chicago: Supporting effective practice.* Chicago: Consortium on Chicago School Research.

Strategic Learning Initiatives. (2004). *Results: Networks of neighborhood schools scaling up best practice.* Unpublished manuscript.

Viteritti, J. P. (2001). Governing big-city school systems. In J. Simmons et al., *School reform in Chicago: Lessons and opportunities* (pp. 177–192). Chicago: Chicago Community Trust.

Wohlstetter, P., & Briggs, K. (2001). School based management. In J. Simmons et al., *School reform in Chicago: Lessons and opportunities* (pp. 271–288). Chicago: Chicago Community Trust.

Chapter Four

In the Driver's Seat: Lessons from Big-City Superintendents

In 2001 when this book was begun, four superintendents and their districts seemed to offer important and quite different windows into the potential role of a big-city school district for transforming its results and closing the gap in student achievement. Each of the districts was showing significant promise.

Tom Payzant had a lifetime of teaching and administration, having served as assistant secretary of education in the Clinton administration and assistant superintendent of the San Diego system, when he was appointed Boston's superintendent in 1995. Kaye Stripling in Houston also had a long career in teaching and as a principal when she took over in 2001 from Rod Paige when he was named secretary of education in the Bush administration. Houston's results in student achievement were featured as "the example for the nation" in the No Child Left Behind law, only to be revealed in 2003 as falsified.

Alan Bersin, former superintendent of San Diego Public Schools and new Secretary of Education, State of California, had been a corporate lawyer and United States Attorney for Southern California, and had no leadership experience with urban school systems when he was selected as superintendent in 1998. Arne Duncan in Chicago was almost 20 years younger than the other three when he became superintendent in 2001, after serving as an assistant superintendent for about 5 years under Paul Vallas, the prior superintendent.

Here are some of the lessons they have learned in trying to transform the results in their districts.

"The work begins with a set of values and aspirations that are supported by the community," Bersin says. "These must be communicated and coupled in turn with a plan for implementation that is sound and sequenced. The key is to identify, develop, and nurture leadership as it emerges at school sites and in the central office. This leadership capacity—among administrators, teachers, and parents—is the crucial ingredient in a reform that seeks to leverage instructional improvement into improved student achievement and to do so at scale."

For his part, Payzant says: "You have to have a sense of what all of the pieces are that you would have to make your puzzle complete, recognizing that you won't necessarily be able to put them all in place at the same time and that you need to figure out where the key levers are for the change effort and focus resources and attention there first. But from the get-go have a sense of what the overall package or puzzle is going to look like and that you are at least doing the first outside perimeter of the puzzle. And that it's all about teaching and learning, so that has to drive it. But you can't do the teaching and learning piece without a lot of these operational pieces. It's resource-dependent, but it is amazing how much opportunity there is if you have the will to do it, to reallocate existing resources in a more effective way.

"Also, find out what is already working, and then build on that for two reasons: One, because it sends the message that there are some good things happening—and there always are in any system—and it sends the message that you want to work with people who are engaged in best practice that predates you. And then, secondly, it doesn't send a message that OK, here I'm the savior riding in and my agenda is it."

For Kaye Stripling, the key is in "setting the high expectations for each of the people in your organization so that they understand number one, the expectation you hold for them. And second, to give them the support they need to get the job done. And then to reward them, even if it is a thank you. . . . I think when people like you, they tend to work harder for you. I have this great feeling that the integrity of every individual has to remain intact. I think [the other lesson is] to promote people and to help them feel valued in the organization and that their work is valued and that they are valued as human beings."

For Arne Duncan, the issue is leadership. "One of the constant challenges—I try to push myself in this all the time—is the use of my time. There are so many demands and only so much you can do and really trying to, every day and every week, to map out and focus and spend time on those things that truly helped the school system improve and take us to the next level.

"I think, first and foremost, you have to lead by example. You can't talk about working hard if you don't have a good work ethic. You can't talk about being responsive if you are not responsive yourself. And you can't talk about listening if you don't listen. You can't preach being focused if you don't focus. The best way you can lead is by trying to live by those principles that you honestly believe are really important."

None of the four superintendents believe that their rate of progress is adequate. None of them have closed the gap in student achievement.

Superintendents are responsible for all aspects of the change process, from the most mundane to the most elusive. The two case studies that follow offer close looks at each end of the spectrum—one discusses improvements in business practices, including updating the nuts and bolts of procurement, and the other explores the difficult business of getting a wide constituency to engage in the rough road of change.

CASE STUDY—IMPROVING BUSINESS PRACTICES—SUPERINTENDENTS ALAN BERSIN, TOM PAYZANT, AND KAYE STRIPLING IN SAN DIEGO, BOSTON, AND HOUSTON

When Bersin took over the San Diego schools, "the district's business practices were both anachronistic and inefficient." Such practices included activities like warehousing supplies rather than ordering them over the Internet on an as-needed basis. Bersin predicts that San Diego's business modernization will generate at least $100 million in efficiencies over the next 5 years—money that will be rechanneled into teaching and learning in classrooms.

Bersin hired two retired admirals to tackle the district's central office operations: a former head of naval support operations to oversee business operations and the head of navy construction worldwide to oversee the district's facilities program. Bersin says the district is "attempting a very sophisticated merger of military and educational cultures."

The two cultures have some parallels, Bersin explains: "In the military, when a new officer takes command, that leader is not able typically—as a corporate executive is—to quickly remove people, but rather is required to train and team-build the people in place based on the expectation of high performance and customer service. The same is roughly true in the public education context. The challenge is to work with people and train them so intensively that two results obtain: The large majority of people who are effective public servants actually rise to the occasion while those who are hiding out from real productivity leave the system. But those results are more a function of the team that is created than they are of dictates from the top."

In Boston, Payzant wants to expand the district's fee-for-service program. The idea is to grant the schools the same flexibility to buy back services from the central office—or go elsewhere if the central office can't meet their needs, forcing the system to become more efficient and competitive in the process. The program is currently used with the pilot schools (essentially in-district charter schools) and may be expanded to include the system's 26 Effective Practice schools (so designated for having raised student test scores and successfully implemented the district's improvement plans).

Payzant has also overhauled human resources at the central office—moving up deadlines to get hires in place quicker to better serve schools and giving principals more hiring freedom—though he says there's still much to be done. "It was a paper-and-pencil operation," he says. The human resources function is critical and has a direct impact on what happens in the classroom "because 80% of your school budget is for people. If you don't recruit and select the best people, efforts to improve all schools will be very hard to pull off."

Houston has outsourced many of the central office's management functions: Service Master runs maintenance operations and Aramark has taken over food service, for example. Much of the district's technology needs are outsourced. The district's print shop is based on a fee-for-service model. Stripling would like to see other areas, such as professional development, follow suit.

Stripling says Houston's central office has undergone an evolution in hiring practices. The "old" idea was that you must always promote from within the system, so someone from the educator ranks would be bumped up to administration. Now, Stripling says she feels free to go outside the system to get specialists who understand management issues. "For instance, for as long as I can remember, we have had textbook problems. And everyone felt like the textbook problem was pretty much like world hunger—we didn't know if it would ever be solved. So I went out and hired what I call the Textbook Czar, somebody who understood warehousing, someone who didn't know anything about textbooks, but who understood how to distribute, how to manage a distribution process. This is the first year that I can remember that I think we are going to have all the textbooks in all the children's hands on the first day of school. And this sounds like a small feat, but with 210,000-plus kids, that's a biggie."

For a look at a system where 92% of the district dollars are controlled by the schools—schools "buy" services from the central office in a "cost recovery" model, which means that the central office only produces what the schools actually want—see the essay by John Simmons and Judy Karasik in Chapter 6.

CASE STUDY—MANAGING RESISTANCE TO CHANGE—FORMER SUPERINTENDENT ALAN BERSIN, SAN DIEGO

With the job of managing all the pieces of change comes an additional task: managing resistance to change.

In San Diego, former Superintendent Alan Bersin instituted the Blueprint for Student Success, outlining a reform plan that relies on intensive professional development of teachers and principals, including peer coaches, and zeros in on literacy and math instruction with extended study blocks. Bersin reorganized the central office so that all things instructional are housed in the Institute for Learning, headed by Anthony Alvarado, the acclaimed former District Two superintendent in New York City. During his appointment, Bersin enjoyed broad political support, particularly from the San Diego business and civic communities, as well as significant support nationally from foundations and institutions of higher education. But he faced a divided school board and rocky relations with the teachers union. Test scores released in 2004 showed a steady rise in the percentage of elementary students performing at or above grade level in math and reading. There was little progress for high schools except for High Tech High, which has become a national model for high school redesign under the leadership of Larry Rosenstock.

The local teachers union criticized Bersin and his team for discounting teachers' concerns over some of the reform changes. Bersin says, "There is an emotional component that will spark strong reaction as it creates personal anxiety and insecurity. . . . Obviously it is always preferable to proceed by agreement and consensus. The dilemma in the urban public education context is that the magnitude of change required, if all children are to be given an ample opportunity to succeed, means that consensus, particularly at the outset, cannot regularly be reached. To the contrary, many of us adults must be taken out of the comfort zones with which we are deeply familiar and to which we are even more deeply attached. In those circumstances, if agreement and consensus remain the overriding values, the necessary result will be a watered-down change that cannot, over time, produce significant capacity for continuous improvement in student achievement.

"We are dealing with a mountain of past practice and received wisdom on the subject that has been in place for generations. Ways of seeing and methods of proceeding tend to be congealed through a series of financial allocations and corresponding political arrangements that produce an enormous inertia in support of the status quo. For this reason, the existing state of affairs is exceedingly difficult to change. In addition, the culture—particularly where "collaboration" has come to be viewed as conveying to every stakeholder a veto over any change—contributes to this tendency toward paralysis."

Despite all the headlines on school reform, the former San Diego school chief thinks the public still doesn't really understand what standards-based reform means. "The notion of what standards-based reform is, the place that it has in replacing the bell curve in American public education, is something that has not been gotten across, either to the opinion elite or to the parents or voters, and so the entire effort suffers from a lack of support."

"The communication link we need most is at the school site with information and points of view circulating back and forth among site leaders, parents, students, teachers, and the local community on a whole variety of matters. This takes enormous effort, critical insight, and local leadership to build effectively. And as schools are in the process of learning themselves how to implement new instructional strategies, there are significant resource limitations on the time, energy, knowledge and insight that can be invested usefully in disseminating information effectively to parents. . . . Our Parent University, the quarterly Parent Congress involving two parent delegates from each school, and the Parent Academic Liaison teachers devoted full time to parent/teacher communications are helping us to make substantial progress here."

But Bersin and some other outside observers say San Diego is close to a "tipping point," where the tide is shifting toward large numbers of teachers buying into the reform, seeing results and seeing improvements being acknowledged by the broader community (Hess, 2005). "I have been out at two schools a week talking with teachers and meeting with parents, and I think there is a real distinction between those who do not like the personalities involved, including mine, and the positive assessment of the work that is being accomplished here by our teachers and principals. I daresay there is hardly a teacher in San Diego, even among those who have most resisted, who would not concede that the intensive professional development has been beneficial to their teaching practice."

WHAT THEY SHARE: A FINAL OVERVIEW

These school superintendents share many common elements in their strategies. While we have been focusing on their differences, Table 4.1 illustrates the commonality of the components these leaders have used. The components frame the key areas the superintendents considered important during their interviews. They included governance, leadership, teamwork, planning, communication, budgeting, personnel, and accountability. The table does not quantify the results the district leaders have achieved with each component.

What's missing from the strategy that these superintendents are implementing when compared to Figure 1.1? While Boston has started the process, one missing piece is a full partnership with the unions. Corporations with unions have not been able to transform their performance without such partnerships.

Another missing ingredient includes regular feedback on the satisfaction of the stakeholders, parents, teachers, principals, students, and employees. Arne Duncan states above that he wants to "dramatically improve responsiveness [of the central office] and cut down the paperwork." But Chicago doesn't have in place either the system to collect the data on

TABLE 4.1. Strategy for Transformation: Big-City Superintendents

Governance	Houston	Boston	San Diego	Chicago
Give principals the authority and support they need to do their job		x	x	x
Reduce middle management at central office		x		x
Empower everyone to take more responsibility for improving quality of their daily work		x		x
Schools get autonomy either from the beginning or as they improve their results	x	x	x	x
Systemwide leadership team that includes principals	x	x	x	
Develop parents and teachers as full partners		x	x	x
Leadership	**Houston**	**Boston**	**San Diego**	**Chicago**
Develop and communicate a shared vision of the new system and how to get there	x	x	x	x
Focus on improving student achievement	x	x	x	x
Encourage leaders at all levels to set measurable objectives and recognize people when they are achieved	x			
People systemwide learn about change and how to lead and manage it	x		x	x
Create a high-performance culture at central office based on high expectations, honesty, openness, trust, collaboration, and thinking outside the box	x		x	x
Develop alignment of core activities around expectations		x	x	x
Establish new strategy for assessing student learning and design framework for whole-school improvement		x		
Emphasize collaborative learning and teamwork within the schools and across stakeholders in the system		x		x
Schools improve their results by working together in clusters and networks		x		
Sense of urgency	x		x	x
Strategic focus that is sustained	x	x	x	x
Encourage people to talk back to the boss!	x			x
Teamwork	**Houston**	**Boston**	**San Diego**	**Chicago**
Break down isolation among and across teachers, principals, parents, and central office departments	x	x		

Encourage the development of teams at all levels to define and solve problems and make decisions				
Provide the training needed for effective team leaders				x
Create networks for people to learn and share best practice				x
Planning	**Houston**	**Boston**	**San Diego**	**Chicago**
Use data to improve decision making	x	x	x	x
Set a limited number of priorities	x	x	x	x
Encourage innovation and experimentation	x	x	x	x
Communication	**Houston**	**Boston**	**San Diego**	**Chicago**
Develop effective and sustained communication, both within and outside of the district—the right information at the right time to the right people	x	x	x	
Deepen public understanding about school reform		x	x	x
Budget	**Houston**	**Boston**	**San Diego**	**Chicago**
Schools make budget decisions: Houston: 66% now, 80% the goal; and Chicago about 25%	x			x
Schools buy services from either central office or other sources		x		
Bring transparency to the budget process		x		
Generate and direct an increasing percentage of resources to schools and instructional improvement		x	x	x
Personnel	**Houston**	**Boston**	**San Diego**	**Chicago**
Schools hire their own principals				x
Principals get responsibility for hiring and assigning teachers		x		x
Development of new knowledge and skills of teachers and parents	x	x	x	
Outsourcing more central office work, e.g., building maintenance, food services, technology, and printing	x			
Hiring outside the system for management specialists, e.g., purchase of textbooks	x		x	
Accountability	**Houston**	**Boston**	**San Diego**	**Chicago**
Monitoring the shift from compliance to service, e.g., use surveys and committees for regular feedback from schools		x		

Source: Interviews with the Superintendents Tom Payzant (Boston), July 2002; Kaye Stripling (Houston), July 2002; Alan Bersin (San Diego), September 2002; and Arne Duncan (Chicago), June 2003.

responsiveness and paperwork, nor has the CEO communicated that they have a corrective action plan that they are implementing. Until the feedback loops are in place to report on progress, it is difficult to accelerate the pace of district change.

Surveys are a key feature of providing feedback in high-performance systems, like regular surveys of the principals and LSC chairs. Often absent is the process of benchmarking practices against an organization with a best practice, for example, the time a principal needs to hire a teacher.

While teamwork is essential for sharing leadership and thinking outside the box, the skills, training, and the recognition of effective teams and networks are virtually absent in most districts.

Finally, the four districts are missing a process for scaling-up best practice, as will be discussed in Part Three, to close the achievement gap in all district classrooms.

Clearly, every school district leader faces political and organizational realities that he or she must confront in trying to effect systemic change. And each leader brings his or her own personality, unique background, and management style to the task. But, as we've seen, there is striking similarity in many of the strategic elements, listed in Table 4.1, that four of America's top urban superintendents identify as being essential to improving schools. When combined, their strategies offer an important, but incomplete, model for leading the transformation of a district and for beginning to close the gap in student achievement. Next, the four key strategies are discussed in detail by leading authors in the field.

REFERENCE

Hess, F. M. (2005). *The San Diego Review*. Cambridge, MA: Harvard Education Press.

PART TWO

NO TIME TO WASTE: EXPERT STRATEGIES FOR ACCELERATING CHANGE

> "The major challenge for leaders in the 21st century will be how to release the brainpower of the organizations."
> —Warren Bennis, "Becoming a Leader of Leaders," (1996)

The lessons learned in Chicago and other cities have brought public school systems to a point that suggests to us a comprehensive strategic framework for large-scale change. That framework, made up of four core strategies, is not created from abstractions and imposed on the schools from above. It comes directly from the experiences on the ground, from years of working in school systems and large organizations in the private sector, seeing what works and doesn't work. And this framework is shaped by the urgent need to solve the problem of how to successfully scale-up best practice. It articulates what researchers, educators, foundations, community members, parents, and students know best: A handful of high-performing urban schools is not enough.

It's not enough to just take the successful elements of one school and replicate them in another. We need a process for diffusing the innovations and the organizational structure and culture needed to support the process, plus the leadership to design and implement it. The infrastructure has to be built into the school system so that the process of creating success on a large scale is viable, continuously improving, and cost-effective.

As Michael Fullan argues in his Chapter 6 essay:

Schools have been plagued by piecemeal innovations that come and go. . . . In the short run, these models provide focus, well-developed designs, and support for implementation. In many cases there is evidence of a positive impact on student learning. As a whole, they represent some of the best advances in school reform in the past quarter of a century. But adopting models is not the main point. The main point of schoolwide reform is reculturing the professional community at the school level and transforming the infrastructure that supports and directs schools.

When Fullan talks about "reculturing," he is talking about altering a school's capacity for continuous learning, which then leads to continuous improvement. That capacity rests on the "knowledge, skills, and dispositions of teachers as individual staff members" (Elmore, 2000). It also requires elements of organizational development, program coherence, instructional improvement, and quality leadership.

The core strategies that make up our framework for change speak to the elements of capacity that Fullan highlights. They also work toward what he considers the other criterion for successful reform: system sustainability. As he says, "You can't get serious reform without an increase in school capacity, and you can't get an increase in school capacity without transforming the system infrastructure." Reform efforts have to work simultaneously on changing individual schools and on changing the larger social, political, and financial universe in which those schools are situated.

The strategies are designed to function fractal-like at the classroom, school, and system levels. Each strategy carries the underlying principle that the individual school community is the critical unit for improving and then sustaining changes. Each one sends the message that school communities need to carry out coordinated initiatives to improve, receive support in the improvement process, and be held accountable for performance. At the same time, the strategies in the school district infrastructure generate changes that allow for sustained relationships with school partners, participation in networks with other schools, long-term foundation support, decentralization, problem solving and decision making at all levels, and quality professional development.

REFERENCES

Bennis, W. (1996). Becoming a leader of leaders. In R. Gibson (Ed.), *Rethinking the future.* London: Nicholas Brealey.

Elmore, R. (2000). *Building a new structure for school leadership.* Washington, DC: Albert Shanker Institute.

Chapter Five

Create More Effective Leaders at Every Level

As Judy Codding, former high school principal in Scarsdale, New York, and Los Angeles, and CEO of America's Choice, says, "You can't put good leaders in place if the whole system is shoddy. And you can't have a good system without good leadership. An entirely new synergy has to be created from the inside out" (Codding, 2001, p. 334).

With an effective, properly aligned central office, the leadership should develop an infrastructure that supports the work of good leaders. Our experience in Chicago has taught us that when the system supports and extends the effectiveness of leaders, leaders in turn support and extend the effectiveness of the system. The schools that have improved the most through Chicago's years of reform also showed the most effective leadership. In these schools, the principals created a culture of trust among the adults and served as instructional leaders. They set high standards and actively engaged parents in supporting their children's learning. They had a regular presence in their classrooms and gave their teachers the authority and skills to influence decisions about instruction and schoolwide issues. They developed an effective partnership with their Local School Council (Simmons et al., 2001) (See Chapter 1).

An essential step toward creating effective school leaders is identifying a process that engages school leaders in developing and understanding the system's goals and objectives so that the whole system focuses on results and the process for learning how to obtain them. Effective district leaders support the system's participation in this process in order to clarify and align the work at all levels of the organization. Codding writes:

> If we borrow from the experience of high-performing organizations and corporations, there must be goals and objectives in place before anything coher-

ent can happen. Secondarily, and just as important, there must be agreement about goals, objectives, and strategies (methods) for coherent results to be achieved (See her essay with Marc Tucker in this chapter) (2001, p. 333).

When leaders at all levels, including key stakeholders such as the principals and the teachers unions, have ownership of the goals, they take more responsibility for implementation and are more accountable for results, as Adam Urbanski emphasizes in his essay in Chapter 6.

Effective school leaders, then, retain a sharp focus on the goals and objectives laid out by the central office and school councils—primarily instructional excellence—and motivate others to do the same. Codding and Tucker offer several practical suggestions for creating a system that supports effective leaders, including the following:

- Selecting principals based on their ability to lead
- Linking principals' training to the task of providing good instruction and improving student achievement
- Crafting a process for identifying and developing leaders in schools
- Focusing on training principals with their school leadership teams as soon as principals begin at their school. This is a best practice from the private sector and military.

Ultimately, though, such steps will lead to measurable improvement only if the system in which they occur is designed to strengthen the things the leaders bring it. The system built with an architecture that supports achievement of results will encourage leaders to focus on the ways their own skills and knowledge reserves can be put to use in reaching the goals. This allows "hidden" leaders to emerge at all levels of the system. As Richard Elmore writes in Chapter 6:

> Accomplished teachers need to be able to "lead" other teachers in the improvement of their practice and to help create the generation of teacher leaders who will replace them in these leadership roles. Heads of schools need to be leaders of practice themselves, but also practitioners of orchestrating the talents of people who bring knowledge to the improvement process. System-level leaders need to be able to create the pool of talent that will work across schools and to marshal the resources and create the accountability structures that will make the work of these people greater than the sum of their individual efforts.

Continuous school improvement is suffocated when school and district cultures foster dysfunctional values and beliefs such as dishonesty, mistrust, fear, low expectations, isolation, and mediocre performance. Continuous improvement of teaching and learning requires people to take risks by trying new strategies, collaborating with colleagues, and looking critically at student and school data to uncover problems that need to be honestly addressed. This most challenging work will not succeed without eliciting the latent creativity and energy in everyone. None of these activities can be effective without a culture of trust within the school and district. That is the basis for teamwork and scaling up best practice. (For the recent history of continuous improvement, see Imai, 1986.)

Students have their own ideas about improvement, and their ideas and support are a significant lever for school improvement. School leaders should empower students—and give them the skills—to become leaders in school improvement efforts.

RECRUITING AND TRAINING EFFECTIVE SCHOOL LEADERS: WHAT WILL IT TAKE?

JUDY CODDING AND MARC TUCKER

High-performing schools require effective leaders. With so many principals leaving the profession and a serious deficit in the number of educators interested in entering the field, what can districts do to strengthen recruitment and training efforts to ensure every school is led by a top-notch administrator? The author offers strategies for transforming school leadership.

Instruction is the core business of schools. Principals who are expected to keep everyone happy first and foremost must be good politicians. But principals who are expected to raise student achievement first and foremost must master the core business of schooling: instruction. This does not mean knowing more about the subject matter than the teachers who specialize in their subjects. It means knowing how to develop and implement coherent, powerful strategies for mobilizing all the school resources on behalf of an instructional design that will result in top student performance. It means getting the faculty to believe their students can actually perform at high levels and getting the students to believe that the faculty is solidly behind them. And, finally, it means giving the faculty the skills and knowledge they need to do the job, motivating them to give it everything they've got. Until now, principals have not been selected to do that, they have not been trained to do that, they have not been coached to do that—that is not how the job has been defined.

Some 80,000 people serve as public school principals in the United States today. About 15% of these turn over every year. Forty percent of the nation's principals are nearing retirement. The need for school administrators through the year 2005 will increase 10% to 20%. Most principals have advanced degrees. The average annual salary for high school principals is $75,000.

Few Choose to Become Principals

The typical principal is White, male, 50 years old, and earns $60,285 as the leader of a suburban elementary school enrolling 425 students. He supervises 30 professionals and 14 support staff. There is no assistant principal.

Here are two other facts: Among the teachers who take the coursework to become principals, a great many decide to remain teachers. Among those who decide to become school administrators, few choose to become school principals. Let's look beyond the statistics to see why.

Begin with the typical principal described above. The principal in the typical school has 44 people reporting more or less directly to him, a span of control vastly exceeding the norms in any other field. All day long, these people and parents are making a beeline for the principal's office to resolve the problems they face. Principals refer to themselves as "1-minute decision makers" because they have only a minute to decide one issue before they are confronted with the next. Besides having to deal with the stress produced by this situation, the typical principal works an average 60-hour workweek compared to 45 hours for the typical teacher.

You would expect principals to make much more than teachers, but it isn't so. Salaries for public school principals are typically similar to those of teachers at the high end of the scale. Teachers who take on additional responsibilities (such as coaching) often make more than their principal. And there's more. Because most teachers work on a 9-month contract and principals work on a 12-month contract, on an hourly basis, most principals make no more than teachers do.

Why would anyone want a job that requires them to work half again as many hours as the job they have now; be on call 7 days a week, 52 weeks a year; and deal daily with 40 or 50 direct reports—as well as deal with a central office that treats principals as "errand boys" and many others who want immediate redress for their grievances? While these conditions have been true for a long time, what is new, and what is driving good people away from this job in greater numbers than before, is the existence of state accountability systems that carry consequences for school principals. The principal is caught in a vise. Produce results, but you cannot select your staff to help you do so. You cannot fire anyone who is already on your staff. You cannot award or withhold a bonus from anyone. Teacher seniority rights mean that overnight you can lose people and have them replaced by people who couldn't care less about your agenda.

You may have little control over the instructional materials that are used. Someone else controls the training agenda. Someone else controls how all but a small amount of your budget is spent. Someone else controls how federal program money is being spent. Some people who work in your school report directly to people in the central office rather than to you. School site governance policies force you to take direction from people who are not being held accountable for the results.

Despite all this, if your students do not make progress on the state accountability measures, your school likely will be put on a public list of low-performing schools. If performance does not improve, your school could be closed, the faculty disbanded, and you fired. You will be held responsible for the whole mess.

You, in short, have most of the responsibility and little of the authority needed to perform. When you add all this to the conditions that have prevailed all too long, it is a wonder that any competent people are still in the job. The fact is that many such people, far more than we deserve, continue in these positions. But it should not surprise us that fewer and fewer are volunteering to take it on.

We know something now about who is in the job, what the job is like, and why fewer people are going into it. The next question is: How does one get to be a principal?

The Principal Pipeline

Most states require that people hired as principals have at least 3 years of prior service as a teacher. Seventeen states require that the candidate pass an exam to get a state license to be a school administrator. But many of these tests are just basic skills tests, and all of them are quite easy (though not all candidates pass them).

Almost all states require that principals have an advanced degree in educational administration. These programs are usually offered by educational administration departments in university graduate schools.

Recruiting for these programs typically does not involve selection criteria related to the candidate's potential as a school principal. Candidates are not interviewed. There is no effort to identify potential school leaders. The programs offered typically have little or no coherence. Very little is expected of the students in these programs by way of performance that would shed some light on their suitability as school administrators. The program is often based on textbooks taught by people who have never taught or administered in schools or by former school administrators who tell war stories about their experiences. There is very little connection between the curriculum as taught and the actual demands, conditions, and problems of everyday practice.

When principals who are generally regarded as outstanding are asked to identify some connection between their ability and the way they were prepared in graduate school, they are unable to do so, pointing instead to personal characteristics and what they learned on the job and from colleagues.

There are exceptions. But when we looked at these programs closely, we found they were small, they depended on the charisma of their leaders, they had little institutional support, they were poorly funded, and virtually all suffered from lack of investment in the development of powerful curriculum materials. None had all the elements one would look for in a successful program.

The Iron Triangle: Job Training, Job Assignments, and Career Advancement

Virtually everyone we talked with in business and military education told us that they could not conceive of successfully doing their job unless certain systems were present in the place where the people trained, worked, or would work. Among those systems is what we came to call the iron triangle. We will illustrate the point using the military. Military officers, like professionals in a large civilian accounting firms, either move up at a predetermined pace or are expected to leave the service. Progress through the ranks is determined by promotion boards, which decide, on the basis of the written record, whether the officer moves to the next stage of his or her career. That decision is made on the basis of the assignments the individual has had, how he or she has done in those jobs, the training that person has had, and how he or she has done in that training. Promotion to the next step involves both a promotion to a new rank and job and the right to take the next appropriate training program.

In this system, jobs and the training for those jobs go hand in hand. Careers are laid out as a series of progressively demanding assignments. All officers are expected to counsel the officers reporting to them and to participate in their education as coaches. Promotion depends in part on how well one has performed this function. The military does not simply send an individual to a particular school or training program just because he or she wants to go any more than it would give that person an assignment simply because he or she volunteered for it. The qualifications for each job and career are known. One has to have the requisite training and previous assignments to qualify, along with the recommendations of one's superiors and, frequently, the right sort of results on the relevant diagnostic tests. In short, the military sees job training and job assignments as integral and highly related elements in a unified, coherent system of career advancement.

Universities admit individuals to master's business administration programs, but increasingly participation in executive development programs is a function of an application by a firm, not an individual, and the firm sends a team, not just one person, to the training. Moreover, the university's executive education program is increasingly likely to include a major project created by the firm for its employees to do. The project has real commercial value to the firm and is in that sense very real. More and more, both in business schools and—even more so—in corporate training centers, the people functioning as teachers are corporate executives, right alongside the academics.

This happens because the continuing training of leaders and managers, both in the military and in business, is seen as a way to drive military (or corporate) goals and strategy down through the organization. The firm's top executives understand those goals, are in a position to create the culture they want to pervade the organization, and have invented the strategies that will be used to reach the goals.

The Ascendancy of Strategy

Not so long ago, business education was largely a matter of increasing the technical proficiency of managers in the functions and disciplines for which they were responsible. It is still necessary to be in command of those functions and disciplines, but that is no longer the heart of the matter. Everything has come unglued in the business world and, increasingly, in the military world, too. It is no more possible to survive by "keeping school" in the military and business than in the school building itself.

Now the game goes to the executive or field commander. He or she, in a rapidly changing context, must figure out the appropriate goal, think strategically about how to marshal all the functions and disciplines on behalf of the goals, command the moral authority to get everyone behind that strategy, and execute it better than the competition. Strategic thinking to achieve overarching goals is now the heart of the matter.

Our aim when we began our investigation was to find a way to produce principals who could design and lead schools that would produce much better student performance with little cost increases—principals who could lead a revolution, who would be prepared to do far more than just keep school. The goal of modern military and business education seems to be on the same track.

And Now, by Way of Contrast

Everything that we have just described could not stand in sharper contrast to public education. In this field, professional education is virtually severed from career development and career advancement. School districts typically make no organized attempt to identify people with high potential for leadership. They have no defined career ladders for school administrators, no system for forecasting principal vacancies, no way to develop and groom people for leadership positions through a nested series of assignments and training opportunities, no organized development or deployment of coaches, no way to take both training and job performance into account side by side as promotions through the system are made.

There simply is no system. Individual teachers decide to enroll in university-based preparation programs, whether or not their district thinks they have any potential. The university makes no attempt to determine whether the district might be interested in hiring or promoting individuals admitted to the university administration program. The training of school and district administrators might just as well take place in Siberia for all the relationship university programs have to the needs, culture, or goals of the school district in which the school administrators work.

The standards for school administrators are simply lists of tasks. Far from focusing on the single goal of improving student performance, they encompass all the things that define the keeping of school. Nothing in the preparation of school administrators prepares them for strategic leadership. There is no joining of district strategies with the professional education of the people who are expected to carry them out.

And there is another matter. When we talked with people at the National War College and leading U.S. business schools, we learned that they simply could not imagine how they would provide effective training if the organization that employed the people they trained did not have clear goals, good measures of progress toward those goals, and strong incentives for the managers and leaders to meet the goals.

Here, too, the contrast is important. The literature on education reform is littered with the stories of school leaders who naively pursued strategies for improving student performance and came to grief when that goal collided with superiority in the sports arena, or the established privileges of a powerful group in the community, or the needs of some groups of adults employed by the district itself. It is probably unproductive and possibly dishonorable to train someone to succeed at the overt goal when other goals are actually more important to the people in charge. This may be the most important reason to make sure that if the training is going to be designed to focus relentlessly on results, the training should take place in collaboration with employers focused relentlessly on results.

Implications for District Policy

Putting a lot of money on the table for schools, districts, and states to purchase services from schools of education to train school principals will not solve the problem. What will help?

1. *Raise principals' pay.* Low pay is the main reason principals give for opting out of the job. Training principals will not address the problem of people unwilling to do the work because the pay is so low.
2. *Train principals for the job ahead.* We have offered a pointed cri-

tique of existing methods. We believe that funding would be largely wasted if it simply went toward more of the same kind of training by the same institutions. Some thought should be given to ways that legislation might be used to attract new kinds of institutions to the work of training school leaders and to stimulate both for-profit and nonprofit institutions to make major investments in new curricula and technology-based delivery systems. It is important to make sure that new training programs draw on what business and the military have learned about the training of leaders and managers, as well as on the best work in education. It also is important to keep in mind that the majority of people who will be principals 5 years from now are principals today. Whatever effort is made to better train school principals should be directed at both current and prospective principals.

3. *Build a first-class curriculum* to develop first-rate courses for web-based delivery. Graduate schools of business, corporations, and the military are investing millions of dollars per course to develop first-rate courses for web-based delivery for the preparation of leaders and managers. The largest amount we could find being spent on course development for school leaders is $6,000 per course. Philanthropic organizations could make grants for the development of high-quality educational administration courses and courseware to educational institutions and nonprofit organizations singly or in consortia with other organizations, including for-profit organizations.

4. *Build strong human resources systems in our school districts.* As we pointed out, few school districts have modern systems in place for identifying and developing their managers and leaders. Without such systems, training is not likely to make much impact. Funding groups could help districts build modern human resource systems for accurately forecasting requirements; identifying promising candidates; sequencing executive career ladders of progressively greater responsibility; providing training matched to the job requirements; coaching candidates and incumbents through the system; and promoting, evaluating, and retiring incumbents.

No school is any better than its leadership. We all know that, but in recent years we seem to have forgotten. It is now imperative to act on what we know.

DEVELOPING SCHOOL LEADERS:
ISSUES AND IDEAS IN PROFESSIONAL DEVELOPMENT

KENT D. PETERSON AND CAROLYN KELLEY

In their roles as instructional and organizational leaders, principals must be able to develop a mission focused on student learning, to conduct analyses of student performance, to design and implement effective teaching and learning structures, and to reinforce and enhance the professional culture in the school. In short, they need the professional development and ongoing training and resources to make a positive impact on student learning. The authors describe several models of professional development and present strategies for improving the training of our nation's school leaders.

Today's press for educational accountability has fallen squarely on the principal's shoulders, as school success or failure is increasingly being measured as the level or growth of schoolwide performance. This adds to the variety of roles that principals must play, and the knowledge, skills, and competencies they must possess to carry out their multiple roles effectively.

Some of these new roles and pressures include the variety of management roles associated with decentralized management structures, such as resource allocation and reallocation, staffing, and the development and management of school improvement plans. In addition, principals are responsible for managing and leading collaborative planning and decision-making with staff and parents, thus increasing their political and governance responsibilities. Principals also must operate under significant accountability pressures, emphasizing the importance of their skills and abilities as instructional leaders, data managers, and change agents. And finally, principals are expected to work in increasingly diverse, fragmented, and pluralistic communities. This means that they must be able to manage the often-competing interests of many stakeholders.

Instructional leadership was identified in the early effective schools literature as an important skill of school leaders. But a variety of advancements in educational policy (staged licensure, results-based accountability, assessment), cognitive science and pedagogy (instruction designed with content knowledge and theories of learning and cognition in mind), and teacher evaluation (focused on evaluation for ongoing growth and development, even for teachers who are already highly skilled) have significantly raised the bar and heightened the importance of instructional leadership skills.

Skills and Knowledge

Numerous individual researchers and professional associations have attempted to delineate the specific knowledge and skills needed for principals to be effective. These include the following:

- A variety of leadership skills, including instructional, transformational, moral, participative, managerial, and contingent leadership (Leithwood & Duke, 1999)
- The ability to both manage and lead, attending to both structural and cultural features of the organization (Deal & Peterson, 1994)
- The capacity to promote the success of all students by advancing vision, culture, organizational structure and management, connections to the community, ethical practice, and participation in the larger political context (Council of Chief State School Officers, 1996)
- The ability to appropriately and accurately identify critical problems that are often complex, ambiguous, and nonroutine—and resolve them appropriately (Leithwood, Jantzi, & Steinbach, 1999).

These requirements likely play a role in the current shortage of qualified candidates for principal positions. Studies of the shortage suggest that a variety of factors may be at play, including insufficient compensation compared to the levels of responsibility required, the stressful nature of the job, the time commitment required, the challenge of satisfying parents and communities, societal problems that challenge the instructional goals of schools, and testing and accountability pressures (Educational Research Service, 1998).

Some districts, such as Chicago, have addressed the compensation issue by raising principal salaries significantly above teacher salaries, and providing training programs to support principals in the development of skills needed to be effective. A number of states have also adopted licensure standards such as the Interstate School Leadership Licensure Consortium standards for teacher licensure (Council of Chief State School Officers, 1996). These standards were designed to provide a clear, organized set of performance standards that could be used to drive principal preparation, professional development, and licensure.

Professional Development Programs

Professional development programs serve a variety of potential purposes, including the following:

- Developing knowledge and skills unique to the organization, such as district norms, culture, and management strategies and approaches
- Providing ongoing investment in knowledge and skill development for occupations requiring significant time and investment, in conjunction with experience on the job, to achieve high competency levels
- Keeping up with rapidly changing knowledge bases, such as emerging research findings, technological skills, and policies
- Giving principals needed time for personal and professional renewal when their jobs typically allow little time for such reflection

The professional development landscape includes a huge variety of institutional arrangements, program structures, and content. As such, various program structures and strategies serve one or more of these strategic purposes with varying degrees of success.

The variety of possible arrangements includes:

- District-sponsored programs such as the training program in the St. Paul, Minnesota, school district, which provides 3 weeks of off-site training in summer along with additional work during the schoolyear.
- District partnerships such as the Chicago Leadership Academies for Supporting Success in Chicago; the Mayerson Academy in Cincinnati, Ohio; or and the Gheens Leadership Development Center in Louisville, Kentucky.
- Reform model programs such as Accelerated Schools, the Coalition for Essential Schools, the Comer School Development Program, Success for All, and the Modern Red School House. All have training modules designed to develop principals' skills related to the comprehensive school model.
- Government-sponsored programs such as the California School Leaders Academy, the North Carolina Principal's Executive Program, the Kentucky Principal Internship Program, and workshops sponsored by the federal educational laboratories.
- Professional association programs such as the National Association of Secondary School Principals, The American Association of School Administrator, and the National Staff Development Council. These associations hold annual conferences and workshops, provide keynote speakers, and offer opportunities for professional networking.
- University-based, nonprofit, and for-profit providers such as the Vanderbilt International Principals' Institute, the Harvard Princi-

pals' Center Institutes, and the variety of short-term high-profile speaker sessions advertised routinely in publications such as *Education Week*.

Best Practice Models

Best practice in the professional development of principals follows the principles of any good professional development generally. It is relevant to principals' specific knowledge and skill needs; it is grounded in practice; and it provides opportunities for learning, application of new knowledge, reflection, and renewal.

The models described here are not the only effective programs, but they provide well-structured and well-run examples.

New Principal Programs. For new principals, programs such as LAUNCH and LIFT in the Chicago Leadership Academies and that run by the Mayerson Academy with the Cincinnati Schools provide good models. The programs provide opportunities for principals to learn the district's culture, leadership, and management approach. They also provide opportunities to develop support networks with other principals and opportunities for mentorship from experienced principals.

California School Leadership Academy. The California School Leadership Academy serves experienced principals; with three programs that address a variety of leadership needs. The multiyear core program provides aspiring, new, and experienced principals with an opportunity to develop and practice instructional leadership skills. Principals participate in 10 related seminars that require them to practice what they are learning and to work over time on developing and refining their instructional leadership skills. Students develop a portfolio of their vision, organization and leadership, and change activities.

The School Leadership Team program is designed to build the capacity of communities of leaders to lead school restructuring to enhance student learning. Teams participate in a series of seminars over a 2- to 3-year period on the development of vision, curriculum and assessment design, change, shared decision making, and culture.

The Ventures program for experienced principals focuses on transformational leadership. Over a 3-year period, participants document the process of transforming their schools' culture and their own skills as change agents. The three-stage program targets first defining the principals' theories of action and focus-of-change efforts, implementing a transformation strategy, and exhibiting their work.

Chicago Leadership Academies for Supporting Success (CLASS).
Chicago hosts one of the nation's best and most comprehensive sets of principal development programs.

Part of the Chicago Principals and Administrators Association, CLASS provides a set of four programs that serve aspiring, first-year, and experienced principals: the Leadership Academy and Urban Network for Chicago (LAUNCH), Leadership Initiative for Transformation (LIFT), Illinois Administrators' Academy (IAA), and the Chicago Academy for School Leaders (CASL).

The program's content is research-based, aligned to the needs of the Chicago Public Schools, and based on a clearly defined set of seven standards that reflect best practices, with attention to visionary leadership skills and effectiveness in urban settings.

Unlike many programs that string a group of one-shot workshops together, most of the CLASS programs provide in-depth, sequenced training combined with follow-up, practice, and coaching (Peterson and & Associates, 2000, CLASS evaluation report).

While these programs are some of the best around, continued refinement, material development, curriculum mapping and linkage with other programs, and use of newer information technologies could significantly enhance their impact. Programs such as these need to be continuously expanded and refined. New ideas, research, and practical needs should be embedded in existing curricula.

Opportunities and Ideas for Scaling-Up Training Programs

Given the importance of school leaders and the number of new hires, quality leadership training is central to school success. Unfortunately, some obstacles exist. Expansion of these programs to serve larger numbers of principals may be inhibited because of the following situations:

- Some programs are too localized or locally focused to be readily applicable to other settings.
- There is a lack of highly knowledgeable and trained facilitators.
- There is limited linkage and knowledge of professional development from other sources (especially comprehensive school reform design programs).

- There is a lack of clear rewards, incentives, or funding for professional development and learning.

Nonetheless, a number of districts and states have found ways to link with foundations, existing programs, and other agencies to expand leadership training opportunities. (For examples, see Peterson & Kelly, 2001.)

Recommendations for District Policy

This is a time of rich experimentation and opportunity for the improvement of principal professional development. We recommend that urban districts do the following:

1. Expand and enhance the instructional leadership focus of principal training. With the current federal legislation (No Child Left Behind), principals will need new and deeper skills in data-driven decision making, design of curricula and instructional programs, and the professional development of teachers.
2. Investigate the new modules, approaches, and materials of other programs around the country. Adapt or incorporate these into existing programs or use them as enrichment activities.
3. Develop increased use of new information technologies (Internet-based learning, streaming video, videoconferencing, list-serves) into the training programs. Test and evaluate these approaches for efficiencies and impact on learning.
4. Develop an enhanced website for participants and graduates that could, for example, provide extensive links to knowledge, make available reviews of current research and best practice, provide networking and interaction for participants, and offer interviews and presentations on Internet video.
5. Work with the Institute for Educational Leadership (IEL) in making use of their e-Lead website, which describes effective leadership programs.
6. Convene yearly meetings with program leaders, researchers on school leadership, and nationally recognized urban practitioners to examine new and emergent issues and ideas that could be used in improving training's impact.
7. Collaborate on training initiatives with local universities offering educational administration certification programs as well as state administrator associations.
8. Map the leadership training concepts, models, skills, and ideas that principals receive from the multitude of programs available

(certification, association workshops, conferences). All participants in a program could keep a list of the training they had received, which could identify future directions for their professional development.

9. Expand programs to all school leaders (principals, assistant principals, teacher leaders) in a district to increase and deepen leadership skills.

In conclusion, this is an extremely important era in the design of professional development for principals. Many approaches, models, and programs have been designed and implemented. It is incumbent upon all who provide leadership programs to learn from these efforts and to find ways to share, support, and link with others seeking to enhance the quality of school leaders.

SCHOOL DISTRICT LEADERSHIP IN A TIME OF ACCOUNTABILITY

SUSAN MOORE JOHNSON

Collaborative leadership is key to sustained education reform in to-day's education world. By involving personnel at all levels of the education process—from teachers to principals to district administrators—superintendents can ensure a positive learning environment and a climate of collaboration and cooperation. The author emphasizes how vital it is that superintendents take on this role, ensuring accountability for themselves and demanding accountability from others.

Reformers across the nation are searching for a model of effective school district leadership that can ensure that all students achieve academic competence. Those who think of the district as a bureaucratic organization with established lines of authority and accountability see effective leadership as a straightforward problem of management. Superintendents, they say, need only exercise formal authority and allocate resources strategically so that principals and teachers will rely on best practice and achieve established goals. However, for several reasons, such top-down management and control procedures seldom deliver the intended results.

First, public education is difficult to manage because it is fundamentally a decentralized enterprise. Not only are school boards locally elected, school budgets locally funded, and labor contracts locally negotiated, but individual school communities feel entitled to define their own educational priorities. There is only modest agreement from state to state, district to district, and even school to school about what the purposes and goals of public education should be or how best to achieve them.

Second, within schools, decisions about curriculum and instruction are further decentralized because teachers work behind closed doors, deciding for themselves how best to use time, select materials, and organize instruction. Rarely do those in schools look to district, state, or federal officials for direction or guidance. Their attitude toward central office initiatives and edicts is far more likely to be one of superficial compliance or quiet defiance rather than genuine endorsement.

Third, professionals disagree about what constitutes best practice. Even in literacy, the one curriculum area about which there is emerging consensus, experts still disagree about the appropriate balance of phonics and whole language. In mathematics, there is even less accord, with some experts advocating greater attention to problem-solving strategies while others promote teaching students how to apply algorithms. In social studies and literature, too, expert panels disagree heatedly about curricular content and pedagogy. Given such lack of consensus, district administrators find it hard to convince skeptical teachers to adopt ready-made answers to complicated instructional problems.

Three District Leadership Models

One response to such uncertainty and lack of conformity is for the superintendent to adopt a laissez-faire approach to leadership, allowing decentralization to run its course. In the best of circumstances—for example, when a school has agreed-upon goals, knowledgeable teachers, an able principal, involved parents, and plentiful resources—this can lead to rich and challenging learning environments that are responsive to students' varied needs. In the worst of circumstances—for example, when goals are contested, teachers are unprepared, the principal is neglectful, parents are disengaged, and resources are scarce—laissez-faire leadership can lead to barren, regimented, or chaotic instructional experiences for children. While allowing each school to go its own way may work for some schools, it will not likely rebuild failing schools or improve student performance districtwide.

Alternatively, the superintendent can act aggressively to install effective practice in all schools. Responding to intense public scrutiny introduced by the standards and accountability movement, many districts officials have sought to impose curricula and instructional practices that will yield consistent, predictable results. This approach to leadership is far more top-down than bottom-up. However, the superintendent cannot possibly specify everything that teachers and principals must do. Moreover, reliance on top-down leadership fails to generate creative and cooperative initiative in others, which is necessary if all schools are to be infused with the sort of commitment to change that leads to improvement.

There is a third model of leadership, which seems to stand between laissez-faire management and top-down control, but in fact is fundamentally different from both. The model of collaborative leadership is one of reciprocal influence, through which individuals holding different roles collaborate to improve education (Moore-Johnson, 1996). Principals and teachers are not dutifully complying with central office edicts but instead are actively drawing on districtwide visions and plans as they diagnose needs, reinterpret goals, and redesign strategies for use in their own classrooms and schools. The superintendent identifies strengths and shortcomings throughout the district and works with schools to improve their performance. Ultimately, the central office functions as a support center organized to expand, not constrain, the schools' capacity for independent action.

The Challenge of Building School Capacity

At the center of today's accountability movement stands an agreement between government and school officials to trade greater resources and autonomy for improved academic performance and documented results. Implicit in this exchange is the notion that schools fail because educators lack will and commitment. To remedy this seeming lack of effort, superintendents and their staff became more explicit in the late 1990s about their expectations. They sought to align curricula with state frameworks and dictated instructional schedules so that core, tested subjects (typically reading and mathematics) would receive substantial periods of teaching time. They restricted the textbooks teachers could use, called for systematic review of lesson plans, required more frequent class observations, and tested students more often. However, insisting on harder work and inspecting it more closely has not provided the lift that public education needs. Teachers and principals have not failed to comply. Rather, they lack the skills and knowledge needed to organize their efforts so that all students achieve at high levels.

Building instructional capacity among teachers and principals requires continuous professional learning, and it is well established that the cafeteria model of professional development falls far short of what is needed to meet the complex demands of classrooms and schools. Today, a small number of districts, including San Diego and District 2 in New York City, are demonstrating the positive effects of intensive, classroom-based professional development for teachers. Their organized strategy for providing sustained support by instructional experts has come as a result of a new approach to district management called "distributed leadership," which is rapidly gaining credence and converts in urban districts. [The ideas of "distributed leadership" were initially laid out by James Spillane (Spillane, Halverson, & Diamond, 2001) and subsequently developed by Richard Elmore (1996, 2000) through his research with Anthony Alvarado, superintendent in District 2 of New York City and, more recently, chief academic officer in San Diego.]

In contrast to traditional, top-down management, which assumes that knowledge and expertise reside at the top of the organizational pyramid, distributed leadership features interdependent relationships among various educators at the district, school, and classroom levels. Everyone's responsibilities are clearly specified. The superintendent exercises leadership by focusing all resources on the instructional improvement, ensuring that all decisions follow from the district's instructional priorities, and seeing that teachers and principals can develop the expertise and knowledge they need to achieve those priorities. Overall, these approaches have succeeded in improving student performance, particularly in literacy at the elementary level.

However, while the model of distributed leadership acknowledges the expertise of teachers and principals, it is essentially a structural model that relies on roles, formal relationships, and positional authority to achieve consistent results. The process of scaling up best practice is seen as controllable, predictable, and uncontaminated by politics and culture. In fact, advocates of distributed leadership tend to dismiss the cultural and political sides of district life, holding that practices grounded in tradition, rather than demonstrated best practice, are misguided and that interactions driven by organizational politics are inappropriate or dysfunctional. However, declaring organizational culture and politics counterproductive does not make them irrelevant or impotent. In contrast, the model of collaborative leadership incorporates not only the structural dimensions of good management but also the cultural and political elements of change that are central to effective school improvement.

The School as the Locus of Change and Accountability

Research continues to reveal that school-site success depends on much more than adopting district-recommended programs and practices. Recent reports about school improvement in Chicago (Newmann, Smith, Allensworth, & Bryk, 2001; Bryk, Camburn, & Louis, 1999) are only the latest in a long list of studies demonstrating the importance of a coherent and socially functional school in achieving student results.

The successful school organization does not simply replicate the district's model of an effective school but is itself organic, dynamic, and independent. It has its own distinct culture and political realities. The school adopts and adapts those practices that prove to be effective in its particular setting with its students. The school's continued well-being depends as much on the independent leadership exercised collaboratively by teachers, the principal, and parents as it does on the adoption of proven practices.

If students are to make steady progress, those in the schools must work together, diagnosing and interpreting their students' needs, adapting the curriculum to address their students' strengths and weaknesses, devising ways to engage parents in their children's learning, sharing responsibility for tracking students' progress across grades and subjects, and knowing how to call on the support of the district office. School districts should be organized to build such capacity for independent action and consistent improvement systemwide.

Recommendations for District Leadership

What, then, does this analysis imply for school district leadership? First, effective leadership should not be a forced choice between centralized control and decentralized empowerment of schools.

Second, the central office should be lean, flexible, and organized to focus the district's resources on school improvement. It is a service center, not a control center. Central office administrative functions that directly support instruction (e.g., finance, human resources, and research) should be assigned to a tier of importance and be judged by the extent to which their activities advance student learning (by providing accurate budget information to schools, recruiting strong teachers to the district, or assisting schools as they interpret test data). Remaining administrative support services, such as building maintenance, transportation, and food services, may be contracted out. A central office should be organized to send clear messages to the schools and the public not only about the district's goals and values but also about the service orientation of the central office staff.

Third, the school remains and should be recognized as the essential unit of change. There is no uniform plan for change that can be applied to all schools. Scaling-up best practice does not mean replicating a plan that proved successful elsewhere. Rather, it means developing the capacity *within* schools for teachers and administrators to adapt promising practices and to draw on the unique features of each school and community in effecting change.

Fourth, the superintendent should be a collaborative leader who recognizes that the district cannot achieve its goals unless teachers and principals have the skills and the authority to identify the needs of their own students and community, devise and test new approaches, and assess their own progress. Superintendents should have a deep and extensive understanding of curriculum, instruction, assessment, and professional development. They must also be versatile managers, insightful analysts of culture, and astute politicians. They must recognize that instructional goals can only be met by a well-run organization that promotes leadership among others and enjoys broad internal and external support.

Barriers and Opportunities

There are several barriers to enacting this approach to collaborative leadership and change. The first involves personnel matters. Superintendents adept at collaboration are uncommon, as are school boards that are ready to hire and support them through the uneven process of improvement. The leadership model of command and control remains the norm for most superintendencies, even though it is less effective than collaborative leadership in effecting school improvement. Because the superintendent inevitably fails to produce the quick and dramatic results promised during the search process, this approach also leads to frequent turnover. By contrast, a superintendent who engages a district in constructive change does so not by providing answers as the educational expert but by participating as an educator among educators—asking good questions, helping to clarify purposes, and drawing out others' perspectives on the work to be done. Programs that train superintendents rarely prepare them for these complex leadership challenges.

Also, central offices are filled with long-term civil servants who lack the instructional expertise and coaching skills needed to develop school-site capacity, yet they remain secure in their positions. Further, principals who have been promoted not for their instructional expertise but for their political connections or reputations as reliable managers seldom have the knowledge and skills to model expert teaching or to recognize and promote the work of master teachers. School district leaders must have and exercise greater discretion in hiring, assigning, and firing personnel so that there is competent support for instructional change in all schools. What they cannot hire, they must develop in a sustained, systemwide program of professional development.

Collective bargaining presents a second set of barriers. Some teacher contracts rely on seniority rather than teaching qualifications to allocate teaching positions. Others inappropriately constrain meeting times for professional development, limit the number of classroom observations, or prescribe a weak or irrelevant evaluation process. However, there are local districts—such as Montgomery County, Cincinnati, Rochester, and others participating in the Teacher Union Reform Network (TURN)—where labor and management are working together to open the way for reform. They can provide models and encouragement for others. (See Adam Urbanski's essay in Chapter 6).

Probably the most challenging barrier, however, is created by the expectations of the public, community officials, and school employees, because these expectations are grounded in years of skepticism and dashed hopes. With any new superintendent, there are inevitably unrealistic demands for rapid change and visible results. City and district officials must continue to emphasize the importance of steady, if measured, progress. Teachers and principals, disillusioned by successive, unrealized agendas for change will not quickly commit to a new approach. Yet superintendents have the opportunity to educate the public about the process of change and prepare staff for the excitement of developing new capacity and commitment.

REFERENCES

Bryk, A., Camburn, E., & Louis, K. S. (1999). The professional communities in Chicago elementary schools: Facilitating factors and organizational consequences. *Educational Administration Quarterly, 35,* 751–781.

Codding, J. (2001). Recruiting and training effective school leaders: What will it take? In J. Simmons et al., *School reform in Chicago: Lessons and opportunities* (pp. 333–342). Chicago: Chicago Community Trust.

Council of Chief State School Officers. (1996). *Interstate school leaders licensure consortium standards for school leaders.* Retrieved April 16, 2001 from http://www.ccsso.org

Deal, T. E., & Peterson, K. D. (1994). *The leadership paradox: Balancing logic and artistry in schools.* San Francisco: Jossey-Bass.

Educational Research Service. (1998). *Is there a shortage of qualified candidates for openings in the principalship? An exploratory study.* Arlington, VA: Educational Research Service.

Elmore, R. (1996). Getting to scale with successful educational practice. In S. H. Fuhrman & J. A. O'Day (Eds.), *Rewards and reform: Creating educational incentives that work* (pp. 294–329). San Francisco: Jossey-Bass.

Elmore, R. (2000). *Building a new structure for school leadership.* Washington, DC: Albert Shanker Institute.

Imai, M. (1986). *Kaizen: The key to Japan's competitive success.* New York: McGraw-Hill.

Leithwood, K., & Duke, D. L. (1999). A century's quest to understand school leadership. In J. Murphy & K. S. Louis (Eds.), *Handbook of research on educational administration* (pp. 45–72). San Francisco: Jossey-Bass.

Leithwood, K., Jantzi, D., & Steinbach, R. (1999). *Changing leadership for changing times.* Philadelphia: Open University Press.

Moore Johnson, S. (1996). *Leading to change: The challenge of the new superintendency.* San Francisco: Jossey-Bass.

Newmann, F. M., Smith, B., Allensworth, E., & Bryk, A. S. (2001, Winter). Instructional program coherence: What it is and why it should guide school improvement. *Educational Evaluation and Policy Analysis, 23*(4), 297–321.

Peterson, K., & Associates. (2000). The CLASS programs of Chicago: A critical review and recommendations. Unpublished manuscript.

Peterson, K. D., & Kelley, C. (2001). Developing school leaders: Issues and ideas in professional development. In J. Simmons et al., *School reform in Chicago: Lessons and opportunities* (pp. 343–356). Chicago: Chicago Community Trust.

Simmons, J., et al. (2001). *School reform in Chicago: Lessons and opportunities.* Chicago: Chicago Community Trust.

Spillane, J. P., Halverson, R., & Diamond, J. B. (2001, April). Investigating school leadership practice: A distributed perspective. *Educational Researcher, 30*(3), 23–28.

Chapter Six

Transform the Structure and Culture of the System

In Chicago we have learned that building trust is a major driver to re-culture a school and improve results at the school level (Bryk & Schneider, 2002).

Viteritti (2001) has argued that a school governance system based on a balance between local control at the school level and accountability to a central authority may well be the model of the future for urban schooling. But as we have seen in Chicago, that model can be weakened if there is a power struggle between local control groups (such as Local School Councils) and the central office. One of the most fundamental strategies for scaling-up improvement in a large urban system, then, must involve redesigning the relationship among the central office, the unions, and the other system elements. That means reconsidering the central office's mission, structure, policies, and practices so that it operates harmoniously within the whole system, not as a counterproductive force, and ensuring that it provides the resources schools need, including quality assistance.

Because research shows that children learn more when decision-making power is located at the individual school (Moore, 2001; Wohlstetter & Briggs, 2001), the central office should focus on holding schools accountable for their decisions and providing the support they need while acknowledging the division of authority between the central office and individual schools (Hallett, 1995; Viteritti, 2001).

Two other key steps help redefine the mission of the central office and, subsequently, of the entire district's education philosophy. One strategy is an increased focus on early education readiness. Step one is improving children's readiness to learn from birth to age 5 and focusing additional and higher-quality resources on prekindergarten through third grade—especially in underperforming schools. This intervention provides cities with the highest rate of return on education investment.

Step two is transforming the typical high school experience for all students, not just in selective-admission schools. We must ensure that students have a link to higher education, good jobs, and effective citizenship by redesigning all underperforming high schools at the same time.

Undertaking large-scale school improvement requires that educators—whether at the school or district or state level—not only ask the hard questions but also be willing to take the risks necessary to ensure a strong, effective system. The following essays from leading school reform experts address the importance of looking at districts as systems and changing the culture, vision, and workings of those systems. These experts provide insight into the challenges and successes of some of the largest school systems and, in doing so, provide us with lessons about how to move forward.

LARGE-SCALE IMPROVEMENT IN URBAN PUBLIC SCHOOL SYSTEMS: THE NEXT GENERATION OF REFORM

RICHARD F. ELMORE

Creating a public school system focused on learning and improvement requires replacing the most fundamental structures and cultural norms of the existing structure and reforming accountability systems, districtwide improvement strategies, social networks, and the definition of leadership. The author describes how districts can approach this seemingly daunting challenge.

The typical urban school is a composite of "programs" addressed to the special needs of groups of children—remedial, special, bilingual, gifted, and so on—as if the categorization of children were an adequate acknowledgment of society's responsibility to these children. Each category of child, of course, comes with its own funding sources and its own set of professionals whose identity is defined by the category of child they serve. Each category of child has a corresponding set of central office administrators whose job it is to advocate for the interests of teachers and children in that category and an external constituency of professionals and parents dedicated to preserving the identity of these children in the school and system.

Urban schools also display the residue of previous state and local administrative "reforms"—school-site councils from past periods of "decentralization," detailed manuals from central administrative offices providing guidance for responding to problems that no longer exist (or that exist in a dramatically different form), curriculum guides that sit on shelves in mute testimony to some ambitious past assistant superintendent (now, more likely than not, a superintendent in some other district), teacher committees whose origin is in the language of some past collective bargaining contract, and so on. Principals of these schools gain and hold their positions by learning how to appease the multiple constituencies created by these structures and how to protect teachers from the incoherence they create. This problem of incoherence in the organization of schools is compounded by the fact that the policy environment around schools typically changes with changes in local leadership and shifts in state policy every 18 months to 3 years. Hence, the people who work in schools are given different signals—often fundamentally different— about what is expected of them before they have had time to respond to the last set of signals. The depth and extensiveness of this cyclical shift in policy is well documented (Hess, 1999; see also Lezotte & Peppel, 1999). It is a system designed to fail.

Reform in American public schools, especially urban schools, has historically made schools more complex, less understandable, less stable, more fragmented, less personal, more politically charged places for children and adults to live and work in. Would anyone willingly create such a structure from scratch? Almost certainly not. Such mindless incoherence arises only from the accretion of small strokes on a large canvas with no overall sense of design or coherence of expression.

This culture of school reform has spawned its own pantheon of countercultural heroes—the Grant Wiggins, Ted and Nancy Sizers, Debbie Meiers, and Dennis Litkys—whose reputations have been made by wrenching coherent and caring educational communities out of the chaos and incoherence of the existing institutional structure. That these heroes are countercultural, however, says it all. They exist because they exploit the pathologies in the larger system, *not* because the larger system learns from them how to fix itself. In fact, such heroes may be important to the continued existence of the pathologies of the larger system, siphoning off the system's most active critics and placing them in settings where they can be happy in their own practice and inveigh harmlessly against the system from which they have escaped. Meanwhile, the typical child in the typical school—especially the poor child of color in the urban school—lives in an educational environment of deep and pathological incoherence and ineffectiveness.

Principles of Action: Accountability, Instruction, Improvement

Much of the current debate about school reform is an attempt to expose and rectify this pathology. Whatever one might think about the idea of standards- and performance-based accountability for schools—and there is much to be critical of—this idea is countercultural. It says that schools and the people who work in them should measure their success against demonstrable evidence of what students have learned and that it is reasonable to expect *all* students to learn at much higher levels than those at which they are currently learning. It further says that giving schools clear targets, in the form of measurable student performance goals, with consequences for adults and children, will focus schools' attention on improving teaching and learning.

Seen against the background of incoherence and muddiness in the existing structure of schools, these themes look stark, simple, and appealing. Performance-based accountability carries its own kind of complexity, however, and herein lies the danger—that reforms that are meant to simplify and focus will, in the end, be consumed by the complexity and incoherence of the existing structure or simply add to the pathologies of the existing structure. It is this issue of breaking the existing pattern of school reform and school culture that I address here. I will presume to state a few principles that, I think, push against the existing culture of incoherence in schooling and that can be used to design school reform strategies that break the previous pattern.

Principle 1: Internal Accountability Precedes External Accountability. In our research on accountability, we have discovered a fairly powerful and robust principle, which is that schools are unlikely to successfully respond to any external demands for demonstrable student performance unless they have their own internal environment for holding people accountable (see Lezotte & Peppel, 1999). For the most part, performance-based accountability systems have what I would call a "black box" approach to schools. States and localities set performance targets for students and schools, they administer assessments (of varying utility and quality), they collect and publish data by school, they often administer rewards and sanctions based on school performance, they sometimes provide assistance to schools that are failing to meet performance targets, and they often threaten to close down or reconstitute failing schools. The part of the accountability model that pertains to what schools are actually supposed to do in order to improve their performance is invariably left unspecified in a box labeled "and then a miracle happens."

This unwillingness of policymakers to get involved in what schools are actually supposed to do to improve their performance is partly—wisely—the result of their recognition that they are institutionally incompetent to make detailed instructional decisions and partly—less wisely—the result of the assumption that improving instruction can't be all that difficult anyway. The result of this avoidance of the black box, however, is that some schools figure out how to respond to the policy and others don't. The schools that figure it out are, of course, disproportionately those with the fewest students at risk; those that don't figure it out are, of course, disproportionately those with the largest populations of at-risk students. So a policy designed to equalize opportunity for high-quality educational experience ends up, in all probability, increasing the distance between the highest-capacity, highest performing schools and the lowest capacity, lowest-performing schools.

Internal accountability, in our view, consists of clear expectations about what constitutes high quality instruction—classroom by classroom, subject by subject, grade by grade—and a reasonable system for getting teachers engaged in learning how to meet those expectations, as well as a system for monitoring whether teachers are actually meeting those expectations. This conclusion is consistent with research on effective schools dating from the 1970s through the present. What is different about our work is its connection to external accountability. At least in our initial research, we found that it is much more important that a school have a well-articulated internal accountability system than that it be tightly aligned with external requirements. Strong organizations seem to do well whether or not they are tightly aligned with the external systems in which they work.

This principle suggests that any attempt to reverse the pattern of previous school reform efforts must start *within* schools and work outward, rather than assuming that external pressure on schools will cause a miracle to happen in previously low-performing schools. The miracles, if they happen at all, happen disproportionately in the schools that least need them. The work that's required to construct an internal accountability system is literally the work of getting people to agree on the specifics of instructional practice, to focus on improving common content areas, to develop clear expectations for one another (teachers for teachers, teachers for students, administrators for teachers, etc.), and to agree to have their work directly inspected. These practices are at odds with the existing culture of most schools, and the work of getting them in place requires skilled leaders and external facilitators. If this capacity doesn't exist, internal accountability won't happen.

Principle 2: It's About Instruction. This principle follows from the first. Internal accountability has to be primarily *about* instructional practice, not, as in past school reform efforts, about such things as the color of the gym mats, the decorum of students in the hallways when they are going to lunch, or the composition and rules of the school-site council.

Internal norms and expectations have a tendency to drift away from instructional practice to factors unrelated to the classroom—and therefore outside of the traditional zone of teacher autonomy. The culture of schools is based on the myth of teacher autonomy, which in turn is based on the hugely destructive belief that good teaching is a result of the personal qualities and traits of individuals rather than their demonstrable knowledge and skill in content and pedagogy (Elmore, 2000).

Site-based management experiments in the 1980s and 1990s demonstrate this tendency clearly—school teams would do virtually anything to avoid confronting instructional issues because teaching practice is regarded as a matter of individual teachers' taste and preference rather than a matter for serious inquiry and discussion and common expectations. The existing structure is predicated on turning instructional decisions over to specialists who operate more or less in isolation from one another and who more or less determine their own practices, without any but the most general overall set of expectations or norms.

Principle 3: Teaching Is a Public Profession. Isolation is the enemy of improvement. Improving practice is a collective effort requiring collective work and public disclosure. Learning—for students, teachers, and administrators—is an inherently social activity.

Most weak instruction is the result of weak knowledge and skill on the part of teachers; it is not the result of personal traits or qualities or deliberate choices by teachers to do things they know are ineffective. So the presumption is that teachers, given the opportunity to learn how to practice more effectively, will, over time, take advantage of the opportunity. They will learn, despite the isolationist tendencies of existing organizational and cultural norms, that there is power in collaboration with other professionals around a common task of improvement. But schools will not improve systematically by working within the existing culture of isolation around teaching—there is simply no way to get improvement at scale without confronting isolation.

Principle 4: Don't Bet on a System That Doesn't Have a Strategy. In the old structure of school reform, school systems were simply the organizational accretion of the policies they had earlier implemented. The organizational chart was a geological map of the strata of past reforms, frozen in time, box by box, layer by layer, budget item by budget item. Organizations that take this form are "systems" in name only—that is, they do not represent purposeful expressions of a set of goals, they do not treat structures as instruments for making things happen in the world, they do not behave coherently in response to external pressure or incentives. Performance-based accountability systems presume that systems are, to a large degree, capable of reorienting themselves to become purposeful, deliberate expressions of the aim of improving student learning. Most school systems are light-years away from achieving this form, but many are at the stage of having recognized, in some way, that they have to move in this direction.

School systems that don't have a strategy for improving instruction are unlikely to make any systemic progress toward increased student learning. They are unlikely to make adequate use of funding from government or private philanthropies.

What is a strategy? Briefly, it is a theory of action that states how system resources will be used to affect the internal accountability of schools, the quality of instructional practice in specific content areas, and the use of new skills and knowledge to improve teaching and learning. If these components are not present and clearly stated, it is unlikely that a system will do much to influence student performance in schools at all. If these components are present, there is no guarantee that the system has chosen the right strategy, but at least there *is* a strategy, one to be revised in light of experience.

Principle 5: Strategy Is About Continuous Learning and Improvement. Underlying old notions of school reform is a fundamental misconception about the nature of organizational improvement—that improvement occurs, essentially, when schools "implement" new practices, structures, or processes, and that when the new idea is fully "implemented" (which it virtually never is, but that's another discussion), the goal of reform is accomplished.

There are at least two fundamental problems with this view of reform: First, the idea that reform is about "implementing" something suggests that good practice can be *installed* when, in fact, as we have seen, it has to be *learned,* and learning is a vastly more complex and continuous process than installation. Second, the idea that the goal is accomplished when the reform is implemented doesn't acknowledge that schools operate in a social environment in which their clientele—students, parents, and community members—is constantly changing. So the demands of good practice are constantly changing.

These misconceptions need to be replaced—institutionally and culturally—by the expectation that schooling is not so much about implementing something as it is about continuous learning and improvement. And improvement here means improvement of everyone in the organization, measured against ever-more-ambitious goals for student learning. Hence, the strategies school systems use—including the investments they make in human skill and knowledge, the ways in which they target their resources around these investments, and the ways in which they define and organize accountability—must be subject to continuous adjustment in response to evidence about the quality of instruction and evidence about the effect of instruction on students' academic performance.

In the literature on management and organizational development, these ideas are captured by the terms *continuous improvement* and double-loop learning (learning in which one develops not only new skills and knowledge but also the capacity to reflect on whether they are appropriate to the goals one is pursuing and whether the goals need to change in light of experience). A system without a strategy is not likely to be an improving system. But a system that is locked into a strategy, without adequate knowledge and feedback about whether it is working and how it needs to be redesigned, is likely to be a system that stalls in the early stages of improvement.

Principle 6: Scale Is the Replication of Shared Norms and Practices Through Social Interaction. The central problem of the old structure is that it was/is constitutionally incapable of capitalizing on its own successes. Every school system, no matter how dismal, has its successes—remarkable people doing remarkable things in isolated settings, working against the grain of the existing structure, often at considerable risk. The problem with large school systems is not that they are incapable of spawning successes—even against their dominant institutional norms—but that they are incompetent and incapable of learning from success in one place and moving it to another.

Most problems of internal accountability and instructional practice are problems of skill and knowledge. The job of administrators in improving systems is to find the sources of the requisite skill and knowledge—either inside or outside the system—and design the processes by which they become the norm for expected behavior in the system at large. One way in which educational organizations are probably different from others in our society is that the knowledge and skills required to make schools more effective rely heavily on *skills of human or social interaction.*

Effective instruction in reading or math, for example, requires grasping the substance and structure of disciplinary knowledge, developing a complex repertoire of skills in understanding students' prerequisite knowledge (the knowledge they bring with them into the classroom), adapting a curriculum to the specific starting place for a specific student, working through the stages of understanding required to reach a higher level of performance, and so on. These skills of human interaction have to be learned through processes of interaction—modeled, observed, critiqued, rehearsed, modeled again, and so on. There is no other way to learn to do this work effectively than by watching it being done by someone who is better at it than you are—and then being watched by someone who can see things in your practice that you can't. Face-to-face relations are the only reliable processes of social replication, and social replication is the only way to achieve any kind of scale (Elmore, 1996).

The implication is that the job of administrators is the continuous development of human talent and the teaching of others to achieve progressively higher levels of skill and knowledge. In any given group of teachers, some will be the teachers of others and some will be the administrators charged with teaching teachers in their schools. In any given group of principals, some will be the teachers of newly recruited principals and the advisors to experienced principals learning new skills. And so on. Creating this capacity to put people together around new skill and knowledge requires the disposition to make hard judgments about who knows what. Experience and expertise are not always highly correlated, especially in systems what have a long record of poor performance; experience is often the cumulative residue of failure.

Principle 7: Leadership Is the Practice of Improvement. Systems in the process of improving generally have strong leaders, and lots of them. Improving systems acknowledge that some people in the organization—or outside—know more than others about how to get the work done effectively; such a philosophy runs heavily against the culture of established public schooling. Improving systems—especially school systems, where the work is very complex and the demands of the work vary a great deal depending on the children and the community a school is serving—have large numbers of people with "local" knowledge (specific knowledge of context) that can be linked to "general" knowledge (knowledge about overall goals and effective practices in other settings).

In other words, there are some people closer to a given problem than others, and these are the individuals who should be responsible for finding solutions to that problem. Accomplished teachers need to be able to "lead" other teachers in the improvement of their practice and to help create the generation of teacher leaders who will replace them in these leadership roles. Heads of schools need to be not only leaders of practice themselves but also practitioners of orchestrating the talents of people who bring knowledge to the improvement process. System-level leaders need to be able to create the pool of talent that will work across schools and to marshal the resources and create the accountability structures that will make the work of these people greater than the sum of their individual efforts. Simple bureaucratic, line-management models of leadership won't work if the task is improvement, not control. Neither will models of leadership work that are based on "experience" or "charisma," without a strong underpinning of the leader's actual knowledge and skill around teaching and learning.

Leadership premised on the large-scale practice of improvement is what James Spillane and his colleagues call "distributed leadership" (Spillane, Halverson, & Diamond, 1999). In this view, leadership functions on the assumption that the skill and knowledge requirements for improvement of instructional practice are acknowledged as the basis for accountability and authority in an organization. Moreover, it assumes that people in various roles are authorized (not "empowered") to lead based on their capacity to produce results and that different leadership roles are knit together around common assumptions about what constitutes high-quality practice and performance. Coherence in improving systems comes from shared norms of practice and accountability for performance rather than from bureaucratic rules and structures.

Conclusion

The disease of the current institutional structure of public education is incoherence. We have gotten to this place through the deliberate accretion of programs and reforms designed to remedy specific problems for specific groups of children. The residue of this approach is an institutional structure in which everyone thinks they are doing good but few, if any, are doing well. The treatment for this pathology is a focus on direct accountability of professionals and the schools they work in for the quality of instructional practice and performance for all children and the construction of deliberate strategies of instructional improvement in schools and school systems. Deliberate improvement requires breaking the norm of privacy of teaching practice and the construction of face-to-face networks of practitioners engaged in the common task of improving instruction, subject to the discipline of measured student performance.

Creating a public school system focused on learning and improvement requires replacing the most fundamental structures and cultural norms of the existing structure—substituting accountability systems based on skill, knowledge, and performance for ones based on bureaucratic process and control; creating and continuously revising a systemwide strategy of improvement that puts the problem of instruction at the center and demands evidence of continuous improvement; focusing on the creation of social networks that bring teacher learning out of the privacy of the classroom into public view; and understanding the definition of leadership as the distributed improvement of practice rather than the exercise of control.

THE SILENCE OF THE SYSTEM:
WHY ORGANIZATIONS CAN'T LEARN

W. Patrick Dolan

Why, time and again, do organizations—including school systems— make the same mistakes? Why can't we get the "reform process" right? The author examines various reform strategies, identifies obstacles to success, and offers a framework for awakening the "silent" system.

Everyone needs a simple key that unlocks the enormous complexity of educational reform that has grown up in the last 5 or so years. We also need some understanding of the system's resistance to or silence about all reform. This resistance originates in a culture of distrust, which often begins with the poor relationships among the major actors in the educational system. Understanding this underlying condition unlocks the door of learning for an organization. It is only with the door unlocked that we can move from individual examples of excellence—a classroom, a school, on a network of schools—to systemic reform.

To sort out the various reform strategies and see their relationships, I use the following three frames:

1. There seems to be a critical *relationship* between the "anchors" in any school system that helps make these complex changes captured by the phrase *higher standards*. These anchors are the board, unions, and management. In addition, parents surely represent a major group with direct and powerful claims on the system from outside. When the relationship of these responsible agents is open and trusting, the work of improvement can proceed.
2. Then there is the work of education itself, the *pedagogy* and *curriculum*. This is really the educational content and the type of engagement and reflection a teacher is able to effect day in and day out.
3. Finally, there is the *culture of measurement* and ongoing improvement that a data-driven system implies. So, the culture of trust, truth telling, and problem solving, surrounding constant measurement for the improvement of teaching and learning, is the goal. Without a strategy for each of these, one is bound to come up short (Dolan, 1994).

If we concentrate on good practice and demanding material, bring effective principals and teachers together with a vision and passion, embrace parents and include them in decision making, we can create exemplary schools that use powerful examples of best practice. We then try to create training centers to offer these practices and use school sites as pilots to show the way. Yet, time and again, nothing moves. In fact, the system sees these pilot schools as a dangerous indictment and does its best to isolate and diminish them. Why?

Or the union and management, after years of conflict, begin to move to a culture of openness and cooperation and life becomes more considerate and respectful. They begin listening to each other's interests, and the community and parents applaud this change and encourage it. Yet the peace never leads to the hard work of redesigning teaching and learning, and this calm leads to another type of stagnation that is friendlier but no more productive: good process with no demanding substance.

Finally, we embrace a Baldrige-like process of rigorous alignment and immersion in data that started in the private sector and is now spreading through schools (Schmoker, 1999). But neither the high-trust culture nor the readiness to embrace best practice is present. Organizational will and courage are lacking. Nothing actually happens to effect higher academic achievement.

Each of these scenarios occurs every day in America, and passionate camps form around each strategy. Yet without all three strategies operating in harmony, we cannot escape the gravitational pull of the old practice, the old culture, and the old system.

The System in Place

Why is it so hard to scale-up best practice from one school to most schools? Maybe it's the nature of schools, somehow, or the folks who choose the profession, who like to work in private. Or maybe the work itself is non-replicable, more like pure art than anything else. Industry has been on a powerful restructuring curve of its own, with some impressive results, so perhaps there are some lessons to be learned there.

Joining me on a panel of experts on organizational change in 1976 was a person from General Motors whose job had been "technology transfer" from the joint GM/Toyota plant in Fremont, California. He told the following story. Some 15 years earlier, GM was struggling with every corporate devil: bad quality, a fast-changing market, bad labor relations, and poor supplier support. He argued that at the same time, GM had, in its own system, two of the best automotive plants in the country—in the world, for that matter. Teams visited the Fremont plant daily from competitors in Japan, Europe, and the United States to see its just-in-time process, teams, and culture of quality and excellence. Meanwhile, the UAW and

GM had created—against a generally lousy corporate environment of distrust—a powerful example of partnership in their then-new Saturn plant in Smyrna, Tennessee. Running seminars for visitors around the world was a full-time job for four union/management leaders.

Everyone came to observe and learn *except* managers from the other GM plants. The corporation finally forced them to visit. The general tone of the GM questions was skeptical, filled with denial, and just as passionately determined to show that all of this was due to special circumstances and hence not transferable anywhere else. Try as he would, no matter what division sent teams, he could not overcome this denial and determination not to learn.

The inability to transfer learning *within* a system is not new, and it is not particular to education. But the phrase *going to scale* has a tendency to frame the direction of the answer incorrectly. It makes us think that somehow it is a question of us convincing others, making a stronger case, broadcasting more powerfully. Or we think those who are not picking up the clues are either thick or ill-willed, since everyone outside the system seems to see the results and pursue the learning.

I argue that the supposed "inability to learn" is actually the system doing something that is ingrained, intelligent in its own terms, and based on sound self-interest as defined by the resident culture. To change the learning ability, one must change the culture of relationships: central office to site, site to site, principal to teacher, teacher to learner, and all of these to parents.

The Deep Culture

Powerful forces flow out of the command-and-control, top-down culture that prevents the system from acknowledging its successes or learning from them. Layers of reporting, decisions made far from the work, distrust of the teachers (and learners, for that matter), and an attitude that the customer/parent is a bother all join to form this culture. As a result, the following behaviors flow:

- The less the central office knows about changes—especially successes at the sites—the better. The central office does not set off to suppress, but it standardizes with a vengeance, all in the name of fairness and equality. If you are a site operating at the edges of policy and standard practice, the last thing you need or want is central office attention. So you learn to keep changes to yourself.
- Union politics compound the issue. The union has an enormous stake in its own "one-size-fits-all" principle, and any exception is

historically seen as weakening the solidarity of the whole. Even if there are exceptions, it is far better to ignore them (whether they work or not) than to disturb the equilibrium.

- Parents, especially empowered ones, feed this "silence-of-the-system" behavior, often without realizing it. When they hear about an effective practice, they naturally demand the same where they are. Sometimes this makes sense, sometimes not. But their reactions strengthen the system's reluctance to talk about specific work, successful or unsuccessful. This culture of power, control, and sameness is frequently attributed to the district's central office alone, but the union and, to some extent, active parents also contribute to its strength and resistance to change.

Motivational Seepage

Finally, there is the silence of those who do the actual work in the schools: teachers and students. Life in an organizational structure of hierarchy and separate, poorly integrated functions creates an alienation that saps power and intelligence from otherwise healthy communities. By the time a child has been in most schools for 4 or 5 years, he or she will have learned that silence and not making waves is the best policy.

We have understood for some time now that to build "accountability systems" that set goals from above, evaluate constantly, give one-way feedback, and keep records of it all sends the message that the work and its quality and productivity are always the responsibility of the organization's hierarchy. So if my work (or learning) is your responsibility, you'd better motivate me and make all the right choices. Good luck.

This denial and displacement of responsibility is profound and all-encompassing. Teenagers have enough energy to constantly prove that the equation is backward in powerful ways. So do unionized employees, when the occasion arises. The message is that those who do the work (learning) are stupid, irresponsible, and can't be trusted. They rise up to state the opposite from time to time, but it is usually discounted by the hierarchy as more proof of irresponsibility and untrustworthiness. Meanwhile, day-to-day, boring, and poor-quality work continues, with the general attitude being that it can't be changed and it's someone else's problem anyway.

So the alienation from the system grows deeper. The relationship that shapes the culture and defines the roles of the players in these systems is based on mutual distrust and fear. To not understand the depth of this displacement, then, leads us to enormous simplification of change strategies. Naively, we trust that good content will pull the system toward excellence. All we have to do is expose the folks to the success and they will embrace it. That's a fallacy. They will not and cannot. They are doing exactly what an intelligent agent would do. They are protecting themselves with the deep knowledge that this work, no matter how wonderful, is not *their* work and that it will be used to damage them, manipulate them, prove somehow they were not intelligent or thoughtful enough to do it without the "authorities."

These issues are brought into focus by a key question: Whom do you work for? For corporations this is a routine question. In education this question is translated into the perspective of the learner: Whom do you learn for? And in a wrong kind of pedagogy—one of control and demand—the unsubtle message is, "You learn for me." It eventually creates powerful resistance. The harder question is how the natural, quite driven little learner of 5 is transformed into the sullen and resistant learner of 12. One can sometimes hear them say in thousands of ways, "I do not learn or live for you." Then prove it.

Strategic Options for Improvement

So the system is deeply divided. Those who do the work are separate from those who set objectives and assign, measure, and constantly "evaluate" the work. The assumption that everyone is ready, willing, and enthusiastic to improve if they are simply exposed to the correct practice and given support and a challenge is nonsense. People in the system (including children by a certain age) trust neither those giving the new direction nor the process by which it is done. In addition, even if these players were willing, the system is locked up in the name of standardization by both the central office and the union. Even when good change seeps out, they cannot and will not own it and celebrate it, for in their minds that would create the conditions of chaos. Now, ask the question again about why these systems won't replicate good practice, known successes, or "take things to scale."

To take this on, the mantra ought to be: The process of change must be as open and authentic as the content improvement we are suggesting. Best practice means changing not only instruction but also mind-sets. Addressing the alienation and beginning to move to a culture of trust and learning have to be as conscious and well designed as the instructional innovation that is the content of the change.

Ideally, a districtwide team of about 20 should be formed with five top managers, five members of the union executive committee, five principals, and five community leaders to listen and learn how the instructional strategies would be presented and implemented. The numbers are not magic, but the intent is to show that three "pathologies" of the system are addressed immediately. The union–management distrust, the inside–outside wariness, and the vertical chain of command's fear of hard information are all gathered together in a "we" that must own a common system. The team's main focus would be overcoming the alienation; keeping all players focused on good practice and school change; and moving their systems quickly toward support and flexibility, away from rigid control and standardization.

This committee has real and important work. It ought to meet regularly, visit schools, and ask questions of an informative and systemic nature: Where could you use more help? What are you learning? How are you measuring what you're trying? What's in your way? They need to find and celebrate sites pushing toward excellence as well as understand what roadblocks those sites encounter. Early on, this team needs someone with experience in organizational development to help them ask systemic questions, lead them into more open truth telling, and constantly reflect with them on how to be more tough-minded about the resistance and its causes.

This team should be known as something like the "District Learning Team." Its role is to steer the learning process of the district—and therefore the schools. It may need to retool a curriculum committee into a "design committee" whose job it is to open all sorts of avenues and access to sources of best practice. It may need to ask a group to look at alignment strategies such as a Baldrige or an ISO 9000 process. But it definitely needs to be the coordinator of the change process itself, so that all this is seen or experienced not as a series of unintegrated activities but rather as a powerful, robust opening of the entire system to a culture of trust, experimentation in teaching and learning, and measurement and realignment of work. This is what the team coordinates and steers. It needs to be felt as a single, focused movement forward. All professional development supports it, and all communication refers to it.

Finally, this work ought to be backed up with good written communication to share what is learned with all the actors, speaking in one voice to the public. It pulls the major stakeholders together, creates a common agenda, and says to everyone that this is *their* work, *their* journey, and *their* responsibility. What this does is rewrite the story of the system into a collaborative one, one about children, teachers, and parents achieving together.

Until the culture is rewritten and retold, a learning system that tries to replicate the success of another can't get a foothold. Each attempt at improvement in the old system exposes me to danger from union and central office alike. And your success indicts me, shows me up, in a culture where that is dangerous to both of us.

The argument here is that there is an intimate connection between a public process of collaboration—involving community, union, and management—*and* the implementation of best practice of teaching and learning for children. An authentic process allows all the actors to overcome the resistance and dedicate themselves to the improvement. A school district can then become a learning system that can and will embrace constant improvement.

"PEOPLE TREAT YOU DIFFERENTLY
IF YOU HAVE MONEY":
SCHOOL-SITE DECISION MAKING IN EDMONTON

JOHN SIMMONS AND JUDY KARASIK

Mike Strembitsky came to the job of superintendent for the Edmonton school district in 1973. He had been a teacher and a principal and believed that the system he had been hired to run worked against school improvement, largely because it failed to trust the front-line people. Strembitsky began a process that gave responsibility and control of funds to principals, starting with seven schools in 1976 and districtwide in 1979. Today 92% of all district funds, excluding bond retirement, are allocated to the schools in lump sums; each school creates its own budget from its total, controlling allocations for instructional, facility, leadership, and technical needs. In an interview with the authors in March 2005, Mike Strembitsky described the system and discussed some of the advantages—and snags—of the Edmonton model.

Pre-Reform Edmonton

Historically, the Edmonton school district was organized, as are most North American districts, on the basis of central authorities making most of the school budget decisions. "When I was in a school, as a teacher, the kids and the community were great, but as a teacher, you ran into something called *The system*," recalled Strembitsky. "You no sooner got to be a school administrator, where you were supposed to be a leader and in charge, but as a principal you could do very little because of *the system*. It was always Us, in the schools, against Them, in the central office. When I was in a school, the things you needed were either free or you couldn't get them. Schools sent in requisitions, and if they were filled, you had no idea what the items cost. Budget was not a school responsibility. Second, if you were turned down, and then you wrote a letter justifying the school's need, your chances of success were better. Failure got rewarded. We had control agents in the district office, and we in the schools were held harmless regarding budgets. There was a very limited framework within which schools could exercise any decision making." When he went to work in the central administration, he saw the operation from a different perspective. No matter how central authorities tried to make something work, the people in the schools had little incentive to do so: "We were so far away from serving a community and its children." Strembitsky was of the community, not a high-flying outsider coming in to do a quick fix and disappear. He, along with a group of determined individuals in leadership positions, knew the system didn't work and was determined to change it.

"By involving the schools in a very real way," he recalled, "we gave them an arena for their creative energies to be exercised."

How the Budgeting Process Works

"The premise behind the approach was that people treat you very differently if you have money," Strembitsky commented. The district calculated allocations—a fair amount to go to each school, based largely on the number of students. It provided the allocations, and the schools made all of the budgeting decisions. People said that this method wouldn't work, that the schools would always try to get more money out of the district. To these people it was as if the central office people were the bankers and the schools were the bank robbers. Strembitsky wanted the bank robbers to become the bank managers.

In the Edmonton model, schools allocate their funds based on the school's needs. They find ways to economize because they make their own choices, their own compromises—because it is "their" money, they find ways to make it go farther.

Reversing where budget choices are made also means that the district will always stay within budget: the choices are made by schools, who know exactly how much they spend on each category, instead of being made at the district level, where amounts for categories were estimated in the hope that they would be spent as budgeted.

Culture Shock and Procurement

To Strembitsky, it is absurd for a large school district to make budget decisions in categories ranging from desks and chairs to salaries. "McDonald's doesn't have a single budget line in headquarters for lettuce. Each franchise figures out how much it needs to spend for lettuce. In Edmonton, one high school needs $10,000 for computers and another one needs $400,000. They should make those decisions to best achieve their results."

Schools buy goods from the central office or from other approved sources (approved so that the schools don't have to vet every vendor). In the early years, this resulted in some culture shock. One central office staff member came to Strembitsky shocked: "I told you this kind of thing would happen! This school has ordered an electric typewriter of the level reserved for the central office! Selectrics are much too expensive for school secretaries!" Strembitsky told them to provide the Selectric—a clear sign that the school valued this particular secretary so much that they were willing to cut back in another area to give her what she wanted and needed.

One school, looking for a paint job, got a bid to do the job as it had always been done: three coats of paint every 17 years. Instead, the school chose a provider outside the system who would paint only one coat, but paint more often, leaving the walls fresher looking. District operations began to realize that they needed to accommodate the needs of the schools and provide the best value for the dollar.

Personnel

When the schools controlled their budgets, they were able to choose their staff. The problem was that they weren't willing to buy what the central office's personnel department was offering. They wanted a say in the selection. The people in personnel reacted as though their candidates were merchandise—and the schools were customers rummaging through the merchandise and messing it up. Then, however, personnel began to ask the schools, "Well, if you don't like the selection, what *would* you buy?" Schools went on recruiting trips, the quality of the pool rose, and schools happily chose teachers available through personnel.

As it turned out, the central office has not withered away. The central office provides more services than before—and now they are providing exactly those goods and services that the schools need, learning from their customers to improve selection and performance. Many of their people are now acting more as consultants: schools that can choose, it turns out, want to make those choices with the benefit of second opinions from experienced people in the central office, many of whom feel more valued as a result.

Schools have created distinctive communities. Some spend funds on purposeful professional development. Others allocate for equipment, libraries, and technology. Teachers self-select, going to the schools that provide more of what they need as individuals.

Impact of Budgeting on Instruction

Under this system, principals have truly become instruction-focused. Once the Edmonton principals controlled the money, they could fix the problems that could be fixed with money—which freed them up to focus on things, most notably instruction, that can't be fixed by money but need to be fixed by principals getting in at the ground level and finding out what's going on in classrooms and supervising instruction.

Paradoxically, when principals didn't have the money, they focused on the money. Once they were given the money, it became a means to an end. "It's what I call a necessary but insufficient condition for achievement," says Strembitsky. "Now they can apply themselves to the issue of instructional quality."

The district tried not to mandate the processes of improved instruction, although it did create mechanisms for sharing effective practices. "We felt that if it doesn't work, we don't need to pass a rule against it," Strembitsky comments. "If it does work, people will copy it. Although what works in one school may not work in another."

How to Get It Started

According to Strembitsky, the best way to get school-site decision making started is to do the following:

- Start with a small-scale project within a district or a state.
- Convene a small group of your own people who are dissatisfied with the present way of operating, people who want change and are willing to work hard to make it happen.
- Find someone who can shepherd you through the necessary changes, including the interface with the existing order of doing things—that existing order being a group who will not take kindly to the proposed changes.
- The goal should be to create something that works in the local culture and local circumstances. Successful experiences from other places are less convincing than a home-grown project that works in the local environment.
- Scale-up from a local success is much more likely to succeed than wholesale implementation from elsewhere.

Though the above strategy holds great promise it is seldom followed. Why?

- People who have contemplated this for a long time, and who are finally ready to make this kind of radical change, often do not want to start small. Once they are convinced, they are so excited that they want to go full-tilt.
- If they start something systemwide, it is highly likely that they will be swamped by a counterwave of resistance. This is virtually guaranteed to result in failure.
- Also, to start something systemwide, they would have to find a very large group of people who can buck the existing culture when that means working harder, working longer hours, and going to

the trouble of learning how to do many things differently; it is hard to find many of these risk takers.

Mike Strembitsky had this advice for leading this process:

- The superintendent should believe that his or her future lies with the people in the front lines.
- The superintendent should be willing to share *all* information publicly—the good, the bad, and the ugly. "I told people that if they didn't have time to share all the information, to follow the principle that the need to share information is inversely proportional to your comfort level in sharing it," says Strembitsky. If it is something that is embarrassing or awkward to share, then you need to share it.
- The superintendent should share information with the board. The more information boards receive, the more those boards will stop micromanaging. "Our board in Edmonton did not approve the allocations, which was unusual; they delegated the creation of the allocations to the district," Strembitsky recalls. "The function they chose for themselves was to be a court of appeal for the allocation system. People would come to them to appeal the allocation, even though they had not approved the allocation system."
- The superintendent should not ask for support from the existing establishment in initiating change. Rather, get support for the willing to try something new and provide the elbow room so that they don't snuff out during the trial period. "When it comes to change, the best you can hope for from an existing structure is benign neutrality," says Strembitsky. "Don't ask them to believe in this. Because most people will only believe it when they see it."
- The superintendent should recruit the people who will believe it *before* they see it. Recruit people who are willing to learn as they go, who will last through a long arduous process and come to really understand how this approach works.

Trust

The Edmonton story of reform describes how effective leadership by the superintendent makes the difference in transforming the results in a school system. Strembitsky—and his colleague and successor Angus McBeath, who has carried on this work—provided the vision and had the courage of their convictions to do what effective principals in urban school districts around North America have been asking for, and the research has confirmed, for decades: trust (McBeath, 2001). The superintendent trusts the principals, teachers, and other front-line personnel, and the board trusts the superintendent. The board, having picked this person to do the job, now lets the superintendent figure out what is best for the teachers, students, and parents in the school, and holds the superintendent accountable for the results.

The tragedy is that trusting people who are skilled and closest to the problem is not a new idea among people who work in high-performance organizations around the world. Most superintendents, once teachers and principals themselves, have forgotten that they felt the same way when they were in their schools.

The Edmonton Model Today

The Edmonton model has spread to Australia, New Zealand, and England. In the United States, Hawaii passed a law in early 2005 that will require 50% of the state's school funds to be controlled by the schools. Cities such as Seattle, Houston, Cincinnati, Pittsburgh, and San Diego have tried parts of the Edmonton model. Finally, in what may yet prove to be the implementation that demonstrates the effectiveness of the Edmonton model for U.S. schools, California is considering a pilot of 15 school districts to voluntarily implement such a program over a 5-year period.

Where the Edmonton model has been used, and principals and their leadership teams received both the authority and the resources to identify and apply best practice, reading and math scores have made steady and significant progress.

WHOLE-SCHOOL AND SYSTEMWIDE REFORM: PROBLEMS AND PROMISES

MICHAEL FULLAN

You can't achieve serious whole-school reform without increasing school capacity, and you can't increase school capacity without transforming the system infrastructure. Fullan outlines strategies for overcoming dysfunctional infrastructures so educators can focus on systemic reform.

Schools have been plagued by piecemeal innovations that come and go. One answer has been the development and implementation of whole-school reform models such as Success for All, Expeditionary Learning Outward Bound, and CO-NECT Schools (Berends, Bodilly, & Kirby, 2001). In the short run, these models provide focus, well-developed designs, and support for implementation. In many cases there is evidence of a positive impact on student learning. As a whole, they represent some of the best advances in school reform in the past quarter of a century. But adopting models is not the main point. The main point of schoolwide reform is reculturing the professional community at the school level and transforming the infrastructure that supports and directs schools. The flaw of whole-school reform models is hidden in their implementation track record. In one study of 16 initiatives involving more than 300 schools, Datnow and Stringfield (2000) observe that in several instances, "educators adopted reform models without thinking through how the model would suit their school's goals, culture, teachers, or students. Even when opportunities to gather information were available, educators seldom made well-informed choices about reform designs" (p. 14).

Policy and political decisions at state and district levels also often influenced schools' adoption of external reform designs, which caused some local educators to adopt models quickly and without careful consideration of "fit" (Datnow & Stringfield, 2000).

Their findings also suggested that strong district support is important to sustained implementation. Schools that were unable to sustain reforms were sometimes located in districts that welcomed new programs but did not provide ongoing support. In other cases, support was provided for a time but waned as district leadership changed. It is instructive to note that after 6 years, only 4 of the 13 schools were still implementing the chosen reform models.

One could conclude that the solution would be to strengthen the commitment and conditions necessary for initial and continued support, but this view masks the fundamental problem. As long as you have external models coming and going, there will never be more than a small proportion of schools and districts involved, and any pockets of success will be short-lived.

Let me be very clear about this fundamental point. First, the primary goal of school reform is not to adopt or even internalize a valuable external model. The primary goal is to alter the *capacity* of the school to engage in improvement. Second, sustainable reform of this kind can only be achieved when working with *whole systems*. By whole systems I mean an entire school district, state, or country. By and large, the 3,000 whole-school re-form models are not operating in whole systems but rather in pieces of systems—in individual schools.

You can't get serious reform without an increase in school capacity, and you can't get an increase in school capacity without transforming the system infrastructure. Whole-school reform models possibly could be one stepping-stone in this direction, but they do not represent the solution.

School Capacity

For successful whole-school reform, you have to strengthen the fundamen-tals, starting with school capacity. Newmann, King, and Youngs (2000) defined school capacity as consisting of the following:

- Principal leadership
- Teachers' knowledge, skills, and dispositions
- Professional community
- Program coherence
- Technical resources

School capacity is seriously undermined if it lacks quality leadership. The role of the principal is to focus on the conditions and strategies for continuously improving results. This involves developing in concert the four elements of capacity identified by Newmann and his colleagues, namely: teachers' knowledge, professional community, program coherence, and resources.

In addition, there must be organizational development because social or relationship resources are key to school improvement. Thus, schools must combine individual development with the development of schoolwide professional communities, the second element of capacity.

But this must be channeled in a way that combats the fragmentation of multiple innovations by working on program coherence: "the extent to which the school's programs for student and staff learning are coordinated, focused on clear learning goals, and sustained over a period of time" (Newmann et al., 2000, p. 4). Program coherence is key to organizational integration.

Finally, instructional improvement requires additional technical resources (materials, equipment, space, time, and access to expertise).

In addition to Newmann's definition of school capacity, I would add the ability of schools to develop a strong, mutually influential relationship with the community.

In any case, whole-school reform models are at best short-term solutions because they do not directly work on these basic school capacities. The case could be made that strong implementation of given models will indeed strengthen the capacities identified by Newmann and colleagues, but there is no evidence that this is the case. I am not suggesting that whole-school models have no value. While they often contribute to capacity, this contribution will always be short-lived. Models come and go, and the whole systems are not involved. Therefore, schools considering a whole-school reform model should ensure it is part and parcel of strengthening school capacity.

The clearest examples of school capacity are at the elementary school level, but there are examples at the secondary level as well. One of the best studies of high schools was conducted by McLaughlin and Talbert (2001), in which they investigated the role of professional learning communities in 16 high schools in California and Michigan.

McLaughlin and Talbert found that "a collaborative community of practice in which teachers share instructional resources and reflections in practice appears essential to their persistence and success in innovating classroom practice" (p. 10). In other words, teachers who were successful with all students, especially those traditionally turned off by school, were constantly figuring out and sharing what works. These teachers "taught in schools and departments with a *strong professional community* engaged in making innovations that support student and teacher learning and success." (McLaughlin & Talbert, 2001, p. 34).

In recent analyses focusing on successful case studies in business and education, I found that strategies and mechanisms for "creating and sharing knowledge" are crucial to success (Fullan, 2001b). Yet in all schools, especially high schools, this aspect is notoriously weak. It may not be possible to create learning communities in the large-scale industrial models of high schools (1,500–3,000 students or more) that we have inherited. In this sense, reculturing (increasing school capacity) and restructuring (reducing the size and structure of high schools) may have to go hand in hand.

Finally, school capacity studies usually produce only a snapshot at one point in time, which inadequately captures the district and state context. We can, however, draw references about the impact of district and state infrastructure on school capacity. Intentions aside, in the vast majority of cases the infrastructure not only does not help, it often (presumably unwittingly) makes matters worse (see Fullan, 2001a). Hatch (2000) found that multiple innovations frequently collide. Hess (1999) talks about "policy churn" and "spinning wheels" in reference to the school boards' instability. One of the main starting points of whole-school reform, then, is to identify the problem as one of "overcoming dysfunctional leadership and policies" at the district and state level. Why is this important? Because it is not possible to accomplish large-scale, sustainable reform in the absence of the infrastructure's active involvement.

Overcoming Dysfunctional Infrastructures

Large-scale reform requires what I call an "accountability pillar" and a "capacity-building pillar." The former refers to standards of performance, transparency of results, monitoring of progress, and consequential action. Capacity building concerns training, resources (time, expertise, and materials), and incentive-based compensation as well as recognition for accomplishments. These pressure and support pillars must act in concert to produce large-scale reform. When done effectively, integrating pressure and support with a focus on results for students creates pride, greater trust, and tremendous motivation and energy.

Large-scale improvement requires new and different two-way relationships between each school and the district, and new relationships across schools as the district develops a new professional learning culture. This involves reculturing the district.

What to Do

The current dilemma in schools and school systems is that the infrastructure is dysfunctional. We are at the early stages of tackling this problem, so there are few models of how to go about this reform. The preliminary examples at the district level (New York's District 2, San Diego) and at the national level (England) are not yet fully developed. Figure 6.1 illustrates some of the district-level key components. The themes in this figure would be pursued within schools, across schools, and between schools and the district. As we go about this work, I suggest four fundamental elements:

1. Get the Conception Right. The conception of reform needs to be developed and constantly refined. It is a conception of "coordinated decentralization" applied systemwide. In this sense, business and educational re-

FIGURE 6.1. District Reform: Within and Across Schools

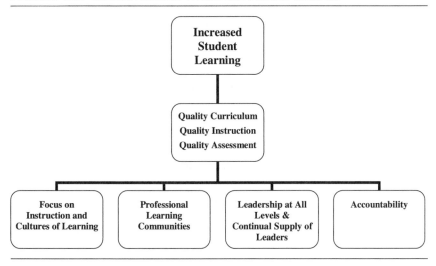

form have much in common (Fullan, 2001b). In a corporatewide model, decentralization and self-managing change are valued but they are played out with constant interaction and identity with the corporation as a whole. Similarly, the school principal should be just as concerned with the fate of other schools and the district as a whole as with his or her own school. Purposeful interaction or what we call "learning in context," fosters districtwide identity as it increases everyone's capacity. Thus, the goal is to constantly foster shared identity with room to be innovative.

2. Focus as Much Attention on District and State Reform as on School Capacity. Schools have received a great deal of attention over the past decade or more, and rightly so. Now we need to balance this with the same kind of attention on district and state policies, programs, and practices insofar as they help or hinder school capacity. We need to reorganize the role of the district and district leadership so that it focuses primarily on instruction, building capacity at the school level, and fostering lateral exchanges across schools. We also need to institute regular feedback from schools as to how the role of the district and state helps or hinders reform. There should be regular assessments of school capacity and performance as well as regular assessments of the district role.

3. Invest in Leadership at All Levels. If we are to scale-up, there needs to be a tremendous investment not only in school and teacher leadership but also in district leadership. If we do not do this, highly effective leadership will always be the exception rather than the rule. Until leadership is widespread, we will never get more than episodic, small-scale success.

4. Form Permanent Endowments. With all the tens of millions of dollars going into district reform, we have to ask whether one-shot expenditures (even over 5 years) will ever have any lasting effect. We need an increase in investment in people and system improvement, as the private sector does on a permanent basis. This means that states need to invest more in capacity building, but we should consider whether states and foundations could also match contributions in order to establish permanent endowments that would provide support (e.g., for leadership development) on a continuous basis. For example, one could take a percentage of large-scale investments from external sources and have them matched—say, $25 million from foundations, matched by $25 million from a state or district to form a 10-year fund to support capacity building on an ongoing basis.

If we do not fundamentally improve the district and state infrastructure in tandem with school improvement, we will never get large-scale, sustained reform. The next few years provide a critical opportunity to try to get this right.

Implications for Superintendents

There are direct implications of these findings for what superintendents should and should not do. I summarize these here (for more elaborate treatment, see Fullan, 2003a).

First, set your targets on large-scale, sustainable reform. Whatever is done, it must focus on all or the majority of schools in the district, with a view to developing capacity for continuous improvement.

Second, there are no shortcuts. Don't rely on external innovations as the solution. Even in districts where this has been done more systematically, such as Memphis, the innovations have a relatively short shelf life (Fullan, 2003a).

Third, do focus on building school capacity to make improvements in instruction as it relates to student learning. We already know how to do this with respect to literacy and numeracy at the elementary school level. My colleagues and I have been engaged in basic capacity building in several districts. This means helping to establish professional learning communities at the school level and having multiple schools involved—all in the service of improving teaching as it relates to student learning (see Rolheiser, Fullan, & Edge, 2003).

Fourth, invest in leadership development and the leadership pipeline. If you want large-scale, sustainable reform, leadership is to this decade what standards were to the 1990s. Investing in the development and support of school leadership is especially crucial (Fullan, 2003b).

In short, superintendents are in a position to move school districts from "managing innovations" to "becoming innovative"—that is, having the capacity to engage in collective continuous improvement with all schools in the district and across schools.

EARLY EDUCATION, CARE, AND SCHOOL SUCCESS

MARGERY WALLEN AND GAIL GOLDBERGER

(This essay was principally authored by Margery Wallen and Gail Goldberger, with contributions by Joan Costello, Chapin Hall Center for Children at the University of Chicago.)

Studies have shown that early education programs such as Head Start improve academic achievement later in school. Unfortunately, many factors undermine our nation's ability to deliver quality early education and care. The authors examine the problem of and suggest an action plan for meeting the needs of young children before they enter the classroom.

While there is a general consensus on the importance of attention to the early years of child development, consistent funding of sufficient scope has not materialized. And yet, given the increase in the numbers of very young children in child care, growing numbers of parents who want educational opportunities for their preschool children, and the pressures to improve students' academic performance, the goal of ensuring that all children have access to high-quality early learning experiences remains an important public policy priority. As schools and districts are pressed to annually improve student results, that pressure will be translated down the age continuum to demands for more and better early childhood care and education—so that all children enter primary school ready and able to learn.

There is a huge gap between what we know and what we do. Cost is generally seen as the prohibitive factor, but nothing is more expensive than what we are doing now: spending more and more money addressing the results of our neglect. In fiscal year 1999, for every $1 Illinois spent on early childhood education and preventive health and social services, $13 was spent on prisons, special education, child protection, and Medicaid. The human costs associated with the neglect of early care—extremely high school dropout rates, low levels of literacy, poor health, and violence—severely limit children's chances of becoming vital, contributing adults (Wallen, 1998).

The Importance of Quality Programs

Good early care and education services offer young children opportunities to build their social, emotional, physical, and cognitive skills so they can enter school ready to learn and thrive. With good services, children have frequent interactions with well-trained teachers who listen as well as talk, guide them to expand their thinking and problem solving, and read to them. Higher-quality care and education are associated with stronger thinking, attention, and social skills; fewer behavior problems; and higher scores in language and math tests, at least through second grade. Good care offers the opportunity to develop friendships and begins to teach social skills needed to sustain them. Good early care and education settings offer diverse opportunities for safe, playful engagement with a world beyond family.

The Child–Parent Centers (CPC) project in Chicago provides stimulating experiences for children ages 3–9 in tandem with educational opportunities for their parents, who are required to participate in preschool and school-age learning activities and family and health services with their children. Since 1985, the project has followed 550 pupils and 989 graduates. At age 5, CPC pupils had a 10-point increase in IQ compared with a control group. At age 19, all CPC graduates (i.e., those children who were participants in only preschool and those who were both preschool and school-age participants) had a 25–30% lower rate of special education needs, a 30–40% reduction in grade failure, and a 25% reduction in high school dropout rates. CPC graduates and pupils had 35% fewer arrests than the comparison group (Reynolds, Temple, Robertson, & Mann, 2001).

Quality early education and care not only promote the healthy development of young children but also enable working parents to have more stable employment. Balancing work and child rearing is a complex endeavor for parents with preschool children. Disturbances in children's education and care arrangements can cause parents to miss work or leave their jobs. Several large surveys of working parents report that an absence of stable education and care reduced parents' job performance.

Creating a Balance. Early childhood professionals are all too familiar with the challenge of balancing quality, affordability, and accessibility and the trade-offs required to achieve that balance. A change in any one of these three factors affects the other two.

Quality. Researchers have identified the essential components of a quality early education program, the most important of which is the relationship between the child and caregiver or teacher. Aspects of program design such as teacher/caregiver education and training, the number of children per teacher, the number of children in a group, and caregiver continuity contribute to making positive relationships more likely.

Even more important than research on the positive benefits of quality care are the negative impacts of low-quality care. The chronic shortage of qualified early childhood teachers due to low wages, lack of benefits, low status, poor working conditions, and limited opportunities for advancement can impair the development of children in their care.

Quality programs also attend to the basic issues of safety, physical and mental health, and parental involvement. Numerous studies of the long-term effects of high-quality early childhood intervention and Head Start programs have found that parents who were provided meaningful opportunities for involvement in these programs became better teachers, motivators, and advocates for their children.

Affordability. The market price of quality early education and care is increasingly high. Estimated costs for full-workday, full-year care for infants and toddlers in the Chicago area range from $8,500 to over $15,000 for licensed center-based care, and from $5,500 to $11,000 in licensed family day-care homes. For 3- to 5-year-olds, costs can range from an estimated $6,100 to $12,000 in licensed centers to $5,100 to $8,500 in licensed homes.

The early childhood education system faces a perverse equation: The amount families can pay for early education and care affects how much providers can charge, and high-quality care is rarely available at a price most parents can afford. Thus, many child-care centers and homes reduce expenses by eliminating components that contribute to quality. Additionally, all higher-quality early childhood services rely on qualified staff who work for wages that are far below the value of their services as measured by wages in occupations with comparable requirements for knowledge, skills, or credentials.

There is serious underfunding in the entire early care system, which has an impact on all families but a greater impact on low-income families. With positive proof that early education and care give children a head start, the reverse is also true. Children from low-income families that lack access to higher-quality early education are often behind when they enter kindergarten and are unable to catch up as schooling proceeds.

Families pay about 60% of the overall cost of care, and 39% is paid by federal, state, and local governments through tax-based and expenditure-based subsidies. Private-sector businesses and foundations pay less than 1%. Obstacles to private-sector (i.e., employer) involvement range from attitudes that work and family life should be separate, to fiscal constraints, to lack of information. Strategies that businesses can use to be more supportive include operating on-site or nearby child-care centers or family-care homes; offering after-school, summer camp, and sick child–care services; and subsidizing services chosen by parents.

Accessibility. Families choose early education and care arrangements based on a variety of factors: their child's age and developmental needs, proximity to home or work, cost, days and hours of operation, philosophy or educational approach, services for siblings, and availability of special services.

Although most parents want care close to home, space is not always available in those programs. This is true in both overcrowded urban communities and in rural communities. Low-income communities generally have significantly fewer licensed early education and care slots than do higher-income communities, and the cost of constructing new centers and schools is often prohibitive (Collins, Layzer, Kreader, Werner, & Glantz, 2000).

Superintendents' Role in Promoting Early Childhood Education

As public schools continue to expand early education programs, school leaders need a synthesis of the best research and practice to develop these programs and enhance existing ones. Building on efforts at the state level, the following recommendations are offered for superintendents, in partnership with school and community stakeholders, to plan and provide the necessary information and resources to prepare young children for success in school.

• *Convene a Local Early Learning Council.* Today's early childhood programs are often discouraged from working together because of conflicting goals, regulations, and funding approaches. Local Early Learning Councils offer opportunities to develop and implement strategic plans for building a more coordinated system that stresses collaboration across programs so that communities can better meet the needs of families and make the most efficient use of existing resources. Many communities, with superintendents at the helm, are moving forward to convene Early Learning Councils with a broad array of members representing a cross section of the community. Councils often include parents and representatives of programs serving children from birth to age 3: child-care centers and homes, the local child-care resource and referral agency, early childhood special education, Head Start and Early Head Start, institutions of higher education (community colleges, colleges, and universities), regional offices of education, school boards, and state prekindergarten and kindergarten programs.

• *Establish program partnerships between preschool, early childhood special education child care, Head Start, and higher education.*

Most preschool programs that seek to deliver high-quality services and meet the scheduling needs of working parents need to blend funding from federal, state, and local sources. The "silo" approach to funding makes it difficult for providers to deliver and for families to access services. One solution is to develop, document, and disseminate models of collaboration that stretch resources and infrastructure—for example, full-day full-year programs that provide prekindergarten education in a child-care or Head Start setting.

• *Encourage planned transitions from home, child care, and services for children from birth to age 3 to preschool and from preschool to elementary school.* Transitions from home or child-care settings into preschool and from preschool into kindergarten can be extremely stressful for young children and their families. Children often face new expectations for independence and responsibility, goals that are more formal in regard to academic progress, and larger class sizes. Strategies that promote successful transitions include visits to preschools by kindergarten teachers so as to understand the curriculum and plan for individual students; arranging for preschool children to visit kindergarten classrooms; establishing formal transition planning teams; initiating joint transition-related training for preschool staff and school or other agency staff; aligning curriculum and expectations across preschool and kindergarten programs; reaching out to families before children start school through communications with parents, encouraging school visits, and educating parents about the steps they can take to prepare their child for school; and home visits by teachers or transition liaisons.

• *Produce, attract, and retain more well-qualified teachers and administrators in early childhood education.* Research has demonstrated that learning by young children is highly dependent on the educational qualifications of their teachers, with the most effective teachers having at least a 4-year college degree and specialized training in early education. However, in most states child-care teachers need only a high school diploma and Head Start teachers a 2-year associate degree. Not surprisingly, low education and training requirements for early childhood educators translate into low compensation. The average salaries of child-care teachers ($15,430 in 1999) and private preschool teachers ($19,610) are less than half the average elementary teacher's salary, causing high turnover (e.g., 43% every 2 years in Illinois). In order to ensure that all young children have access to high-quality early childhood education, the bar must be raised on teacher qualifications and teacher pay increased. The supply of well-qualified early educators must also be substantially increased. To achieve this, school districts can partner with local institutions of higher education to design early education teacher preparation programs that connect specifically to local school districts. They can also design district professional development plans that align policies and programs in the areas of teacher preparation, recruitment, retention, induction and support, ongoing professional development, and teacher evaluation and leadership.

Despite consensus in the research arena regarding the components and long-term benefits of high-quality early childhood education, this information has not been effectively communicated to the public or to policymakers. Generating greater public and policymaker awareness, particularly with state and local legislators, requires mobilizing politically powerful groups of stakeholders that are beneficiaries of early childhood education—including business, labor, parents, and law enforcement—through targeted advocacy and communications efforts about the essential ingredients and long- term benefits of high-quality early childhood education. These interest groups have proved to be powerful allies at the state level and can be potent forces in making the case for increased investment in early education.

HIGH SCHOOL REDESIGN: WHAT'S WORKING

VALERIE E. LEE

There is a strong consensus among policymakers, educational researchers, and the informed public that U.S. high schools are in serious trouble. The complaints center around several features common to America's comprehensive high schools: a general sense that most high schools are too large; that students are not known well and feel anonymous; that the curriculum is fragmented, stratified, and unresponsive to students' interests and needs; that many students are disengaged and uncommitted to school; and that the organization of high schools is overly bureaucratic, driven by rigid rules, roles, and procedures.

Over the last few years, calls for high school reform have focused on fundamental change—or restructuring—rather than more modest reforms that would tinker at the edges.

Restructuring High Schools for Equity and Excellence

It is important that we examine restructuring's impact on fundamental outcomes of equity and excellence. To address the impact, my colleague Julia Smith and I, under the sponsorship of the Center on the Organization and Restructuring of Schools (CORS), analyzed a nationally representative sample of nearly 800 U.S. high schools—public and private—using data collected by the National Center for Education Statistics. We also studied 12,000 students' progress through high school with data collected at the end of eighth, tenth, and twelfth grades.

Findings About Restructuring

Based on the schools' reports of how many of which types of reform practices they had in place in their schools, we grouped the schools into three categories:

1. Highly restructured schools
2. Traditionally restructured schools
3. Schools not engaged in reform

Highly restructured schools were those that engaged in several reform practices consistent with the CORS definition of restructuring: "fundamental departure from conventional practice." Strategies included interdisciplinary teaching teams, mixed-ability classes, schools-within-schools, common planning time for teachers, flexible time for classes, and students keeping the same homeroom throughout high school.

Traditionally restructured schools also engaged in reform practices, but ones that did not fit the CORS definition. Neither were the schools as uncommon as the highly restructured practices. We were surprised to find some schools that did not report doing any of the restructured or traditional practices.

An analysis of the contrast between restructured schools and traditionally structured schools surfaced four major findings:

- Students learned more in highly restructured than traditionally structured high schools (and a lot more than those in schools not engaged in reform).
- Not only was learning higher, but it was also more equitably distributed in restructured high schools—learning was less stratified by socioeconomic status (SES).
- Learning was greatest in schools that had only a few restructuring practices in place (three or four). When schools adopted too many restructuring practices, learning dropped off.
- Restructuring effects were sustained over students' 4 years in high school. The positive effects we found for school restructuring during the first 2 years of high school were either equally large, or even larger, during the last 2 years.

Restructuring and School Organization

Despite our findings that high school restructuring seems to "work" in terms of both excellence (students learn more) and equity (student learning is less stratified), we wondered if these findings might actually be capturing more enduring and fundamental aspects of the high schools we had called "restructured." So we explored whether high schools' organizational properties were associated with the restructuring practices they used and whether the effects we had identified might be "explained away" once we took these features of high schools into account.

In the book in which this research is summarized, *Restructuring High Schools for Equity and Excellence: What Works* (Lee, 2001), we divided these organizational properties into a few recognizable categories: the organization of the curriculum, instruction, teachers' work, and school size. This is what we concluded from our research:

- Once schools' organizational properties were taken into account, the positive effects of school restructuring on learning and its equitable distribution dropped to nonsignificance in our models.
- The curricular structure mattered. Students learned more, and learning was more equitable, in schools where virtually all students followed a rather narrow academic curriculum, one that offered fewer low-level courses and where most students took advanced courses.
- The type of instruction also mattered. In schools where interactive (or authentic) instruction was common, students learned more and learning was more equitably distributed.
- How teachers organized their work also mattered. In schools where teachers took collective responsibility for their students' learning and where these attitudes were shared widely among the faculty, student learning was both higher and more equitable.
- Students learned more, and learning was more equitable, in smaller schools. In other related explorations, we actually identified an ideal size for high schools—600–900 students—where students both learned more and learning was more equitably distributed. This "ideal" size was similar across schools that enrolled students with different social backgrounds (lower and higher SES, more and fewer minority students). We also found that school size mattered more in terms of student learning in schools enrolling more disadvantaged students.

The Effects of School Size

The study of high school size within the restructuring work has received much attention (Lee & Smith, 1997). Some small-school advocates were critical of our findings because they did not favor the smallest schools. We felt that the 600–900 student range was ideal because it struck a balance: High schools in that range were small enough for students and faculty to know one another well but large enough to be able to mount a credible academic curriculum.

In our conclusions about school size, we offered support for a related reform movement—one that advocates breaking large high schools into several smaller subunits. This is a seemingly inexpensive and feasible way to create small schools without bricks and mortar. Although this type of reform and these smaller schools are labeled in many different ways—small schools, mini-schools, career academies, houses, or small learning communities—we lump these together under the label "schools-within-schools." A major justification for creating schools-within-schools centers on social advantages: smaller settings can personalize learning.

Schools-Within-Schools

We found that "full-model" schools-within-schools (SWSs) were not very common in high schools. In the fall of 1998, we identified only 55 such schools across the country (Lee, Ready, & Johnson, 2001). Most of the 55 schools we identified were inner-city schools with largely disadvantaged students. We tried to identify a school that enrolled a relatively elite student population, but couldn't.

Our findings centered on several issues that emerged during our 2-year study. What were the schools' stated and unstated purposes (what did they hope to accomplish using the SWS model of reform)? How were the schools governed? How did academic and social stratification play out in these settings? How were curricula and instruction structured? How did larger state policy initiatives influence how the schools organized themselves? The following observations emerged from our in-depth case study of five of these SWSs.

- The schools-within-schools reform model seems quite promising. It represents a fundamental departure from conventional practice because it confronts almost every sacrosanct aspect of the comprehensive public high school. The SWS model, although difficult to implement and sustain, is worth the effort.
- SWS high schools seem better able to personalize education for students. Informants in all the schools we studied said that increasing personalism was a major motivation for their having moved to this model and a major advantage for keeping it in place.
- This field-based study was not designed to allow us to draw conclusions about the efficacy of SWS reform in improving student learning. However, all the schools we studied expected this to happen indirectly, through improved social relations. The reform's major purpose is not aimed at raising achievement (at least directly or quickly), so I suggest that those who engage in it should not have high expectations in this regard.
- The SWS we studied seemed to diminish the importance of academic departments, sometimes in favor of an integrated curriculum and project-based learning developed by a small group of teachers

working together in subunits. It seems clear to me that discipline-based departments work, at least in part, at cross-purposes to autonomous subunits. This was not always the case, nor was it always successful. However, as long as the school did not lose academic rigor with the demise of departments, a shift toward more integration of the curriculum seems positive.

- The academic and social stratification that typifies most high schools, occurring mainly through curriculum differentiation and tracking, pops up in other places in SWS high schools, mainly through stratification between subunits. Student choice, exercised as students affiliate themselves with subunits (and teachers do this also), increases stratification. Subunit reputations become self-fulfilling prophecies over time, mostly through choice. Thus, stratification is something to worry about.

- The increasing accountability and standardization in state and federal policy has profound and usually negative effects on the SWS design, at least in the schools we studied. A major underlying framework of this reform—that subunit members have considerable autonomy from the school and district administration in planning their curriculum and their students' experiences with it—is fundamentally undercut by a focus on more frequent and high-stakes testing and a standardization of the curriculum to align with the tests. If *school* accountability is increased, *subunit* autonomy must be sacrificed.

A Few Questions to Ponder

The issues I have discussed seem particularly relevant for urban high schools, for several reasons. First, the high schools that almost everyone agrees need "fixing" are mostly located in inner cities. Second, these high schools are typically quite large, although many suburban high schools are also large. But "largeness" is mostly seen as a problem for inner-city schools. Third, the 55 SWS high schools we located in 1998, and the 5 we chose to study from among the 55, were located in cities. Not all the schools were in America's largest cities, but most were. Fourth, it may actually be somewhat easier to implement fundamental reform in urban high schools than in suburban settings. This is because there is less often an entrenched group of parents and/or teachers who consider that any change challenges their relative advantage. For all these reasons, the directions for "redesign" that I have discussed seem particularly appropriate in urban settings. Let me end this chapter with four questions that flow from what I have written. Hopefully, they raise issues worth considering:

1. Do the reforms described here represent fundamental departures from conventional practice, which is how "restructuring" was defined in the CORS work? My research suggests that changing high schools requires much more than tinkering at the edges, although most reforms do exactly that. The more problematic the setting, the more fundamental the change needs to be.

2. What is (or should be) the role of departments? Are they part of the problem or part of the solution for improving urban high schools? Administrators in the SWSs we studied seemed to feel that departments pulled faculty loyalties away from the subunits and made students' academic experiences more fragmented and less integrated. If departmental structure decreases, where is the focus of academic rigor to be located?

3. How do reforms influence equity? That is, are some students advantaged by them while others are disadvantaged? Who do reforms benefit, and who gets overlooked? Smaller schools seem to be more beneficial for less advantaged students, a major finding from our research. But the SWS high schools we studied that did not direct specific attention to guarding against stratification by subunits within their larger schools usually found that stratification resulted from student choice.

4. Is it possible to reform high schools through efforts that emanate from the top? The Chicago high school reforms discussed by V. E. Lee (2002) that came from within the school were successful, whereas the high school reform directed from the Chicago Public Schools' central office was much less successful. Thus, we must wonder if reforms can only be successful if they bubble up from the bottom (C. D. Lee, 2002; Gutierrez & Morales, 2002). If so, how do the sparks of such reform get kindled? Does every school need an inspirational leader to instigate reform? Is there a compromise? Where does the impetus for change come from, and how is it acted on?

IMPROVING STUDENT ACHIEVEMENT THROUGH LABOR–MANAGEMENT COLLABORATION

ADAM URBANSKI

Central to any effort to improve urban schools is the relationship between school managers and the teachers union. Without union–management collaboration, even the best efforts of district leaders to launch any positive reform are tantamount to one hand clapping. The author offers several recommendations for building labor–management collaboration and focusing it on improving student achievement.

Improving public schools requires hard work, bold ideas, and a commitment for the long haul. It is tough enough to turn around urban schools when all key constituencies are pulling in the same direction. It is virtually impossible in an atmosphere of apathy or adversarial battles. If education is to work for everyone, then everyone must work on improving education. And if the adults in the lives of children can't manage to get their act together, there's little reason to expect that the kids will.

If urban school districts are to yield substantially better results, both the district and union must be open to considering a substantial shift in the role of central office and union headquarters. Both must be willing to restructure themselves to primarily be service centers to the schools and support schools by assuring an equitable distribution of resources while respecting schools' autonomy. Both the district and union must involve teachers and school administrators shaping policies and searching for effective strategies to support student learning.

The following recommendations can help districts and teachers unions accomplish this unity of purpose. While any one of these recommendations may be worth considering on its own, the desired improvement in student learning can best be achieved if the individual reforms are connected in a systemic approach. Random acts of innovation have limited impact.

Recommendation 1: Negotiate "Living Contracts"

For more than three decades, collective bargaining has defined the relationship between organized teachers and district officials. All too often, this relationship has been hostile and the institutionalized rancor has impeded collaboration and reform.

The current approach to collective bargaining has significant problems. It emphasizes a precision that impedes flexibility and often reinforces barriers to cooperation. It assumes that conflict is natural, that everything must be standardized, and that just because all is even, then it must be fair. And perhaps worst of all, the current mode relegates negotiations to a once-in-a-while battle.

This adversarial approach to negotiations has been increasingly yielding to so-called interest-based bargaining, based on three key principles: focusing on issues, not personalities; using reason to make decisions, not power; and sticking to interests, not positions. This collaborative method of problem solving is clearly an improvement. It can lead teachers unions to view the educational and instructional programs as union business and can lead both labor and management to commit to look at issues through the lens of what is educationally best for the students.

But can the collective bargaining process be an effective tool for enhancing learning opportunities for students? Can we finally recognize that what is familiar is not necessarily natural? Can labor–management relations and collective bargaining be conducted in a way that adheres to high standards and be more responsible and more responsive to students' needs?

My answer is yes. But it requires forging an entirely different set of relationships and a different ethic in how teachers unions and school districts deal with each other. Genuine collaboration can exist only in an atmosphere of trust between equal partners. And collaboration does not mean just congeniality. It must be substantive, with the goal of turning goodwill into results.

In Rochester, New York, the parties have sought to move even beyond the interest-based model of collective bargaining. Together, the district and the union developed strategic objectives and engaged in joint problem solving. By changing the process and expanding the scope of collective bargaining to include educational and instructional issues, the parties have negotiated a "living contract" that includes a commitment to do the following:

- Adopt "what's best for students" as the shared value, the common denominator, and the litmus test for any specific proposal advanced by either party.
- Conduct ongoing negotiations as timely problem solving rather than something relegated to once-in-a-while.
- View collective bargaining as collaboration rather than positional and adversarial fights.
- Establish standards, benchmarks, and formulas that serve both parties well and would continue to guide them beyond the life of any individual negotiations.

- Use the collective bargaining process to build a more genuine profession for teachers and more effective schools for all students.

Many important issues of mutual interest can be addressed through the living contract, such as the question of "customizing" additional time in a flexible way to meet the instructional needs of each individual student or a collaborative plan to develop a critical mass of teachers certified by the National Board for Professional Teaching Standards. The living contract can be used for addressing issues that may not have surfaced yet but cannot and need not await the expiration of the existing contract before they are given attention. As a matter of principle, living contracts are an opportunity to achieve greater coherence among policies, practices, and provisions.

By eschewing the "Them versus Us" mind-set, this more flexible approach can nurture the necessary trust and commitment that promote respect and collaboration for the benefit of all students. It can promote the kind of partnership and dynamics that could change the very culture of labor–management relations. The purpose of all this is to improve learning opportunities for all students. In this way, it pays attention to both the bottom line and the horizon.

Admittedly, it is not easy to change the culture of collective bargaining, nor would it suffice to sustain the collaboration only at the central level. We must find effective strategies to extend labor–management collaboration to where it matters most: at each and every school. If we succeed, we will increase our joint capacity to build a more genuine profession for teachers and more effective schools for all students.

Recommendation 2: Focus on Improving Teaching Quality

What impedes effective teaching and learning is not teachers themselves; it is that teachers work within outmoded, unprofessional systems. By taking responsibility for redesigning schools and abandoning unexamined practices and policies, we can restructure the teaching profession in ways that promise more productive schooling.

We must strengthen teaching in ways that reflect the features evident in other genuine professions.

Shared Knowledge Base. While it is important for teachers to care about students, it is not enough that teachers "love to teach." Good teachers must also know their subjects well. They must know how to teach these subjects effectively to all students. They must understand human development, how the brain works, and how learning occurs. They must base their teaching on what is known from research as well as on experience with effective practice. And they must know how to connect learning to students' lives and experiences.

Standards. Teachers must be involved in setting high and rigorous professional standards. These standards must then be enforced through peer review, because nobody knows better the difference between good teaching and bad teaching than the best teachers themselves. "Emergency" or "temporary" licenses in teaching should not be permitted any more than they would be in medicine, law, or any other profession.

Professional Preparation. Teachers must have access to the most current knowledge available to meet their students' needs. All teachers deserve high-quality preparation programs that slight neither disciplinary knowledge nor teaching knowledge and that merge theory and practice in professional development schools.

Induction. New teachers should not have to learn their job by the sink-or-swim method. They should be ushered in under the watchful supportive eyes of experienced and expert colleagues who assist them and guide their practice during the initial year(s).

Continuous Learning. "You cannot teach what you do not model," Deborah Meier, the celebrated founder of New York City's Central Park East secondary school, is fond of saying. Teachers must be learners. They should not stop learning the day that they start teaching. Professional development should become inseparable from the day-to-day work that teachers do—not limited to courses, workshops, or conferences.

Promotion. It should be possible to promote teachers without compelling them to leave teaching. Deserving practitioners should get more pay, more status, and more responsibilities while continuing to teach—for at least a portion of their time. Through expanded career opportunities, highly accomplished teachers should be able to assume roles as mentors to new teachers, as curriculum and staff development experts, as adjunct instructors in teacher education programs, and even as "principal teachers" responsible for leading a school's instructional program. Such "lead teachers" should also assume the most challenging assignments, which are now often relegated to the least experienced and most vulnerable novices.

Conditions. Like other professionals with comparable levels of education and responsibility, teachers need and deserve a professional level of compensation and treatment. They should not be burdened with noninstructional duties and should have the resources necessary for effective practice.

Discretion. Teacher "empowerment" has little to do with transferring administrative roles to teachers. That's the last thing that most teachers want or need. What teachers *do* want, though, is more say about what to teach, how to teach it, and how to assess student learning.

Accountability. Last, but not least, we must replace the current emphasis on bureaucratic accountability (following established procedures) with a new emphasis on *professional* teacher accountability. It is wrong to try to hold anyone accountable for the outcomes of decisions that they do not make. Teachers will disown the results of such a process—as they have been—by saying, "Hey, they make all the decisions, so hold them accountable; I'm just a teacher."

Teachers can and must be accountable, yet this can only be achieved if we can frame systemic accountability features that would be responsible and responsive to student needs as well as to the realities that exist for educators.

Recommendation 3: Create a System of Differentiated Staffing and Differential Pay for Teachers

Developing a more genuine teaching profession also requires the establishment and legitimization of differentiated roles and differentiated pay systems for teachers. One possible model could be the Career in Teaching (CIT) plan implemented in Rochester, New York in 1986. This plan retains excellent practitioners and permits them to achieve leadership roles relating to instruction and the advancement of the profession:

> *Intern teachers* are new practitioners without prior teaching experience. Interns teach under the guidance of more experienced mentor teachers.
>
> *Resident teachers* have successfully completed a year of internship but have not yet achieved tenure or received their permanent certification, tenure, or a master's degree.
>
> *Lead teachers* are selected on a voluntary but competitive basis by a panel that includes other teachers. They teach part time and also work as mentors; as consultants who select textbooks, write curricula, plan staff development programs and direct other instruction-related tasks; or as demonstration teachers who "model" effective teaching. Lead teachers must have at least 10 years of experience, work up to 11 months a year, and receive a salary

differential. They work with students at risk, teach in remedial and/or enrichment programs, serve as adjunct professors in local teacher education schools, and perform other duties that might be required of instructional leaders and expert practitioners.

The purpose of this cooperative plan is to provide structure, career options, and incentives for current and prospective teachers—as well as to enhance their practice, compensation, and opportunities for change, growth, and development within teaching. The CIT plan enables the district to make more effective use of staff. It can increase the reliability and validity of teacher evaluations and reward long-term commitment to teaching. It can also enhance the district's ability to recruit and retain outstanding teachers.

Besides making the teaching occupation a genuine profession, CIT attacks a major obstacle to effective student learning: the need to match at-risk students and the toughest teaching assignments with those teachers who are best equipped to accept them—the experienced and expert lead teachers. Under the current structure and existing practices, the most difficult assignments and the most "challenging" students often fall, by default, to the least experienced and most vulnerable teachers. Veteran teachers can choose to avoid such assignments—largely due to negotiated seniority rules.

The concept of levels of competence among teachers may be uncomfortable for some. A crucial feature of a differentiated staffing proposal like the one implemented for Rochester is fair and equal access for all qualified teachers. Merit-pay schemes have been roundly condemned as "payoffs for pets." Integrity, openness, and equity must drive the selection process for lead teachers.

Differentiated Pay. There are two general categories of approaches to differentiated teacher pay. They can be implemented in tandem: schoolwide incentives and pay for knowledge and skills. Both have been the subject of substantial conversations and work at the Teacher Union Reform Network.

The underlying principle of a school-based performance-award program is that some incentive, typically monetary, is granted to a school or to individual teachers if specified performance goals or improvement gains are met. A school-based performance award is an element of serious accountability programs that attach consequences to results.

To work, accountability programs must ultimately help teachers improve their instruction, because better instruction is the key to higher student achievement levels. So even accountability programs that provide monetary awards to teachers must be inextricably linked to good professional development and a systemwide focus on improving the quality of teaching.

Knowledge- and skill-based pay systems provide salary increases for the demonstration of specified knowledge, skills, and professional expertise. Such salary increases can be focused on beginning, experienced, or mid-career teachers. They can be based on deeper knowledge of content, as represented by a master's degree or doctorate in the content area, or on demonstrated instructional expertise beyond that expected for a beginning teacher. Another form of knowledge- and skills-based pay involves paying additional money to teachers who perform certain functions, such as lead teachers who mentor new teachers. These programs typically have "term limits" so that participating teachers eventually return to classroom instruction, both to maintain and enhance their own instructional expertise and to allow other teachers an opportunity to participate in these new leadership roles.

Finally, some districts allow for teachers in shortage areas (typically science and math) to be placed on a higher salary step. This practice acknowledges both the reality that certain types of skills cost more in the marketplace and the school's interest in hiring and retaining teachers who are knowledgeable about their subject area and can teach it well.

National Board for Professional Teaching Standards. One of the most rigorous efforts to identify and recognize good instruction is reflected in the work of the National Board for Professional Teaching Standards. Teachers in many districts receive some form of compensation or fee support or are granted special standing as mentors, lead teachers, and so on after attaining board certification. In California and Florida, the state provides additional pay to board-certified teachers who mentor other teachers. Los Angeles provides a 15% salary increase for board-certified teachers. Hammond, Indiana, treats board certification as the equivalent of the doctorate on the traditional salary schedule. In some cases the stipend is contingent on the teacher's remaining in the district for a certain number of years; in that way the financial investment in the teacher's professional growth is at least partially offset by the enhanced knowledge and expertise the board-certified teacher brings to the district. And, indeed, board-certified teachers often assume leadership roles in their districts and in their unions—particularly in such areas as professional development.

Recommendation 4: Develop a System of Professional Accountability

Accountability is achieved only when the policies and processes work both to provide good education and to correct problems as they occur. Assessment data are helpful to the extent that they provide relevant, valid, timely, and useful information about how individual students are doing and how schools are serving them.

A professional accountability system seeks to create policies, practices, safeguards, and incentives that result in the following outcomes:

- Professionals pledge their first and primary commitment to the welfare of their students.
- All individuals are competent to practice in their designated roles.
- Where knowledge about good practice exists, it is used as the basis for making decisions.
- Practitioners—individually and collectively, through inquiry and consultation—continually seek to discover the most appropriate course of action.

To accomplish these objectives, a professional accountability system must pay attention to personnel policies governing the hiring, assignment, and evaluation of teachers and other staff. It also must offer opportunities for professional development; assessment tools for students and teachers; safeguards for identifying and addressing problems; and incentives to sustain teacher learning, self-evaluation, and challenge within the classroom and school.

The quality of staff hired and retained is a key component of professional accountability. No system can be accountable if it does not have serious, meaningful standards and safeguards regarding the hiring, assignment, evaluation, and support of professional staff.

The system should commit to hiring only fully qualified staff. If districts have difficulties recruiting teachers who are fully prepared for their teaching assignments, they should adjust incentives rather than lower their standards. Standards should reflect those articulated by the National Board for Professional Teaching Standards. In addition, selection decisions should include teachers' as well as principals' input at the school level for hiring of both principals and teachers.

New teachers should be well trained, not left to learn by trial and error at the expense of the children they serve. An intern program is a key support. Ultimately, the creation of professional development school partnerships between colleges and schools can be the linchpins in professional accountability. They allow teachers to prepare for state-of-the-art practice under the guidance of master teachers and teacher educators.

The assignment of beginning and veteran teachers is also important. If some schools have less senior and less stable teaching forces than others, two strategies are needed to ensure fairness to children. There must be adequate mentoring supports for inexperienced teachers where they are clustered, to reduce turnover and enhance their learning. And there must be incentives—such as improved working conditions, opportunities for teacher leadership, and material/programmatic supports—to attract top teachers to hard-to-staff schools.

Ongoing Development and Evaluation. Meaningful summative evaluation of teachers is needed at key junctures: tenure and movement between career levels. There must also be useful formative evaluation in between.

A specially established committee of teachers and administrators should make all cumulative evaluation decisions about promotions or continued employment. These evaluations need not take place every year except for intern/resident teachers or teachers who are placed on probation/intervention status.

Formative evaluation should focus on teachers' pursuit of their own goals for professional growth. Each teacher should set his or her own professional development goals and a plan for meeting them.

Teachers cannot be held accountable for knowledge-based, client-oriented decisions if they do not have access to knowledge as well as opportunities for consultation and evaluation of their work. School districts should give priority to providing time and money for teachers' professional development as well as knowledge resources in schools.

Client-oriented accountability also requires that teachers primarily be responsible for teaching students, not just teaching courses. This has at least two implications for the organization of schooling. Teachers should stay with the same students for longer periods of time so that they can know what students' needs are and be responsible for addressing them. School problem solving should be organized around the individual and collective needs of students rather than around program definitions, grades, tracks, and other labels.

Recommendation 5: Develop a System of Incentives and Shared Accountability

Rewards and sanctions are often called "incentives" because they are intended to encourage certain behaviors and discourage others. However, there is substantial evidence that such systems may actually function as *disincentives*. The idea is to create incentives that will *motivate* individuals and organizations to pursue the genuine goals of the organization. Using evidence of student learning as part of teacher and school evaluation should provide incentives to assume such responsibility for students. The system should also provide incentives for educators to take on professional challenges. Having master teachers work with schools and students who most need their expertise is one such incentive.

A System of Shared Accountability. Professional accountability systems aim to structure the work so that practitioners can make responsible decisions. Accountability is provided by rigorous training and careful selection of staff, serious and sustained internships for beginners, meaningful teacher and administrator evaluation, opportunities for professional development, and ongoing peer review of practice, buttressed by collegial decision making and consultation.

Each level of the system must assume its appropriate share of responsibility:

- Teachers must be accountable for identifying and meeting the needs of individual students responsibly and knowledgeably, based on standards of professional practice. They must continually evaluate—using assessment information and feedback sources (parents, students, and colleagues)—how well their practices are accomplishing this goal. And they must seek new knowledge and information and continually revise their strategies to better meet student needs.
- The school and its governing structure must be accountable for equitable resource distribution; for adopting policies that reflect professional knowledge; for establishing ways staff can continually gain more knowledge; for establishing organizational configurations that support teaching and learning; for creating problem-identification and problem-solving processes that continually assess and modify its own practices; and for responding to parent, student, and staff concerns and ideas.
- The central office must be accountable for evaluating the utility and effects of all its policies, such as hiring policies and paperwork requirements, and for equitable distribution of school resources, including qualified and highly experienced staff and rich curriculum opportunities. It should also be accountable for creating processes that make the school district responsive to the needs and concerns of parents, students, and school-level staff.

A system of shared accountability can lead to schooling that is inclusive, representational, and more likely to enhance the chances that all students will learn better. Learning and experimentation cannot thrive in an environment of fear. Instead, we should expect schools and educators to "account" by revealing candidly all the information about their enterprise.

This includes negative findings as well as positive. Then educators should be held accountable for shedding what doesn't work and building on what does.

Recommendation 6: Make Public Schools More Like Private Schools

Finally, I wish to offer an idea that could radically change the very structure of public education. It would inject market dynamics in the system, provide for shared accountability, enable schools to enforce standards, and empower students and their parents to choose from among all city public schools the one best suited to their needs.

Such a two-way choice would mean that accountability would be built in: Parents and students would vote with their feet, while public schools would, for the first time, gain the right to actually enforce the academic, behavioral, and parental involvement codes they set. In a way, public schools would gain the capacity and authority that private schools have had all along.

Here are some features of the proposal:

- The current drive to create smaller schools and schools-within-schools would accelerate. Small schools where students are well known are more effective. Also, by multiplying the number of available schools, we could expand the number of choices for parents, students, and educators. Each school should have increased autonomy over its own codes, organization, budget, staffing, and expectations. Each self-governing school should be free to develop its own theme and uniqueness. Each school should be led by a "teaching principal" or a "principal teacher" subject to annual affirmation or nonrenewal by the faculty and parents.
- On an annual basis, schools should report publicly to their communities about school performance—especially about student learning. This would serve to inform parents about the quality of each school.
- Parents could choose the right schools for their children from all available schools.
- The chosen school would gain the authority to require that parents and students who select that school sign a compact outlining behavior codes, academic performance, parental involvement, teacher and school commitments, and other features. Students and parents would have to adhere to this compact to continue in that school—or "shop around" for a school that might be a better match.

- Schools that are not chosen by parents and students would diminish in size. The vacated space could be filled by satellites of more effective schools or by newly developed public charter schools.
- Schools that are chosen by many parents and students could "franchise" themselves by expanding into satellites in spaces vacated in other, less effective schools.
- Approximately 10% of the schools would become "full-service schools." These schools would have health and social services for students who need them, case managers, a lower student-to-adult ratio, more counseling services, and other resources that only some children need. These schools for the most needy children would be staffed by experienced and accomplished teachers and would become the "educational intensive care units" of the district.
- Racial balance would be mandated in all schools—perhaps through the Singleton Formula that is now used for racially balancing the staff in our schools: The racial distribution in any school could not vary significantly from the overall racial makeup of the school district.
- At least one-third of all the slots in each school would be reserved for students in the neighborhood. Also, each school would include a proportional share of special education students.
- The per-capita amount of money allotted for each student would vary. For example, students with greater needs would be allotted a higher per-capita funding support than other students. The same would be true for students in full-service schools and special education students. This would serve as an incentive for schools to seek out these students instead of avoiding them.
- The weighted formula for each student would also include a "margin of profit" so that schools that attract and are successful with more students would have more incentives and could engage in profit sharing. A market-driven system that includes a two-way choice for public schools could offer incentives for everyone, encourage entrepreneurship, lessen the bureaucracy, phase out failing programs, and replicate successful schools. It would be more responsive to students and more conducive to continuous improvement.

Any of these recommendations might be worth considering on its own merits. But to implement them effectively, it's necessary to create a living contract between labor and management. All of these recommendations impact teacher working conditions that are governed by the union contract. To accomplish the next phase of reform, labor and management leaders must forge a relationship of mutual trust and respect instead of an adversarial one. A living contract provides the means to do so.

REFERENCES

Berends, M., Bodilly, S., & Kirby, S. N. (2001, April). *Lessons learned from a longitudinal assessment of the new American schools scale-up phase.* Paper presented at the annual meeting of the American Educational Research Association, San Diego.

Bryk, A. S., & Schneider, B. (2002). *Trust in schools: A core resource for improvement.* New York: Russell Sage Foundation.

Collins, A., Layzer, J., Kreader, J. L., Werner, A., & Glantz, F. (2000, November). *National study of child care for low-income Families: State and community substudy interim report.* Washington, DC: Abt Associates.

Datnow, A., & Stringfield, S. (2000). Working together for reliable school reform. *Journal of Education for Students Placed at Risk, 5*, 12–20.

Dolan, W. P. (1994). *Restructuring our schools: A primer on systemic change.* Kansas City: Systems and Organization.

Elmore, R. (1996). Getting to scale with successful educational practice. In S. H. Fuhrman & J. A. O'Day (Eds.), *Rewards and reform: Creating educational incentives that work* (pp. 249–329). San Francisco: Jossey-Bass Publishers.

Elmore, R. (2000). *Building a new structure for school leadership.* Washington, DC: Albert Shanker Institute.

Fullan, M. (2001a). *The new meaning of educational change* (3rd ed.). New York: Teachers College Press.

Fullan, M. (2001b). *Leading in a culture of change.* San Francisco: Jossey-Bass.

Fullan, M. (2003a). *Change forces with a vengeance.* London: Routledge Falmer.

Fullan, M. (2003b). *The moral imperative of school leadership.* Thousand Oaks, CA: Corwin.

Gutierrez, R., & Morales, H. (2002). Teacher community, biography, and math reform. In V. E. Lee (Ed.), *Reforming Chicago's high schools' research perspectives on school and system-level change* (p. 223–250). Chicago: Consortium on School Research, University of Chicago.

Hallett, A. (Ed.). (1995). *Reinventing central office: A primer for successful schools.* Chicago: Cross City Campaign for Urban School Reform.

Hatch, T. (2000). *What happens when multiple innovations collide.* Mendo Park, CA: Carnegie Foundation for the Advancement of Teaching.

Hess, F. (1999). *Spinning wheels: The politics of urban school reform.* Washington, DC: Brookings Institution.

Lee, C. D. (2002). Cultural modeling and the challenges of Chicago high school reform. In V. E. Lee (Ed.), *Reforming Chicago's high schools' research perspectives on school and system-level change* (pp. 203–222). Chicago: Consortium on School Research, University of Chicago.

Lee, V. E. (with J. B. Smith). (2001). *Restructuring high schools for equity and excellence: What works.* New York: Teachers College Press.

Lee, V. E. (Ed.). (2002). *Reforming Chicago's high schools' research perspectives on school and system-level change.* Chicago: Consortium on School Research, University of Chicago.

Lee, V. E., Ready, D. D., & Johnson, D. J. (2001). The difficulty of identifying rare samples: The case of high schools divided into schools-within-schools. *Educational Evaluation and Policy Analysis, 23*(4), 365–379.

Lee, V. E., & Smith, J. B. (1997). High school size: Which works and for whom? *Educational Evaluation and Policy Analysis, 19* (3), 205–227.

Lezotte, L. W., & Cipriano Peppel, J. (1999). *The effective schools and process: A powerful path to learning for all.* Okemos, MI: Effective School Products.

McBeath, A. (2001). Changing the rules and roles in Edmonton: A primer on school-based decision-making. In J. Simmons et al., *School reform in Chicago: Lessons and opportunities* (pp. 193–204). Chicago: Chicago Community Trust.

McLaughlin, M., & Talbert, J. (2001). *Professional communities and the work of high school teaching.* Chicago: University of Chicago Press.

Moore, D. (2001). Effects of elementary school reform. In J. Simmons et al., *School reform in Chicago: Lessons and opportunities* (pp. 49–54). Chicago: Chicago Community Trust.

Newmann, F., King, B., & Youngs, P. (2000, April). *Professional development that addresses school capacity.* Paper presented at the annual meeting of the American Educational Research Association, New Orleans.

Reynolds, A. J., Temple, J. A., Robertson, D. L., & Mann, E. A. (2001, May 9). Long-term effects of early intervention on educational achievement and juvenile arrests: A fifteen-year follow up of low-income children in public schools. *Journal of the American Medical Association, 285*(18), 2330–2246. Summary available at www.ccfc.ca.gov/PDF/SRI/chicago_cpc_jama.pdf.

Rolheiser, C., Fullan, M., & Edge, K. (2003). Dynamic duo. *Journal of Staff Development, 24*(2), 38–41.

Schmoker, M. (1999). *Results: The key to continuous school improvement.* Alexandria, VA: Association for Supervision and Curriculum Development.

Spillane, J., Halverson, R., & Diamond, J. (1999, April). *Distributed leadership: Toward a theory of school leadership practice.* Paper presented at the annual meeting of the American Educational Research Association, Montreal.

Viteritti, J. P. (2001). Governing big-city school systems. In J. Simmons et al., *School reform in Chicago: Lessons and opportunities* (pp. 177–192). Chicago: Chicago Community Trust.

Wallen, M. (1998, December). Taking the next steps: Focus on prevention by starting early [Paper prepared for Governor George Ryan's Transition Team]. Chicago: Ounce of Prevention Fund.

Wohlstetter, P., & Briggs, K. (2001). School-based management. In J. Simmons et al., *School reform in Chicago: Lessons and opportunities* (pp. 271–288). Chicago: Chicago Community Trust.

Chapter Seven

Improve the Quality
of Instruction

Even if all the other elements of the education system are up and running effectively, student achievement is not possible without excellent teaching. And a system that guarantees anything less than a qualified and effective teacher for every student is inadequate.

How can school systems ensure that every classroom is led by an effective teacher? One key step is examining the distribution of qualified and effective teachers within the district and zeroing in on problem areas to resolve shortages (Humphrey & Shields, 2001). A Northwestern University study found that 48% of teachers in some Chicago public high schools have such poor skills that out of 20 students, they were able to "reach" only 5 or fewer (Simmons et al., 2001).

Steps for increasing teacher quality include analyzing student achievement over time against professional supports offered to teachers; specifying standards for teachers; and crafting a high-quality, continuous, systemwide approach to professional development (Humphrey & Shields, 2001). When asked about the most important conditions that support effective teaching, Chicago teachers provided three primary answers:

1. A supportive school culture in which there is a shared education philosophy, consistent policies, and a safe environment;
2. School leaders who support teachers and hold them accountable for high-quality instruction; and
3. Teaching among a cadre of committed teachers who love to teach (Simmons et al., 2001).

In addition to working toward these conditions, reformers need to invest additional resources to make the immediate improvement in the instruction of low-performing students a high priority. This may mean introducing incentives to attract the district's best teachers and principals to the lowest-performing schools, shifting teachers within buildings, adding instructional time, providing after-school tutoring, or creating smaller classes for low-performing students (Humphrey & Shields, 2001).

If a system's architects have built into it the proper supports for good teaching, like those listed above, then quality teaching is more likely. Underperforming teachers who have been provided coaching and training, yet still remain ineffective, should not be teaching.

URBAN TEACHING: STRATEGIES FOR QUALITY

LINDA DARLING-HAMMOND

The field is ripe for dramatic improvement in the quality of teaching—especially in schools serving our most underserved students—and the demand is urgent. The author examines the major problems and issues in each of several areas related to teacher preparation, what strategies have been proposed and tried for addressing these problems, and the outcomes to date.

Causes of Poor-Quality Teaching

Despite conventional wisdom that school inputs make little difference in student learning, a growing body of research suggests that schools do make a difference, and a substantial portion of that difference is attributable to teachers. Recent studies of teacher effects at the classroom level have found that differential teacher effectiveness is an extremely strong determinant of differences in student learning, far outweighing the effects of differences in class size and composition (Sanders & Rivers, 1996; see also Wright, Horn, & Sanders, 1997).

Students who are assigned to several ineffective teachers in a row have significantly lower achievement—with differences of as much as 50 percentile points over 3 years—and smaller gains in achievement than those who are assigned to several highly effective teachers in sequence. These studies also find troubling indicators for educational equity. Students of color are much more likely to be assigned to the least effective teachers (Sanders & Rivers, 1996).

Studies in California, North Carolina, and Texas, among others, have found that students' likelihood of passing state achievement tests in reading and mathematics is strongly related to their access to fully qualified teachers, both before and after controlling for student poverty and other background factors (Darling-Hammond, 2000a; Fetler, 1999; Fuller, 1998; Strauss & Sawyer, 1986). Yet schools serving low-income and minority students are four to five times more likely to hire teachers who are untrained and uncertified than are schools serving more affluent, predominantly White students (Shields et al., 2001; NCTAF, 1996). This differential is particularly alarming as states enact new standards for student learning that are increasingly used as the basis for grade-level promotions and graduation from high school.

As Figure 7.1 graphically shows, there is a consistent relationship at

FIGURE 7.1. Reading Acheivement by Poverty Level of School and Percentage of Uncertified Teachers, Los Angeles Public Schools, 2nd and 3rd Graders

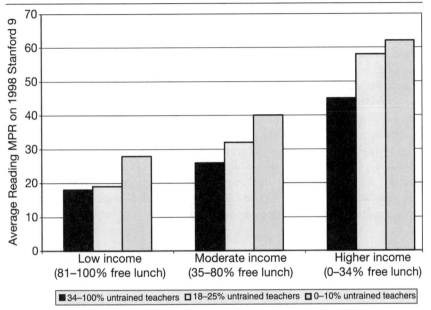

Source: Los Angeles County Office of Education, 1999

every income level between the reading achievement of elementary students and their teachers' qualifications.

The reach of good teacher preparation and of policies that create an adequate supply of well-prepared teachers is particularly important for children who live in poor communities. Because of chronic shortages of teachers, large cities such as New York, Chicago, Los Angeles, and Dallas have filled thousands of vacancies with unqualified teachers. In recent years, at least 50,000 unprepared teachers have been hired annually. These teachers are almost always assigned to teach low-income and minority students in central-city schools. Sadly, in stark contrast to their students' needs, these teachers of disadvantaged students are least likely to have been trained in how children grow, learn, and develop or what to do if these students are having difficulty learning.

Research consistently finds that unprepared teachers are less able to plan curricula that meets students' needs, less able to implement a range of teaching strategies—especially those that support higher-order learning and performance skills—and less likely to know what to do when students are having difficulty (for reviews, see Darling-Hammond, 1992, 2000a). Teachers who are well prepared are better able to use teaching strategies that respond to students' needs and learning styles and encourage higher-order learning (Hansen, 1988; Perkes, 1967–1968; Skipper & Quantz, 1987; Wenglinsky, 2002). Since the novel tasks required for problem solving are more difficult to manage than the routine tasks associated with rote learning, lack of knowledge about how to manage an active, inquiry-oriented classroom can lead teachers to turn to passive tactics that "dumb-down" the curriculum, busying students with workbooks rather than complex tasks that require more skill to orchestrate (Carter & Doyle, 1987; Cooper & Sherk, 1989; Doyle, 1986).

States that have not yet upgraded their licensing standards may not be preparing all of their teachers to support the needs of very diverse learners and to attain much more challenging learning goals than they have ever before sought to achieve. Figure 7.2 shows that schools serving low-income students have a higher percentage of unlicensed teachers.

FIGURE 7.2. Qualifications of Newly Hired Teachers,* by School Type, 1994

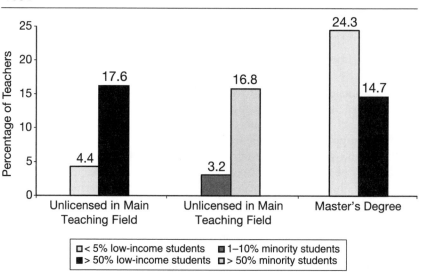

* Newly hired teachers, excluding transfers

Source: Tabulations conducted by the National Commission on Teaching and America's Future from data contained in the NCES's *Schools and Staffing Survey* (U.S. Department of Education, 1994)

   Clearly, expanding educational opportunity for all students requires serious attention to the questions not only of teacher preparation but also of teacher recruitment, distribution, and retention. Over the next decade, districts across the country are expected to hire more than 2 million new teachers as student enrollments grow and teacher retirements increase. The character of this teaching force will in large part determine the opportunities children experience throughout their educational careers. The need to better prepare teachers now is critical since most teachers who will be in classrooms in 2015 will have been hired in this decade.

   That investments in the quality of the teaching force could make a noticeable difference in the student outcomes is suggested by the results of a review of 60 studies that found that, if the goal is to increase student learning, the most productive use of additional education dollars among a number of common alternatives is to improve teacher education (Greenwald, Hedges, & Laine, 1996). Figure 7.3 shows the correlations this study calculated between specific educational investments and gains in student achievement.

   The recruitment and retention of well-prepared teachers and the support of high-quality teaching are the major responsibilities of a principal who functions as an instructional leader. The nature of this leadership af-

FIGURE 7.3. Effects of Educational Investments: Size of Increase in Student Achievement for Every $500 Spent on:

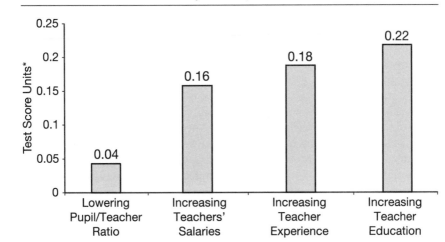

* Achievement gains were calculated as standard deviation units on a range of achievement tests in the 60 studies reviewed.

fects the quality of teaching and the retention of high-quality teachers. The principal–teacher relationship is the most powerful predictor of teachers' willingness to participate in personnel, curriculum, staff development, and administrative decision making (Smylie, 1992). Whether and how schools provide opportunities for involvement in decision making, for collaborative work with other teachers, and for engagement in curriculum building and other professional tasks influence teacher commitment, including whether teachers remain in a school and in the profession (Sclan, 1993).

Study after study has noted that good schools in low-income communities have strong principals who serve as instructional leaders. While resources and working conditions certainly matter, research suggests that teachers who have options choose to enter and remain in schools where they feel well supported by the local administrator and that schools with poor leadership typically have difficulty attracting and retaining teachers (Edmonds, 1979; Sclan, 1993; Anderman, Belzer, & Smith, 1991; NCES, 1997; Peterson & Martin, 1990). In national surveys of teachers about their decisions to remain in teaching, administrative supports matter far more than the characteristics of the student body or even variables such as student behavior and parent involvement (Darling-Hammond & Sclan, 1996).

The question for those concerned about equity is how schools serving poor and minority students can enhance their ability to get and keep well-prepared teachers and capable leaders. This question should lead school district reform efforts. Unfortunately, though, the question of how to improve teaching is often not at the forefront of reforms. Ostensibly simpler strategies, such as mandating new curriculum or using tests to determine promotion and graduation, are often viewed as silver bullets for curing the ills of struggling schools. These approaches, absent large investments in the capacity of educators to teach more effectively, always prove disappointing in the long run.

A study of Chicago's recent reforms is a case in point. Finding that low-achieving students who were retained in grade based on high-stakes tests did not improve their achievement but were, instead, more likely to drop out, the study noted that the failure to invest in improved teaching was an unrecognized problem in the city's reform strategy. The reform's focus on grade retention and a highly scripted, centrally developed curriculum (which assumed students would learn in the same ways and at the same pace) missed the mark. As the researchers noted, "Thus the administration has worked to raise test scores among low-performing students without having to address questions regarding the adequacy of instruction during the school day or spend resources to increase teachers' capacity to teach and to meet students' needs more successfully" (Roderick, Bryk, Jacob, Easton, & Allensworth, 1999, p. 57).

When the failure to learn is a result of inadequate teaching and when the system's primary response is to require children to experience that inadequate teaching again, such a policy even if it is touted under the banner of accountability, does not increase genuine accountability to parents and students.

Developing a Systemic Approach to Improving the Quality of Teaching

Developing quality teaching begins with attracting and recruiting promising candidates, continues with initial preparation that combines theory and practice in powerful ways, follows with support to teachers during the critical induction period in which they begin regular teaching, and continues to provide opportunities for professional growth throughout a teacher's career in schools that are well organized to support success. The problem of attracting and retaining an adequate supply of well-qualified teachers has a number of components that must be understood in tandem. A systemic approach to teaching quality includes at least the following:

- *Standards* for preparation, licensing, and advanced certification that reflect knowledge of best practice, are aligned with one another, and are well-recognized and well-enforced
- *Recruitment* incentives that ensure adequate supply across fields and districts (e.g., compensation that is market-competitive and equitable across districts, scholarships for training with payback options based on teaching in shortage fields or areas, improved working conditions in hard-to-staff schools, and supports for teacher retention)
- *Preparation* that ensures knowledge of content, learning, development, effective teaching strategies, curriculum, and assessment, and that links a coherent program of coursework with extensive clinical training under the direct supervision of expert teachers
- *Induction* that ensures mentoring by expert teachers who are trained and supported for mentoring with release time
- *Professional learning opportunities* that are sustained, continuous, curriculum-embedded, and linked to problems of practice
- *School redesign* to construct settings that support strong relationships between adults and children and in-depth student and teacher learning

Several major reports have outlined how to improve teacher preparation in each of these areas, and many organizations are intently pursuing this agenda. Among the most salient reports were the Carnegie Forum's *A Nation Prepared: Teachers for the 21st Century* in 1986, which led to the creation of the National Board for Professional Teaching Standards, and the Holmes Group of Education Deans' *Tomorrow's Teachers*, also in 1986, which launched new designs for teacher education programs that include more systematic study of content and pedagogy and more supervised clinical experience in settings serving diverse learners. Ten years later, the National Commission on Teaching and America's Future (1996) issued *What Matters Most: Teaching for America's Future*, a "blueprint for recruiting, preparing, and supporting excellent teachers in all of America's schools" (p. 10). This report led to widespread policy changes affecting teacher recruitment, preparation, induction, compensation, and professional development in states across the country.

Enhancing Recruitment

A key strategy for improving the quality of teaching is to expand recruitment initiatives for key fields and locations. Nationally, teaching continues to pay less than other professions requiring similar levels of education, even after salaries are adjusted for differences in the length of the workyear. Wage disparities are greatest for those in fields like mathematics, science, and computer technology, which is one of the reasons shortages are most severe in these fields. Figure 7.4 shows the differences between salaries for teachers and those in other occupations.

While teacher salaries have risen since their low point in the early 1980s, they have shrunk since 1960 as a percentage of overall education expenditures. In many other countries that the United States considers peers or competitors, well-qualified teachers are the major investment of schools, and teacher salaries account for more than 60% of total expenditures (NCTAF, 1996). A number of studies have produced evidence that such investments are associated with better educational results. For example, Ferguson's (1991) analysis of student achievement in Texas concluded that student gains were associated with the use of resources to acquire higher-quality teachers. Another study that looked across states from 1960 through 1990 and across districts in California from 1975 through 1995, found that student educational attainment increased most in states and districts that increased teacher wages (Loeb & Page, 2000).

Given the salary status of teaching, it is particularly important to invest in service scholarships and forgivable loans for undergraduate and graduate teacher education students, so that talented individuals can be

FIGURE 7.4. Beginning Salaries in Teaching and Other Occupations, 1999*

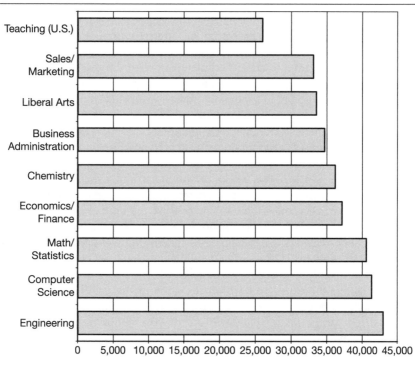

* Adjusted for cost of living
Source: Nelson & Schneider, 1999

recruited into professional preparation and can afford to enter teaching without a large debt load. Such scholarships are paid back through service in public school teaching. Especially crucial are incentives for students who prepare to teach in shortage fields (math, science, bilingual education, and special education) and shortage locations (e.g., central cities or poor rural areas), as well as for prospective teachers of color, who are also in substantial demand.

Alternative Pathways into Teaching

Since the 1980s, 41 states have enacted some type of alternative route to teacher certification to provide options beyond the traditional undergraduate programs of teacher education as one approach to expanding teacher recruitment. Virtually all states now have an array of programs available for persons with a bachelor's degree who want to become licensed to teach. Some of these are high-quality post-baccalaureate programs that are tailored to help mid-career recruits meet the same high standards as other recruits. They streamline preparation by interweaving coursework about learning and teaching with a well-supported clinical training experience. Usually these programs can be completed in 9 to 15 months and often result in a master's degree. A high-quality alternative in Chicago has been Teachers for Chicago (TFC), sponsored by a consortium of universities that work closely with receiving schools to support entrants with pre-service and in-service courses and intensive mentoring. Follow-up studies show that about 75% of TFC recruits remain in teaching after several years.

Other alternative routes are little more than emergency hiring options, however, offering just a few weeks of summer training before candidates are placed as teachers of record fully responsible for classrooms of students. In most cases, the follow-up mentoring is minimal to nonexistent, providing little support for these candidates or their students as they learn to teach. Such teachers are generally assigned almost exclusively to poor and minority students in the least advantaged schools, where they contribute to a chronically low quality of education.

Ironically, these programs often exacerbate the problems of supply and demand rather than solve them. Recent studies have documented that recruits from programs offering only a few weeks training before they assume full-time teaching responsibilities typically leave at very high rates. For example, 36% of New York City's Teaching Fellows left teaching after their second year, more than double the national attrition rate; 46% of recruits from the Massachusetts Initiative for New Teachers [MINT] program left teaching within 3 years; and an average of 80% of recruits from the Teach for America program left their teaching jobs in Houston, Texas, after 2 years (Fowler, 2002; New York State Education Department, 2003; Raymond, Fletcher, & Luque, 2001). Analyses of national data show that individuals who enter teaching without student teaching, which these programs generally truncate or omit, leave teaching at rates twice as high as those who have had such practice teaching (Henke, Chen, Geis, & Knepper, 2000; NCTAF, 2003).

These attrition patterns were reflected in a recent survey of more than 3,000 beginning teachers in New York City (Darling-Hammond, Chung, & Frelow, 2002). Teachers who had completed full programs of preparation felt significantly better prepared to meet the needs of the students in their classrooms and planned to stay in teaching longer than those who had entered through alternative routes. Recruits who had had little or no student teaching and had only a few weeks of training before they started teaching, reported that they did not feel that they were prepared to plan curriculum, assess their students' learning, design lessons to meet their students' needs or teach the state's content standards, or design instruction to meet the needs of special education students and second-language learners in their classrooms.

Feelings of underpreparation and lack of success contribute to very high attrition rates for candidates from short-term alternative programs. Overall, about 60% of individuals who enter teaching through such programs leave the profession by their third year, as compared to about 30% of traditionally trained teachers and only about 10% of teachers prepared in 5-year teacher education programs. Taking into account the costs to states, universities, and school districts of preparation, recruitment, induction, and replacement due to attrition, the actual cost of preparing a career teacher in the more intensive 5-year programs is actually significantly less than that of preparing a greater number of teachers in shorter-term programs who are less likely to stay—and, not incidentally, who are also less successful in the classroom (Darling-Hammond, 2000b). Figure 7.5 illus-

FIGURE 7.5. Average Retention Rates for Different Pathways into Teaching

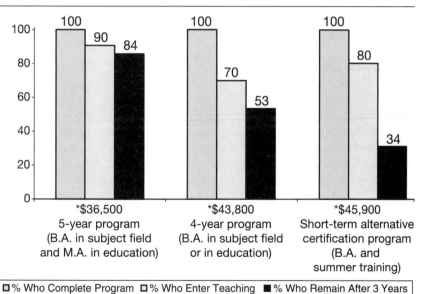

□ % Who Complete Program   □ % Who Enter Teaching   ■ % Who Remain After 3 Years

* Estimated cost per 3rd-year teacher

Estimates based on costs of teacher preparation, recruitment, induction, and replacement due to attrition.

Source: Darling-Hammond, 2002b

trates the actual costs for recruiting career teachers through different pathways into teaching, taking into account their different rates of attrition.

Alternatives that provide only a few weeks of training before placing candidates in classrooms appear to disadvantage both their own recruits and the disproportionately minority and low-income children these recruits teach. Many recruits report that their success, and that of their students, has been compromised by their lack of access to the knowledge needed to teach (Schorr, 1993; Mehlman, 2002).

In the long run, it is more sensible and cost-effective to recruit candidates into high-quality preparation programs than it is to recruit them via pathways that leave them underprepared and vulnerable to dropping out of the profession. It is also critical for the students who will be taught that they have teachers who understand how to teach them well rather than floundering about, leaving high levels of student failure in their wake. Superintendents considering how to improve recruitment need to locate or launch programs that both attract high-need candidates into the profession and enable them to succeed. Funds for service scholarships (free tuition offset by years of service in teaching), subsidized student teaching, stipends to support candidates while they complete a 1-year MAT program, and funds to universities to create or expand such post-baccalaureate programs are important means to improve recruitment, particularly for candidates of color and recruits in shortage fields.

Improving District Management

While labor-force issues and resource inequities often put urban school systems at a disadvantage, the ways in which districts choose to organize their hiring efforts and use their resources also matter greatly. Districts' hiring practices strongly affect the quantity and quality of teachers in the labor pool and the distribution of teachers to different types of school systems. Studies have found that some districts hire unqualified teachers for reasons other than shortages, including cumbersome hiring procedures that chase candidates away, a desire to save money on salaries by hiring low-cost recruits over those who are better qualified, beliefs that more-qualified teachers are more likely to leave and less likely to take orders, and sometimes, out-and-out patronage (Browne & Rankin, 1986; Haberman, 1995; Johanson & Gips, 1992; Pflaum & Abramson, 1990; Poda, 1995; Wise, Darling-Hammond, & Berry, 1987). A RAND Corporation study, for example, found that many districts emphasize teachers' ability to "fit in" and their willingness to comply with local edicts rather than their professional expertise (Wise, 1987). When these and other new teachers leave in frustration because they are underprepared for teaching and undersupported by the current induction practices, the hiring scramble begins all over again.

Furthermore, school districts sometimes lose out on the most qualified and highly ranked teachers in their applicant pool because of inadequate management information systems and antiquated hiring procedures that discourage or lose good applicants in a sea of paperwork.

These are particular problems in large urban districts, where reports of vacancies and information on candidates are not always accessible to district decision makers; hiring procedures are often cumbersome and bureaucratic; candidates repeatedly have their files lost, fail to receive responses to repeated requests for information, cannot secure interviews, and cannot get timely notice of job availability. Late budget notification and union contracts requiring placement of all internal teacher transfers prior to hiring of new candidates often put off hiring decisions until August or September, when candidates have since decided to take other jobs. As a result of these inefficiencies, large urban districts often lose good candidates to other districts and to nonteaching jobs (Wise et al., 1987).

Other state and school district practices can also undermine high-quality teacher recruitment and development. For example:

- Most districts impose a cap on the salaries they offer experienced candidates. As a consequence, highly educated and experienced teachers are forced to take a cut in pay if they move to a new locality and want to continue to teach. Many choose instead to change professions.
- Few districts provide reimbursement for travel and moving expenses.
- Many districts place beginning teachers in the most difficult schools with the highest rates of teacher turnover, the greatest numbers of inexperienced staff, and the least capacity to support teacher growth and development. Without induction supports, many teachers leave.

Just as policies can create shortages, they can also eliminate them. Urban districts that are successful in hiring the teachers they most want and need have developed proactive outreach systems for recruiting from local colleges and from other regional and national sources, streamlined personnel systems using sophisticated information technology to make information about vacancies available to candidates and information about candidates readily available to decision makers, and developed systems for projecting vacancies and making offers early in the spring, as well as strategies for ensuring that those who receive offers are made to feel welcome, wanted, and well-inducted into the school district (Darling-Hammond, Hightower, Husbands, LaFors, & Young, 2003; Snyder, 2002; Wise et al., 1987).

Improving Teacher Education

Long-standing criticisms of education schools have recently spurred reforms in many colleges and universities. Many of these programs have joined with local school districts to create professional development schools (PDSs). Like teaching hospitals in medicine, these schools aim to provide sites for state-of-the-art practice that are also organized to support the training of new professionals, extend the professional development of veteran teachers, and sponsor collaborative research and inquiry.

In urban areas, the creation of PDS models has allowed high-quality training for prospective teachers in settings where they can learn to succeed with diverse learners, rather than fearing urban teaching or failing when they enter. In the most highly developed sites, programs are jointly planned and taught by university-based and school-based faculty. Beginning teachers get a richer, more coherent learning experience when they are organized in teams to study and practice with faculty and with one another. Senior teachers report that they deepen their knowledge by serving as mentors, adjunct faculty, co-researchers, and teacher leaders (Darling-Hammond, 1994). Thus, these schools help create the rub between theory and practice that teachers need in order to learn. Several states, including North Carolina, Maryland, and Ohio, have provided funding and other incentives for the creation of PDS models for teacher education. Some foundations, such as Bell South, have supported colleges in creating these models.

A study of extraordinarily successful teacher education programs by the National Commission on Teaching and America's Future (Darling-Hammond, 2000c) looked at seven teacher preparation programs that are unusually and consistently successful at teaching diverse learners. Located at public and private universities across the country, these programs—at Alverno College in Milwaukee, Wisconsin; Bank Street College of Education in New York City; Trinity University in San Antonio, Texas; the University of California at Berkeley; the University of Southern Maine; the University of Virginia in Charlottesville; and Wheelock College in Boston, Massachusetts—represent a range of program types. Despite their institutional differences, the programs share several features that directly distinguish them from many others:

• *A common, clear vision of good teaching* that is apparent in all coursework and clinical experiences. In contrast to the fragmented courses and agnostic sense of purpose present on most campuses, faculty in these programs have hammered out their view of what matters for good teaching and have constructed a series of courses and experiences that ensure all of the building blocks for such teaching are present and reinforced. This vision includes an ethical commitment to the education of all students along with study of teaching strategies that address the needs of a wide range of students.

- *Well-defined standards* of practice and performance that are used to guide and evaluate coursework and clinical work. Along with a common vision of good teaching are explicit standards for what professional teachers should know and be able to do to meet the needs of diverse students and to teach their subject matter(s) in powerful ways. These standards guide decisions about learning experiences, assignments, and ongoing assessment of students' learning and performance in both the college classroom and the school classroom. Students have many examples of the kind of practice they are trying to develop, and they have many opportunities to get feedback about how they are progressing toward those goals.

- *A rigorous core curriculum.* Unlike programs criticized for "mushy" education courses that have an unclear knowledge base and mostly pass on unexamined teaching lore, these programs have developed a systematic program of study grounded in substantial knowledge of subject-matter content, child and adolescent development, learning theory, cognition, motivation, social contexts, and subject-matter pedagogy, taught in the context of practice. Students do not report that their only valuable experience was student teaching. Instead, they report that their courses were intellectually engaging, theoretically well grounded, and practically useful.

- *Extensive use of problem-based methods,* including cases and case studies, teacher research, performance assessments, and portfolio evaluation. Like the strategies used in good schools of business, law, architecture, engineering, and medicine, these methods help teachers apply general propositions derived from research and theory to real problems of practice, thus supporting their developing abilities to reason pedagogically. Learning to think like a teacher requires the combination of multiple kinds and sources of knowledge with a diagnostic eye on both curriculum goals and student needs. Problem-based methods support the development of teaching judgment and tools for inquiry as they are used in practice.

- *Intensely supervised, extended clinical experiences* (at least 30 weeks) that are carefully chosen to support the ideas and practices presented in simultaneous, closely interwoven coursework. In contrast to traditional programs' weak student teaching experience of 8 to 12 weeks, these candidates have a full academic year to develop, test, and problem-solve more sophisticated forms of practice under the guidance of master teachers. Their practice has an opportunity to take root and grow strong, so that it is not blown over like a thin reed when they enter difficult teaching circumstances as a first-year teacher.

- *Strong relationships with reform-minded local schools* that support the development of common knowledge and shared beliefs among school- and university-based faculty. These partnerships support co-reform of both the school and the university teacher education program and create sites for state-of-the-art practice, training, and research.

Improving Induction

The roles of the resident in medicine, the intern in architecture, and the associate in a law firm illustrate the importance other professions place on an extended clinical preparation period that carefully guides novices into growing responsibilities and increasingly more complex practice. In these and other professions, novices continue to hone their knowledge and skills under the watchful eyes of more knowledgeable and experienced practitioners. At the same time, the novices—fresh from their studies—bring the latest research and theoretical perspectives to bear on their practice, where it is shared and tested by novice and veteran practitioners alike.

The usual conditions of teaching, of course, are far from this utopian model. Traditionally, new teachers have been expected to sink or swim with little support and guidance. Overburdened principals charged with the supervision and evaluation of all teachers, along with their other responsibilities, have typically been unable to provide the intensive mentoring and oversight novices require. In addition to the fact that this leaves new teachers with little daily help, it has also meant that decisions about continuation and tenure have typically been pro forma because they are based on little data (Wise, Darling-Hammond, McLaughlin, & Bernstein, 1984).

With estimates that 30% of beginning teachers leave the profession within their first 5 years (Henke et al., 2000), a means of providing new educators with support is essential. Experience suggests there is a large payoff in establishing a comprehensive teacher-induction program. Beginning teachers who have access to intensive mentoring by expert colleagues are much less likely to leave teaching in the early years. A number of districts—such as Cincinnati, Columbus, and Toledo, Ohio, and Rochester, New York—have substantially reduced attrition rates of beginning teachers (often from levels exceeding 30% to rates of 5–10%) by providing expert mentors with release time to coach beginners in their first year on the job (NCTAF, 1996). These young teachers not only stay in the profession at higher rates but also become competent more quickly than those who must learn by trial and error.

In the best-developed programs, mentors are trained and released from classroom responsibilities so they can visit and observe in beginners' classrooms. Some induction programs involve collaboration between school districts and local schools of education (Debolt, 1992; MacIsaac and Brookhart, 1994; Wisniewski, 1992). In many districts, these partnerships are framed by professional development schools that connect pre-service teacher training, beginning-teacher induction, and ongoing professional development.

An example of how professional development schools can transform beginning-teacher preparation and induction is the configuration of the internship year in the University of Cincinnati's 5-year teacher education program. In collaboration with the university, the Cincinnati Public Schools established nine "professional practice schools" and created a special intern designation at half-pay in the salary schedule. During their fifth year of training, interns teach half time in one of the professional practice schools under the direct supervision of a team of expert veteran teachers who hold adjunct status with the university. The interns also complete coursework and in-school seminars co-planned by school- and university-based faculty. The interns systematically learn the complexities of effective teaching under close supervision. Following their internship year, those who are hired in the Cincinnati Public Schools experience the additional advantages of the larger mentoring and peer review process described earlier.

Induction supports can make an especially significant contribution to quality practice in urban schools, where new teachers often struggle most severely and burn out most quickly, given the demands and difficulties of the job when it must be confronted all alone. And professional development schools that model good teaching can help novices learn to practice competently and confidently in city neighborhoods where they will be most needed when they complete their training.

Strengthening Professional Development

In addition to the problems with teacher preparation and induction described above, professional development investments are often paltry. Most districts' offerings have traditionally been limited to "hit-and-run" workshops and do not help teachers learn the sophisticated teaching strategies they need to address very challenging learning goals with very diverse populations of students. Most school districts do not direct their professional development dollars in a coherent way toward sustained, practically useful learning opportunities for teachers. And teachers have little time to learn from one another: In U.S. schools, most teachers have only 3 to 5 hours a week in which to prepare their lessons, usually in isolation from their colleagues. They rarely have opportunities to plan or collaborate with other teachers, to observe and study teaching, or to talk together about how to improve curriculum and meet the needs of students. In short, many teachers in the United States enter the profession with inadequate preparation, and few have many opportunities to enhance their knowledge and skills over the course of their careers (NCTAF, 1996).

The type of in-service education makes a difference. A large-scale study by David Cohen and Heather Hill (2000) found that mathematics teachers who participated in sustained professional development grounded in the curriculum they were learning to teach were much more likely than those who engaged in other kinds of professional development to report reform-oriented teaching practices. These practices and their professional development participation were, in turn, associated with higher mathematics achievement for students on the state assessment, holding student characteristics and school conditions constant. The professional development that proved effective involved teachers in working directly with one another and with experts on new student curriculum materials related to specific concepts in California's mathematics framework. Teachers collaboratively studied these materials, developed and tried lessons, and discussed the results with their colleagues, treating issues of mathematics content, instruction, and learning simultaneously.

The question is how to make more sustained, in-depth opportunities for teacher learning more widely and routinely available in schools across the country, especially in urban districts where professional development opportunities are generally most needed and least available.

Conclusions

The opportunities for making a major intervention in the life chances of urban children by transforming the teaching and schooling they experience have never been greater. That systematic efforts in overhauling the quality of teaching can make a difference in the outcomes of city schools has been shown in long-term efforts in New York City's School District 2; San Diego and New Haven, California; and El Paso and San Antonio, Texas—where teachers are now carefully recruited, prepared, and supported, and where students are learning at levels far exceeding those generally expected for them. Successful districts do the following:

- Recruit teachers aggressively and hire well-prepared teachers early
- Set competitive salaries and allocate resources to teaching
- Provide mentoring for beginning teachers and professional development for all teachers

- Ensure good working conditions: materials, administrative support, and input to decisions
- Design schools so that teachers and students can build strong relationships and focus on in-depth learning and teaching.

If the interaction between teachers and students is the most important aspect of effective schooling, then reducing inequality in learning has to rely on policies that provide equal access to competent, well-supported teachers. The public education system ought to be able to guarantee that every child who is forced by law to go to school is taught by someone who is knowledgeable, competent, and caring. That is real accountability. As Carl Grant (1989) puts it:

> Teachers who perform high-quality work in urban schools know that, despite reform efforts and endless debates, it is meaningful curricula and dedicated and knowledgeable teachers that make the difference in the education of urban students. (p. 770)

When it comes to equalizing opportunities for students to learn, that is the bottom line.

IMPROVING STUDENT LEARNING
THROUGH ENHANCED TEACHER QUALITY

CHARLOTTE DANIELSON

Recent research confirms what discerning parents have always known—that the quality of teaching matters. School districts have little chance of improving student learning without attending to the quality of teaching. And they can't improve teacher quality unless they operate with a common definition of what quality instruction is. The author describes a framework for teaching that, in its many uses, promotes improved teacher quality.

Of all the influences on student learning over which the school has control, the single most important is the quality of teaching. But despite this recognition, most school districts have not defined what they mean by good teaching. This has been left to the individual and idiosyncratic discretion of each teacher and administrator. Consequently, administrators, when they observe teachers for the purpose of coaching or evaluation, comment that they "don't know what they should be looking for," and their supervisors are concerned that the judgments of different administrators are wildly different from one another. Furthermore, teachers express concern because they must infer, from what an administrator may say in passing, what that person values in the classroom. Therefore, a comment such as "I'll come back when you're teaching"—overheard from a principal entering a classroom for an observation when the students were engaged in a somewhat messy but productive science lesson—speaks volumes. The teacher's response, predictably, is to "play it safe," to conduct the next lesson with the students in their desks, in rows, engaged in something quiet (and quite possibly boring).

One of the principal benefits of any framework to describe teaching is providing a common language for use by practitioners-teachers, administrators, board members, and so on. This common language enables them to describe their work, explore alternatives, and so on. All professions have a language through which practitioners can communicate; in the case of some professions, that language is highly specialized. When professional development experts share their concerns about improving teaching, one of the first items they tend to mention is that educators do not even share a common language. The framework for teaching can address that concern.

A Framework for Teaching

The first step in enhancing teaching quality is to determine what constitutes quality. What does teaching well mean? What is it that excellent teachers know and do? Is it the same in every instructional setting, or is it different with different-aged students and in different disciplines? And when a school or district (or state) has determined what good teaching is, what are the benefits of such a coherent definition?

Components of Professional Practice. The teaching framework offered here organizes the complex work of teaching into four broad areas or domains: planning and preparation, classroom environment, instruction, and professional responsibilities. Each domain is further divided into five or six components, each with anywhere from two to five smaller elements. The framework is summarized in Table 7.1.

The teaching framework offers a coherent definition that can serve as an organizational structure to describe and promote good teaching. The framework is built on extensive research conducted at Educational Testing Service (ETS) in the development of the Praxis III assessments for beginning teachers (Danielson, 1996). Many districts, both in the United States and overseas, have adopted this framework as the structure for defining and describing good teaching in their settings. In a 1997 ETS study, the framework was independently validated for experienced teachers.

The framework attempts to describe the totality of teaching, including those aspects that occur beyond the classroom walls. Thus, in addition to describing classroom performance, it includes such things as communicating with families or contributing to the school and district. This feature sets it apart from other lists of teaching skills, which may confine themselves to aspects of teaching that happen only when teachers are interacting with students. The framework components are not specific to a particular discipline or level; instead, they apply to all instructional settings. They also apply to teachers at all levels of experience, from novice to highly accomplished.

Assumptions of the Framework for Teaching. The growing appreciation of the importance of good teaching in promoting student achievement has been accompanied by an enhanced understanding of cognition and what contributes to learning. This emphasis on learning has also broadened the definition of what is worth learning; educators and citizens alike now recognize that schools must teach more than facts—they must also impart complex skills of reasoning and judgment.

TABLE 7.1. The Framework for Teaching: Four Domains

Domain 1: **Planning and Preparation**	Domain 2: **Classroom Environment**
Includes comprehensive understanding of the content to be taught, knowledge of the students' backgrounds, and designing instruction and assessment.	*Is concerned with the teacher's skill in establishing an environment conducive to learning, including both the physical and interpersonal aspects of the environment.*
The components are: 1. Demonstrating knowledge of content pedagogy 2. Demonstrating knowledge of students 3. Selecting instructional goals 4. Demonstrating knowledge of resources 5. Designing coherent instruction 6. Assessing student learning	The components are: 1. Creating an environment of respect and rapport 2. Establishing a culture for learning 3. Managing classroom procedures 4. Managing student behavior 5. Organizing physical space
Domain 3: **Instruction**	Domain 4: **Professional Responsibilities**
Is concerned with the teacher's skill in engaging students in learning the content and includes the wide range of instructional strategies that enable students to learn.	*Is concerned with a teacher's additional professional responsibilities, including self-assessment and reflection, communication with parents, participating in ongoing professional development, and contributing to the school and district environment.*
The components are: 1. Communicating clearly and accurately 2. Using questioning and discussion techniques 3. Engaging students in learning 4. Providing feedback to students 5. Demonstrating flexibility and responsiveness	The components are: 1. Reflecting on teaching 2. Maintaining accurate records 3. Communicating with families 4. Contributing to the school and district 5. Growing and developing professionally 6. Showing professionalism

If school learning is not simply a matter of learning facts by rote, teaching is not equivalent to telling. The image that many people hold of teachers—the person standing at the front of the room lecturing to a docile group of students—simply does not apply to the vast majority of school settings. Research into cognition emphasizes the active nature of learning and the important role of teachers in structuring learning activities to enable students to, for example, formulate and test hypotheses, extract general principles from a variety of specific instances, and learn to express their ideas succinctly and powerfully. Learning activities to promote important learning are not a random free-for-all; rather, they are structured to maximize student intellectual engagement. School learning, in other words, is not a spectator sport; it is organized, disciplined, and responsive to students' knowledge base and cognitive structures.

The teaching framework offered here does not promote a particular style of teaching. Effective teaching may be accomplished in many different ways and can look very different. For example, group work is not always more effective than a presentation; it depends on the teacher's purpose. The choice of instructional approach depends on what is appropriate to achieve a particular instructional goal.

Context Matters. The framework does not define specific behaviors for teachers. It describes what teachers can achieve in their work, what effect they should be able to produce. For example, the techniques a kindergarten teacher uses to establish an environment of respect and rapport will be very different from those used by a high school chemistry teacher, but the effect will be the same: Every student will feel valued and respected by the teacher and students. Therefore, the framework is not a checklist of specific behaviors; it cannot be, since the behaviors themselves are dependent on the context.

Many factors combine to determine context: the age and developmental levels of the students; the subject being taught; the cultural heritage of the students; the larger environment (urban, rural, or suburban) of the school. Many of the details of what teachers do are determined by these factors.

Levels of Performance. It is not sufficient to list the tasks of teaching; educators and policymakers must be able to differentiate excellent from poor or mediocre performance. A contribution of the framework for teaching is to describe, for each of its components and elements, how it is manifested at each of four levels of experience and proficiency: unsatisfactory, basic, proficient, and distinguished. An example, for the component "establishing an environment of respect and rapport," is provided in Table 7.2.

TABLE 7.2. Levels of Performance

Element	Unsatisfactory	Basic	Proficient	Distinguished
Teacher interaction with students	Teacher interaction with at least some students is negative, demeaning, sarcastic, or inappropriate to the age or culture of the students. Students exhibit disrespect for teacher.	Teacher–student interactions are generally appropriate but may reflect occasional inconsistencies, favoritism, or disregard for students' cultures. Students exhibit only minimal respect for teacher.	Teacher–student interactions are friendly and demonstrate general warmth, caring, and respect. Such interactions are appropriate to developmental and cultural norms. Students exhibit respect for teacher.	Teacher demonstrates genuine caring and respect for individual students. Students exhibit respect for teacher as an individual, beyond that for the role.
Student interaction	Student interactions are characterized by conflict, sarcasm, or put-downs.	Students do not demonstrate negative behavior toward one another.	Student interactions are generally polite and respectful.	Students demonstrate genuine caring for one another as individuals and as students.

Uses of the Framework for Teaching

The framework is a powerful tool with several applications available for institutions and policymakers to bring about coherence in teaching, including professional development and teacher evaluation.

Professional Development. Professional development must be organized around a common definition of teaching. This professional development can take many forms, from study groups, to more formal workshops and presentations, to web support. However, regardless of the form selected (or the range of offerings provided), it is essential that the professional development engage teachers in sustained, job-embedded investigations and analysis of practice within a supportive and professional environment.

Teacher Evaluation. Some of the most innovative applications of the framework for teaching have been in teacher evaluation. Many districts, in virtually every state, have implemented new approaches in which teachers take a more active role in the process, engage in professional conversations with colleagues and evaluators, and document their practice through techniques that mirror those used by the National Board for Professional Teaching Standards. This includes not only teaching observations but also teachers assembling other evidence of their practice in a portfolio of artifacts.

Few educational leaders recognize the potential of using their teacher evaluation systems as a core component in enhancing teacher quality. However, recent evidence suggests that it is an overlooked resource, one that can play a major role in school improvement efforts. The system's design is critical, but it appears that the professional conversations that accompany a well-designed system could promote reflective practice and student achievement.

By making the framework components public, practitioners can engage in open conversations and dialogue regarding good teaching practice. This openness is important for professional dialogue and is essential if the framework is used as the basis for teacher evaluation.

Policy Implications for Supporting Teacher Quality

Individual applications of the framework for teaching can have a significant impact on teacher quality. But their real impact comes from a comprehensive approach, when a school or district incorporates all aspects. Typically, even in small school districts, the responsibility (and frequently the budget) for coordinating student teacher placement, mentoring, and induction; professional development; and teacher evaluation rests with different individuals, each with his or her own sense of the job at hand. In large school districts, this fragmentation is far more pronounced, with each initiative organized completely independently. The framework, if used to inform each of the programs, can provide unity and coherence, tying them together around a common vision of teacher quality.

Policy implications here are clear for leadership, most importantly from the superintendent's office. If school districts are to derive the full benefit of a coherent definition of teaching, one that can provide a "curriculum" for its efforts in supervising student teachers, recruiting and mentoring new teachers, structuring professional development, and evaluating teacher performance, the district must be prepared to exercise the leadership required to pull these efforts together under a single umbrella. The characteristics of districts that have successfully implemented such approaches are the following:

- An uncompromising commitment to student learning, with all components of the instructional program organized to support such learning.

- High expectations for both students and staff, combined with high levels of support to enable teachers and administrators to acquire new skills and use new approaches and organizational structures.
- Redesign of the teacher evaluation system to encourage self-assessment, reflection, and professional conversation.
- Promotion of focused professional learning by both teachers and administrators. This typically takes the form of training in the framework for teaching, training for mentors in supporting beginning teachers, and training for administrators in observing and analyzing teaching and providing feedback.

CULTIVATING ACCOUNTABILITY: CREATING CONDITIONS FOR ALL STUDENTS TO ACHIEVE HIGH STANDARDS

KATE JAMENTZ

With the new climate of increased accountability for results, district administrators are well served by turning their attention to strengthening the relationships and creating the conditions through which students, educators, staff, and parents can do their part to raise the bar on student achievement. The author outlines what districts and communities can do to cultivate accountability.

Today's "education mayors," "education governors," and "education presidents" all champion school accountability. Their various accountability plans call for high standards and swift action to "turn around" low-performing schools. The mental model that undergirds these plans is one of "accounting." Student performance is measured in some way, counts are made of the number of students who have yet to achieve to acceptable levels, and consequences and assigned to individuals or groups who are thereby held to account for those results. Schools that do not make adequate progress are singled out in the local paper and on the Internet. Principals are reassigned and staff is reconstituted or the school "taken over" by a higher authority. Students are retained in grade or denied a diploma.

While many believe these drastic actions are necessary to regain the public trust and jump-start improvement efforts, it is doubtful that these top-down systems can generate the kind of capacity and sustained effort that it will take to close the achievement gap and ensure that all students achieve to high standards. Those critical goals require that we work from a very different mental model of accountability—one that assumes that accountability is embedded not in a management system but in a personal system of values.

An accountable school is one where accountability is an organizational norm, where individuals express a sense of urgency for improvement and work collectively to realize it rather than blaming each other for failure. Accountability cannot be imposed if it is to be effective.

Working from this mental model, the role of district and community leaders becomes one of strengthening the relationships and creating the conditions through which students, professional educators, staff, and parents alike recognize and accept their responsibility for improving student learning.

What do systems do to cultivate accountability? Implementing six strategies is essential for school districts to achieve effective accountability:

1. Articulate standards for student performance
2. Use professional development
3. Invest in quality assessments
4. De-privatize instruction
5. Engage the larger public
6. Define standards for adult performance

Articulate Standards for Student Performance

The recent standards movement was born of the realization that, despite the fact that public schools open their doors to everyone, what students *experience* there varies greatly. America's system of common schools provides anything *but* a common experience for those who attend them.

Traditionally, the teacher's job is to plan engaging instructional experiences that will help students cover the grade-level curriculum to which they are assigned. Teachers choose lessons or learning activities from texts, or make up their own, to address key topics from the curriculum. They individually determine how long they will spend on a given topic, when and how they will test students on what they have learned, and what criteria they will use to determine the quality of the work students produce. What teachers teach and expect of students is a function of what they know about their subject matter, what they like to teach, and what they believe any given child is capable of learning. When the current chapter or instructional unit is finished, they move on to new topics.

From the students' point of view, what they are exposed to, what they learn, and "what counts" in terms of their grade are determined by the teacher they happen to have that year. Other students taking the same course at the same grade level might be required to do very different work or to produce work of much greater or much lesser quality. Typically, students whom the system deems capable of college-level work land in the classes of those teachers who demand the most, while other students experience a range of expectations from the challenging to the "Mickey Mouse."

Unfortunately, districts frequently and vastly underestimate what it takes to organize resources to assure that all students achieve to high standards. Too often, the process of setting district standards for student performance is limited to adopting, or perhaps customizing, and distributing a laundry list of statements about what students should know and do in a range of subject areas. There is little participation of teachers and other stakeholders in system design and thus little ownership by the people who have to improve the results.

District systems that successfully cultivate accountability recognize that standards for student performance put in practice answer the question: *What do we think students should know and be able to do ... and how well do they need to do it?* Systems that support the value of accountability draw on the work of experts in each content area, paying attention to the standards that guide external, high-stakes testing systems to which their students may be held accountable. At the same time, they also involve individuals at all levels in negotiating common interpretations of the standards as reflected in the work students do every day.

Standards in these districts represent hard-won agreements about what is considered *essential* for all students to know and do in order to progress through grade levels and be successful in the world outside school.

Use Professional Development

In systems where judgments of performance are guided by agreed-upon performance standards, professional development is designed to help teachers internalize expectations for quality work at the grade levels they teach. Teachers must be exposed to numerous exemplars of the kinds of work considered adequate for the students they teach. They should be able to analyze student work samples not only in terms of whether they are adequate but also in terms of what they reveal about a student's needs for additional instruction.

Both teacher-induction and ongoing professional development programs should include ample opportunities for teachers to (1) identify the types of assignments and learning experiences that provide adequate intellectual challenge and (2) develop confidence that their own expectations of student work reflect what is known about cognitive development as well as the standards agreed upon by the larger community.

Standards in these schools define clear expectations for student performance and bind teachers and students as teammates in the effort to get each student to those levels. Standards do not confine or limit what teachers teach or students learn; instead, they work as agreements about what schools can and should promise to those who pay for, or depend upon, the fruits of public schools.

Invest in Quality Assessments

At every level of a standards-based system, from policy deliberations to lesson planning, decision makers must have data about student achievement that they trust and can use to make the decisions for which they are responsible. School board members must make policy decisions that reflect an analysis of patterns of achievement over time and throughout the district. Principals need data to understand the efficacy of a given program. Teachers need data they can use in guiding instruction on a day-to-day basis.

Most of the newest state-level accountability systems are based on large-scale assessments that provide data only on an annual basis. Constructed to be efficient and reliable to administer, these tests are much better at assessing discrete skills than in providing data about whether a student *can actually use those skills* to do tasks similar to those they will encounter in the world outside school. They are useful for measuring the progress and achievement of large groups of students against a limited set of important standards. However, these tests fail to measure student achievement against agreed-upon standards and instead measure student performance only in relation to other students.

Far too often these narrow, large-scale assessments are used as the sole or primary criteria for decisions of high consequence in the lives of students or teachers, despite warnings from even the test developers themselves about this inappropriate use.

If educators are to develop norms of responsible data-driven decision making, high-quality, standards-based assessment tools that are valid and reliable enough to serve the purpose for which they are intended must inform their decisions. State and/or district assessments should provide criterion-referenced information about achievement of key standards and be used primarily to indicate patterns of programmatic strength and weakness.

Decisions guiding day-to-day instruction should be informed by (1) local, cross-classroom assessments that reveal what a given student can already do in relation to agreed-upon performance standards, (2) what may be getting in the way of that student's understanding, and (3) what knowledge or skill the teacher can build on to help that student's progress.

High-stakes decisions about individual students, teachers, or schools must be justified by the use of multiple assessments, including both highly reliable large-scale assessments and judgments made by teachers who are trained and held responsible for the credibility of their judgments of student work in relation to the standards.

Because assessment technology does not currently offer a single test that can provide all the forms of data needed by decision makers at all levels of the system, districts and schools determined to cultivate accountability must invest in an accountability *system* that not only monitors large-scale achievement in relation to the standards but also provides regular diagnostic information to individual teachers and students who use it as a guide to teaching and learning.

An assessment system that serves real accountability is judged not only for its reliability and its efficiency but also for its credibility and usefulness to all those who use its data in their decision making.

De-Privatize Instruction

The norms and practices that have supported systems of differentiated standards are deeply ingrained in school practice and professional development. Teachers have been taught, rewarded for being, and sustained as orchestrators of engaging activities from which some students benefited and others did not. The private practice of making assignments, setting standards, and judging performance has been protected in the name of teacher autonomy and perpetuated by the difficulty of finding time for collaborative planning or analysis of student work.

Accountability is fostered in organizations that focus on improving instructional quality by opening instructional practice to professional and public scrutiny. Judgments about quality practice or performance are not left to individual whim, experience, or even expertise. In these systems, standards and assessments are used to focus dialogue and collective decision making on what evidence students must produce in order to "demonstrate understanding" of a concept and what specific characteristics are required of work that is "good enough" to meet the standard. Expectations for performance are not established by individuals who are necessarily limited in what they believe possible by their own experience. They are set (and, as necessary, revised) in consultation with others using evidence of what students can produce in high-quality programs.

The responsibilities of educators are defined not only by what they do alone in their classrooms but also by what they do in collaboration with colleagues. School systems that foster accountability provide time for and expect teachers and principals to visit one anothers' classrooms and to give and receive feedback on instructional practice and the quality of student work. Educators engage in professional dialogue (1) to challenge anothers' expectations for what students should and can do, (2) to give feedback to one another about the effectiveness of instruction, and (3) to adjust or reallocate resources or expertise to address shared programmatic concerns.

Collaboration is supported not just because it creates a desirable working condition but because it facilitates shared responsibility. The infamous "egg-carton" image of schools is deliberately broken down so that teachers have access to the knowledge and skills of their colleagues and information about the needs of students other than their own. Through collaboration it becomes feasible for individuals to see the whole and to behave in such a way that the school becomes more than the sum of its parts. Only then can the responsibility for the success of individual students be owned by all adults and the language of decision making driven by what "*we* will do" for "*our* students." Expert teachers might then accept responsibility for working with students most in need or with other teachers to improve their skills.

Engage the Larger Public

The fundamental school accountability relationship is between educators and the students and families they serve. Yet large-scale state-level accountability systems run the risk of obscuring those relationships, suggesting that the responsibility of the school is to improve scores on state tests. Schools that foster accountability as an organizational norm engage parents and the public in critical questions of school quality and how it might be improved.

Many state accountability systems assume clarity on what makes a good or accountable school, and yet, in reality, no such clarity exists. While the quality of students' academic performance clearly is an important indicator of what the public wants from its schools, it is also clear that that is not all that goes into judging school quality. Parents also want safe schools in which students demonstrate tolerance, respect, and self-discipline—and learn to enjoy learning. Test scores are important, but so are graduation and employment rates as well as student and parent perceptions of the school.

Similarly, there is no real consensus about how student academic performance should be judged. While some argue that performance should be marked in relation to an absolute standard, others want normative information that compares performance to other students and schools. While some systems define school quality in terms of raising the average level of performance, others demand that improvement be defined in terms of "closing the achievement gap" between poor students or students of color and their more traditionally successful peers.

The histories of many high-visibility and controversial school improvement strategies—"alternative assessments," "whole-language," or "new-new math"—indicate that educators often leave parents and their communities behind in advocating for changes in practice in public schools. Parents fear their children are being put at risk by unproven innovations and are increasingly less willing to take at face value what they fear to be the "reform du jour."

Systems that foster accountability as a personal value and organizational norm expand the conversation about school quality beyond school walls. Schools bring parents to the table to help establish performance standards or to consider how a new assessment strategy might provide better data for certain kinds of decision making. They work to amplify the voices of all stakeholders to ensure they are heard in defining the criteria on which the school should be judged and in sharing perspectives on what is and is not working for their students.

In fostering meaningful public engagement, schools bring the accountability conversation home from the state legislature to the local school. When schools create dialogue between and among members of different groups, parents learn to communicate to teachers about the support they need to assist their children. Additionally, teachers talk to parents about the support they need from home and to administrators about the training, materials, or other resources they need to accomplish schoolwide goals. Cross-role coalitions grow out of the opportunity provided to share perspectives and needs.

The participation of parents and community members is not confined to bake sales; instead, their input is welcomed as partners in promoting student learning. Research suggests that schools willing to open themselves up to scrutiny, to be transparent about critical issues of quality and student learning, generate public appreciation and support.

Define Standards for Adult Performance

Implied in these strategies for cultivating accountability are a set of standards for adult performance in schools that differ from our traditional expectations for teachers and site and district leaders. Teachers cannot succeed at the work of assuring that all students achieve to high standards without participating in collaborative efforts to internalize those standards or without having the skills to assess student performance and judge student work in relation to those shared standards. Their work is defined not only in terms of how they work with students assigned to them but also in terms of how they contribute to the success of all students and the ability of the school as a whole to respond to their needs. Skills that at one time were considered "above and beyond the call of duty" for classroom teachers are requisite to systems determined to close the achievement gap.

Implementation of these six strategies is dependent on principals and district leaders who are therefore responsible for (1) creating the conditions that help teachers build and sustain these skills, (2) promoting evidence-based decision making, and (3) facilitating the public and professional dialogue that generates collective action. They are first and foremost orchestrators of individual and organizational learning and guardians of a sense of community necessary to make a set of individuals—teachers, parents, and students—function as more than the sum of its parts.

REFERENCES

Anderman, E., Belzer, S., & Smith, J. (1991, April). Teacher commitment and job satisfaction: The role of school culture and principal leadership. Paper presented at the annual meeting of the American Educational Research Association, Chicago.

Browne, B., & Rankin, R. (1986). Predicting employment in education: The relative efficiency of national teacher examinations scores and student teacher ratings. *Educational and Psychological Measurement, 46,* 191–197.

Carnegie Forum on Education and the Economy. (1986). *A nation prepared: Teachers for the 21st century.* Washington, DC: The Task Force on Teaching as a Profession. ERIC Document No. ED 268 120.

Carter, K., & Doyle, W. (1987). Teachers' knowledge structures and comprehension processes. In J. Calderhead (Ed.), *Exploring teacher thinking* (pp. 147–160). London: Cassell.

Cohen, D., & Hill, H. (2000). Instructional policy and classroom performance: The mathematics reform in California. *Teachers College Record, 102*(2), 294–343.

Cooper, E., & Sherk, J. (1989). Addressing urban school reform: Issues and alliances. *Journal of Negro Education, 58*(3), 315–331.

Danielson, C. (1996). *Enhancing professional practice: A framework for teaching.* Alexandria, VA: Association for Supervision and Curriculum Development.

Darling-Hammond, L. (1992). Teaching and knowledge: Policy issues posed by alternate certification for teachers. *Peabody Journal of Education, 67*(3), 123–154.

Darling-Hammond, L. (Ed.). (1994). *Professional development schools: Schools for developing a profession.* New York: Teachers College Press.

Darling-Hammond, L. (1997). *The right to learn: A blueprint for creating schools that work.* San Francisco: Jossey-Bass.

Darling-Hammond, L. (2000a). Teacher quality and student achievement: A review of state policy evidence. *Educational Evaluation and Policy Analysis, 8*(1). Retrieved June 28, 2005 from http://epaa.asu.edu/epaa/v8n1

Darling-Hammond, L. (2000b). *Solving the dilemmas of teacher supply, demand, and standards: How we can ensure a competent, caring, and qualified teacher for every child.* New York: National Commission on Teaching and America's Future.

Darling-Hammond, L. (Ed.). (2000c). *Studies of excellence in teacher education* (three volumes). Washington, DC: American Association of Colleges for Teacher Education.

Darling-Hammond, L., Chung, R, & Frelow, F. (2002). Variation in teacher preparation: How well do different pathways prepare teachers to teach? *Journal of Teacher Education, 53*(4), 286–302.

Darling-Hammond, L., Hightower, A., Husbands, J., LaFors, J., & Young, V. (2003). *Building instructional quality: Inside-out, bottom-up, and top-down perspectives on San Diego's school reform.* Seattle: Center for the Study of Teaching and Policy, University of Washington.

Darling-Hammond, L., & Sclan, E. (1996). Who teaches and why: The dilemmas of building a profession for 21st century schools. In John Sikula (Ed.), *Handbook of research on teacher education* (pp. 67–101). New York: Macmillan.

Debolt, G. (1992). *Teacher induction and mentoring: School-based collaborative programs.* Albany: State University of New York Press.

Doyle, W. (1986). Content representation in teachers' definitions of academic work. *Journal of Curriculum Studies, 18,* 365–379.

Edmonds, R. (1979). Effective schools for the urban poor. *Educational Leadership, 37*(1), 15–24.

Ferguson, R. F. (1991). Paying for public education: New evidence on how and money matters. *Harvard Journal of Legislation, 28*(2), 465–498.

Fetler, M. (1999, March 24). High school staff characteristics and mathematics test results. *Education Policy Analysis Archives, 7.* Retrieved June 28, 2005 from http://epaa.asu.edu

Fowler, C. (2002, August). Fast track . . . slow going? Research brief. *Education Policy, 2*(1), 1–2.

Fuller, E. (1998). *Do properly certified teachers matter? A comparison of elementary school performance on the TAAS in 1997 between schools with high and low percentages of properly certified regular education teachers.* Austin: Charles A. Dana Center, University of Texas at Austin.

Grant, C. A. (1989). Urban teachers: Their new challenge and curriculum. *Phi Delta Kappan, 70,* 764–770.

Greenwald, R., Hedges, L., & Laine, R. (1996). The effect of school resources on student achievement. *Review of Educational Research, 66,* 361–396.

Haberman, M. (1995). Selecting 'star' teachers for children. *Phi Delta Kappan, 76,* 777–781.

Hansen, J. (1988). *The relationship of skills and classroom climate of trained and untrained teachers of gifted students.* Unpublished doctoral dissertation, Purdue University, West Lafayette, IN.

Henke, R. R., Chen, X., Geis, S., & Knepper, P. (2000). *Progress through the teacher pipeline: 1992–93 college graduates and elementary/secondary school teaching as of 1997.* Washington, DC: National Center for Education Statistics.

Holmes Group of Education Deans. (1986). *Tomorrow's teachers.* East Lansing, MI: Author.

Humphrey, D., & Shields, P. (2001). Teacher quality: Findings from recent research. In J. Simmons et al., *School reform in Chicago: Lessons and opportunities* (pp. 447–458). Chicago: Chicago Community Trust.

Johanson, G. A., & Gips, C. J. (1992). The hiring preferences of secondary school principals. *The High School Journal, 76,* 1–16.

Loeb, S., & Page, M. (2000). Examining the link between teacher wages and student outcomes: The importance of alternative labor market opportunities and non-pecuniary variation. *Review of Economics and Statistics, 82*(3), 393–408.

Los Angeles County Office of Education. (1999). Teacher quality and early reading achievement in Los Angeles County public schools. *Los Angeles: Trends: Policy issues Facing Los Angeles County Public Schools, 6*(2), [entire issue].

MacIsaac, D., & Brookhart, L. (1994, February). *A partnership approach to new teacher induction.* Paper presented at the annual meeting of the American Association of Colleges of Teacher Education, Chicago.

Mehlman, N. (2002, June 24). My brief teaching career. *New York Times.* Retrieved June 28, 2005 from http://www.nytimes.com/2002/06/24/opinion/24MEHL. html?todaysheadlines

National Center for Education Statistics. (1997). *America's teachers: Profile of a profession.* Washington, DC: U.S. Department of Education.

National Commission on Teaching and America's Future (NCTAF). (1996). *What matters most: Teaching for America's future.* New York: Author.

National Commission on Teaching and America's Future (NCTAF). (2003). *No dream denied: A pledge to America's children.* Washington, DC: Author.

Nelson, H., & Schneider, K. (1999). *Survey analysis of salary trends.* Washington, DC: American Federation of Teachers.

New York State Education Department. (2003, June). *Progress report to the Board of Regents: Alternative teacher certification.* Albany: Author.

Perkes, V. (1967–1968). Junior high school science teacher preparation, teaching behavior, and student achievement. *Journal of Research in Science Teaching, 6* (4), 121–126.

Peterson, K. D., & Martin, J. L. (1990). Developing teacher commitment: The role of the administrator. In P. Reyes (Ed.), *Teachers and their workplace: Commitment, performance, and productivity* (pp. 225–240). Newbury Park, CA: Sage.

Pflaum, S. W., & Abramson, T. (1990). Teacher assignment, hiring, and preparation: Minority teachers in New York City. *The Urban Review, 22* , 17–31.

Poda, J. (1995). 1994–95 annual report for the South Carolina Center for Teacher Recruitment.

Raymond, M., Fletcher, S., & Luque, J. (2001). *Teach for America: An evaluation of teacher differences and student outcomes in Houston, Texas.* Stanford, CA: Hoover Institution, Center for Research on Education Outcomes.

Roderick, M. A., Bryk, B., Jacob, J., Easton, J., & Allensworth, E. (1999). *Ending social promotion: Results from the first two years.* Chicago: Consortium on Chicago School Research.

Sanders, W. L., & Rivers, J. C. (1996). *Cumulative and residual effects of teachers on future student academic achievement.* Knoxville: University of Tennessee Value-Added Research and Assessment Center.

Schorr, J. (1993). Class action: What Clinton's National Service Program could learn from "Teach for America." *Phi Delta Kappan, 75,* 315–318.

Sclan, E. M. (1993). The effect of perceived workplace conditions on beginning teachers' work commitment, career choice commitment, and planned retention. *Dissertation Abstracts International 54*–08A (University Microfilms No. 9400594).

Shields, P. M., Humphrey, D. C., Wechsler, M. E., Riel, L. M., Tiffany-Morales, J., Woodworth, K., Young, V. M., & Price, T. (2001). *The status of the teaching profession 2001.* Santa Cruz, CA: Center for the Future of Teaching and Learning.

Simmons, J., et al. (2001). *School reform in Chicago: Lessons and opportunities.* Chicago: Chicago Community Trust.

Skipper, C., & Quantz, R. (1987). Changes in educational attitudes of education and arts and science students during four years of college. *Journal of Teacher Education, 38*(3), 39–44.

Smylie, M. A. (1992). Teacher participation in school decision making: Assessing willingness to participate. *Educational Evaluation and Policy Analysis, 14*(1), 53–67.

Snyder, J. (2002). New Haven Unified School District: A teaching quality system for excellence and equity. In A. Hightower, M. Knapp, J. Marsh, & M. McLaughlin (Eds.), *School districts and instructional renewal* (pp. 94–110). New York: Teachers College Press.

Strauss, R., & Sawyer, E. (1986). Some new evidence on teacher and student competencies. *Economics of Education Review, 5*(1), 41–48.

U.S. Department of Education, National Center for Education Statistics. (1994). *Schools and staff survey, 1994–1994.* Washington, DC: U.S. Government Printing Office.

Weglinsky, H. (2002). The link between teacher classroom practices and student academic performance. *Education Policy Analysis Archives, 10*(12). Retrieved June 28, 2005 from http://epaa.asu.edu/epaa/v10n12

Wise, A. E., Darling-Hammond, L., & Berry, B. (1987). *Effective teacher selection, from recruitment to retention.* Santa Monica, CA: RAND Corporation.

Wise, A. E., Darling-Hammond, L., McLaughlin, M., & Bernstein, H. (1984). *Teacher evaluation: A study of effective practices.* Santa Monica, CA: RAND Corporation.

Wisniewski, R. (1992). On collaboration. *Teacher Education and Practice, 7*(2), 13–16.

Wright, S. P., Horn, S. P., & Sanders, W. L. (1997). Teacher and classroom context effects on student achievement: Implications for teacher evaluation. *Journal of personnel evaluation in education, 11*(1), 57–67.

Chapter Eight

Build Effective Support with Parents and Funding

More and more households in the United States are headed by two working parents, making parental engagement more difficult—especially at the secondary school level. The number of single parents is increasing, too. However, without parent and community engagement, school systems cannot provide all the necessary resources and support to improve student learning. Making parent and community involvement a priority is the first part of our fourth strategy. The second part is to improve student achievement with adequate and equitable financing. Some suburban students get $3 for every $1 spent on students in the Chicago Public Schools.

Parent engagement is a crucial element of any school system; without it, children simply aren't motivated to discover their own abilities and potentials. As Gail Goldberger puts it in her essay: "Research shows that children learn more when their parents are directly engaged in their education. Children achieve better grades and higher test scores, have higher reading comprehension and more positive attitudes about school and homework, graduate at higher rates, are more likely to enroll in higher education, and demonstrate fewer behavioral problems" (see also Simmons, 2001). Research by Linda Darling-Hammond and Ronald Ferguson (1991) points out that the role of parents in improving student learning is equal to that of quality teaching. Chicago principals cited "ensuring parent engagement" as one of their most important responsibilities. Underlying their comments was the belief that unless parents are involved in the education of their children, the system cannot be fully invested in providing that education.

Parents themselves agree. But in a focus group in Chicago sponsored in July 2001 by Parents United for Responsible Education (PURE), 2003 winner of the National Challenge Award for Advocacy, parents cited several barriers that they believe keep them from being fully involved. First and foremost, they said, they feel disrespected and marginalized by schools and the school system. They also believe that they lack information and support from the schools (Simmons, 2001).

As stakeholders in the local school system, community members— including those without children in the schools—should also play a part in ensuring high-performing schools. It is with their support and resources that schools can continue to focus on providing a supportive learning environment.

Parents and community members themselves have many ideas for increasing parent engagement. Here are some ideas that emerged from the Chicago parent focus group:

- Arrange meetings between accountability experts and parents so that parents can learn how to hold teachers and principals accountable.
- Offer equal opportunity and access to everyone who wants to help schools—both individuals and organizations.
- Educate parents and offer them seminars on Local School Councils' rights and responsibilities.
- Create special invitations for parents to get involved.
- Have teachers and administrators go door to door to talk to parents.
- Conduct workshops on engaging parents in student learning.
- Tailor programs to the particular needs and interests of individual communities in order to draw parents in, such as workshops on immigration rights, Section 8 housing, and similar social issues.

Another strategy for promoting community involvement is leveraging learning through cross-school networks of neighborhood parents. Networks help create a synergy among improvement strategies and across a small group of schools. They sustain learning about best practice; encourage teachers, principals, parents, and students to share their ideas; multiply the impact of whole-school interventions; and scale-up best practice cost-effectively.

IMPROVING PARENT ENGAGEMENT

Gail Goldberger

The vital role parents play in their children's education is without dispute. But despite valiant efforts, some schools are not able to get parents involved at more than a surface level. The author outlines the characteristics of effective parent engagement programs and spotlights several proven programs.

Research shows that children learn more when their parents are directly engaged in their education. Children achieve better grades and higher test scores, have higher reading comprehension and more positive attitudes about school and homework, graduate at higher rates, are more likely to enroll in higher education, and demonstrate fewer behavioral problems. When community members get involved, more mentors and role models are added to the mix, providing additional layers of support and inspiration (Riley, 2000).

Students aren't the only ones who benefit. The morale boost teachers receive from active, supportive parents and community members helps them feel more positive. Parents form stronger relationships with one another, with other parents' children, and their communities. Good collaboration among teachers, families, and communities can even foster classroom innovation and creativity, improving school climate and overall performance (Riley, 2000).

All families want their children to succeed. Research shows no significant racial, ethnic, or socioeconomic differences in this regard. What research *does* show is that some parents take an active role in helping their children while others need more guidance and encouragement to do so. Low-income parents and parents from non-English-speaking backgrounds, for example, may have had less formal education themselves or may feel they lack the knowledge and skills to help educate their children. They may have had negative experiences with schools and may be more wary, fearful, or intimidated by teachers and school authorities.

Likewise, some teachers may have had negative experiences with parents and therefore lack confidence in working closely with parents from different backgrounds. Unfortunately, all too often teachers contact parents only when there are problems, creating a climate of blame and defensiveness, counterproductive to cooperation and support. The research also shows that when the influence of teachers and parents is compared on improving student achievement, they are about equal. Ronald Ferguson, at Harvard University, looked at the results of Texas students for 900 districts in grades 3 through 5. As Figure 8.1 shows, he found that 49% of the improvement in math scores were due to parent factors, and 43% due to teacher qualifications. Another 8% was due to class size (Darling-Hammond, 1997; Ferguson, 1991).

Successful parent programs demonstrate that parents can overcome obstacles to effective parent engagement and accelerate student performance.

FIGURE 8.1. Influence of Parents and Teachers on Student Achievement (Proportion of Explained Variance in Math Test Score Gains in Grades 3 to 5)

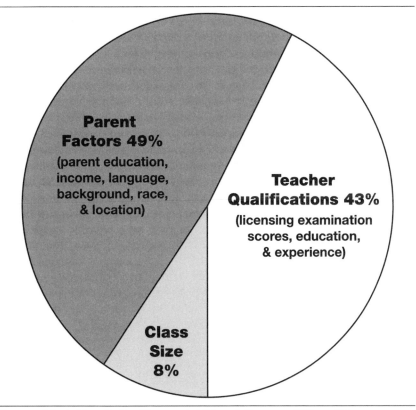

Sources: Adapted from Darling-Hammond, 1997, p. 9; Ferguson, 1991, p. 465

What Programs Get the Best Results and Why?

The most successful programs are collaborations among schools, parents, districts, communities, and students. These collaborations have the following qualities:

- They have good leadership.
- They grow from shared power and the belief that parents are key to a successful educational process.
- They build respectful partnerships between teachers and parents.

The importance of the principle of shared power and leadership cannot be overemphasized. Collaboration requires power, the ability to act. It allows individuals and groups to exercise judgment, responsibility, and control. Parents *and* teachers must have the opportunity to create programs, recommend changes, and eliminate what isn't working. When superintendents, district administrators, and school principals support these collaborations, they are more likely to succeed.

We examine here three models that differ in some important ways yet are all effective in increasing teacher–parent collaboration. Common to all three are some key principles: (1) School districts and principals support and facilitate collaborations between teachers and parents based on mutual respect and trust; (2) teachers and parents in partnership design and put into practice those efforts needed to improve student performance; and (3) all parties receive training so they know how to make relational collaborations work. The three models are the following:

1. The program that permeates Central Park East in East Harlem, New York City
2. The National Network of Partnership Schools that grew out of research at Johns Hopkins University
3. The Alliance Schools, which use the Industrial Areas Foundation model of community and parent engagement

The success of these models is evidenced by replication. More than 100 small schools like Central Park East are operating in New York City, with several thousand more operating across the country. The National Network of Partnership Schools at the Center for School, Family and Community Partnerships, Johns Hopkins University, includes 1,415 member schools, 142 school districts, and 19 state departments of education across the nation. The Industrial Areas Foundation works closely with 200 schools—130 in Texas and the rest scattered from Louisiana, Nebraska,

Arizona, and New Mexico to California. They are funded under an umbrella organization, the Interfaith Education Fund, located in Austin, Texas.

Central Park East: Partnerships for a Learning Culture. In 1974, a school was organized that challenged the notions that poor children can't learn and that unless poverty is eradicated, the disadvantaged are doomed to welfare, bad jobs, or death. That school was Central Park East Elementary (CPE) in East Harlem. According to a survey conducted in 1985, CPE's students were poorer and represented a higher percentage of minorities than the overall population of students in New York City Public Schools. Yet by 1991, nine out of ten students graduated from high school and two of three enrolled in college (Bensman, 2000). Current director Jane Andrias says those same results hold true today (J. Andrias, personal communication, May 30, 2001).

When CPE began, school staff and founding director, Deborah Meier spent much time and energy explaining CPE's theories of teaching and learning through weekly newsletters sent to parents, parent–teacher meetings, and individual family conferences. In the first 2 weeks of school, every teacher met individually with parents to discuss their child's needs and interests. Every communication with parents, verbal and written, included an invitation to get involved and welcomed collaboration.

Today, Jane Andrias also sends out weekly letters to families, and mandatory parent conferences are held three times a year, with students in attendance. Then and now, parents are actively brought into school activities through organized trips, parties, celebrations, potluck suppers, and fund-raisers. Informal opportunities to engage parents are seized as well. When mothers were seen milling around the school in the early morning, for example, a few teachers gathered them and brought them inside to engage in community readings with students before the actual school day began and before the moms went off to work.

Students at CPE go home with three written reports rather than report cards. These reports vary in length but include at least one long and detailed narrative. When a problem arises, family conferences are organized, with the director (rather than the teacher) chairing the meeting. These conferences end with suggestions everyone agrees to try (including the student). A follow-up meeting is scheduled to assess the results of the suggestions and determine if a different strategy is in order. The focus is on the goal of "solving a problem" or "getting the plan right," not on how long it takes to do that (Meier, 1996; personal communication, May 23, 2001).

This working out of problems in a nonblaming way is one of the conditions, or assumptions, that contributes to the success of this school. Howard Weiss, a psychologist from the Ackerman Institute for the Family who worked with the school in its beginning years, has summarized the assumptions that drive the collaborative climate of CPE.

1. From nursery school on, the child is an active participant and decision maker in his or her program of learning. If parents aren't involved with their children's learning, there is something wrong with the invitation.
2. A nonblaming atmosphere is established for problem solving. It is assumed that all individuals—parents, students, and teachers—have been doing the best they can under their particular circumstances.
3. All parents care about their children's education and well-being, and if they don't, then they are not in a position to do so.
4. All staff care about the experiences and accomplishments of their students, and if it doesn't seem that way to parents, then there has been an insufficient attempt on the part of the teacher to establish a relationship with the parents.
5. Educators, parents, and children can restructure opportunities to build collaborative relationships. Teachers can be trained to have participatory parent–teacher meetings, children can be trained to be active participants in their education, and parents are expected and encouraged to interact actively with their children and their children's teachers.
6. Positive interactions generate more positive interactions, and collaboration should always be sought. All messages, newsletters, and bulletin boards should "breathe" collaboration and encourage participation (H. Weiss, personal communication, May 11, 2001).

The key element is the partnership that develops among the teacher, student, and parent. To build trust and effective communication, teachers and parents rarely meet without the student present. Neither the director nor the teachers assume the role of remote authority figure, setting rules and evaluating student progress. Rather, they concern themselves with all of the child's needs, respect and pay attention to each individual child, and take caring beyond the school walls. The director treats teachers like teachers treat their students—with respect, courtesy, and compassion. Parents are encouraged to express their thoughts about curricula, homework policies, and other aspects of the school's policies and programs. Although most parents work full time, there is an unusually high level of parent participation in school affairs.

When Deborah Meier, director of CPE from 1974 to 1985, was asked how parent–teacher partnerships were sustained over time, she replied, "Most parents are delighted to talk with someone who likes and knows their children well. I don't think one needs more than that. It's tougher if a teacher is no longer feeling optimistic, hopeful, or positive about a kid. Then, we set up a process to try to reframe issues so that we'd feel more [positive about] possibilities. We often got discouraged in really tough cases, and so did parents, and sometimes we'd all back away for awhile, but the assumption that working out the tough cases was long term and required persistence was stated up front" (D. Meier, personal communication, May 23, 2001).

A strong CPE parent association meets on its own monthly. The parent association has two co-chairs, two co-secretaries, and two co-treasurers. CPE's director, Jane Andrias, meets with representatives from the association every 2 weeks for 2 hours, at night, to discuss whatever concerns are on their minds. At CPE, parent engagement has become more organized, active, and productive.

All relationships in the CPE community are based on caring, mutual trust, respect, and tolerance. CPE's small size (250 students) helps. It also helps that admissions give preference to siblings of CPE students and children of CPE staff. The entire school comes together on projects, camping trips, and musical and dramatic performances, which forge strong ties among all members of the school community: parents, teachers, students, and alumni.

National Network of Partnership Schools. Established in 1995 by researchers at Johns Hopkins University, The National Network of Partnership Schools (NNPS) brings together schools, districts, and states that are committed to developing and maintaining comprehensive programs of school–family–community partnerships. The network, founded by Joyce Epstein, director of the Center on School, Family and Community Partnerships, offers a research-based framework for schools to think about collaboration, training for districts that want to fund and implement collaborative programs, and a wealth of information for schools that need ideas for ways to engage parents and communities. By joining the network, schools, districts, and states have access to workshops and publications, an extensive website with a menu of action plans and programs, and a powerful system for networking with the staff at Johns Hopkins and other partner schools, districts, and states (National Network of Partnership Schools, home page). A structure for every aspect of involvement at every level (school, district, state) has been mapped out and delineated in publications and on the website, making the network the most accessible of models described here. Every partner uses a common framework and standard structures but chooses site-specific practices in order to tailor collaboration to its community.

In Chicago three networks of elementary schools draw on the NNPS and other models, and they are getting strong results. In the Pilsen Education Network, 50% of families are participating after three years—more than almost seven times the average rate of family participation for the city's elementary schools. Parent engagement is part of a strategic school improvement model used by networks of schools in the same neighborhood (Strategic Learning Initiatives, 2004).

Epstein (2001) has developed a framework of six types of engagement in which schools, parents, and communities can partner:

1. Parenting (positive home conditions parents can provide to support children's learning)
2. Communicating (the responsibility of the school to provide parents with information about school progress and children's academic progress, to be welcoming to parents and open to feedback)
3. Volunteering (parents and others assisting academic progress by tutoring, reading inside and outside the classroom, and engaging in other activities to encourage social growth)
4. Learning at home (helping parents monitor and assist their own children with homework and academic decisions)
5. Decision making (parental involvement in school decision making, governance, and advocacy)
6. Collaborating with the community (coordinating resources from the community for family/ students/school and providing services in the community).

Epstein stresses that efforts to support these programs should be recognized in principals' and teachers' annual professional evaluations. The model does not require a reorganization of the school or school system, nor should it spark a political power struggle.

The Industrial Areas Foundation (IAF) Model. The Industrial Area Foundation (IAF) is a national organization that operates locally in many communities around the country. Begun in Chicago over 50 years ago, IAF is a network of broad-based, multiethnic, interfaith organizations in low- and moderate-income communities.

In the late 1960s, educational leader Ernesto Cortés Jr. was trained by IAF in Chicago. He returned to his hometown of San Antonio, Texas, in 1973 and began his organizing with churches on a parish-by-parish basis and addressed neighborhood problems ranging from lack of sewers and an abundance of rats to odors from processing plants and failing schools.

To understand how IAF organizes communities, it is important to understand how Cortés and the cadre of trained IAF organizers think about power. For them, power is not an entity that is traded with or held over one person or another, but a capacity for being able to act. Power emerges from reciprocal relationships and grows from associations among neighbors, co-workers, parishioners, and parents, and their common interests in changing the status quo. This concept of power includes developing relationships with current adversaries and leaving the door open to become allies in the future.

IAF organizers develop new leaders who continue to identify and address the greatest needs in the community. What distinguishes the Texas IAF from other parent engagement models is that it develops school leaders among parents, teachers, and community members. Student learning is supported by cultivating school leadership among the children's parents and neighbors. In this way, IAF extends parental engagement beyond transforming the students' education and the school to transforming the adult community and the school system at large.

IAF also makes a distinction between parent involvement and engagement. Involvement means attending bake sales, performances, open houses, and generally maintaining the school culture. Engagement, on the other hand, means that parents play an active role and are genuinely interested in affecting the school culture and promoting change and improvement (Shirley, 1997a).

An example of the effectiveness of IAF is the change that happened in Ysleta Elementary School in El Paso, Texas, after IAF organized the school community to take charge of an issue that lay outside student learning. In the spring of 1992, parents and staff determined that traffic safety around the school was a major concern. After a girl from a local parochial school was killed by a truck, the parent coordinator of Ysleta Elementary gathered more than 400 signatures on a petition that called for action by the city government to resolve the dangerous traffic situation. Ultimately, this led to the creation of school crossing zones, a one-way street, and a traffic light. It was the first time the school had reached out to parents, and it represented a breakthrough in parent–school communication.

This success created a higher level of trust between the school and the community as the two groups worked together. The school moved the parent room to a more central and visible location. It got a grant to equip the room with comfortable furniture and educational materials, started pre-K classes, and made recommendations about a new building.

In addition, teachers began organizing portfolios of student work for parents to see and return with comments, and opened two multiaged dual-language classrooms for 5- to 8-year-olds. A wellness center with health screenings has been integrated into the school, as well as innovative projects that more closely involve parents with in-classroom projects alongside their children.

As a testament to the link between parent engagement and achievement, in just 1 year student achievement increased dramatically. In 1993, only 27% of Ysleta's fourth-grade students passed the reading portion of the state's criterion-referenced test; in 1994, 61% passed the same portion. From 1993 to 1994, the percentage of fourth graders who passed the writing test increased from 49% to 70%, and those who passed the math test increased from 21% to 51% (Shirley, 1997b).

Similarities and Differences

Certain requirements for successful parent-engagement strategies emerge from these three models:

- *Schools* need to reach out respectfully to parents so they know they are valued, welcome, and have a voice in their children's education. Or parents need to demand that their schools listen to them and respect their input and participation.
- *Educators* need to communicate to parents what children need from them to help them get results in school. Parents need to let educators know what they need in order to help their children get results in school.
- *Parent leaders* need to be identified and supported. Parent leaders (and students) need to make their wants and needs known to schools and districts.
- *Principals, superintendents*, districts, and boards need to support teachers *absolutely* in their efforts to forge relationships with parents and to help find funding for them to do that.
- *All parties* need to put aside their fears and previously acquired attitudes about parent engagement and parent–teacher–school collaborations.
- *All parties* should have training in how to make relational collaborations work. Parent-engagement education should be mandated in teacher certification requirements.
- Outside partners must realize that it is never helpful to do for people what they can do for themselves. Partners should work with schools, districts, and states to *facilitate* their leadership and participation in collaborations.

Implications for District Leaders

For parent engagement to succeed, districts must support schools' efforts to adopt proactive and collaborative relationships with parents and abandon a top-down approach to change. Districts must provide the vision, the resources and the funding—in other words, they must be the center of support that enhances the schools' capacities to build engagement strategies. The one district that has scaled-up the John's Hopkins model is Baltimore, between 1994 through 2000 (Epstein, 1997, personal communication, May 9, 2001).

The models and experience are available for assisting parents to be much more effective in accelerating student learning. Can district and union leaders provide the commitment that is needed for engaging their community's most underutilized educational resource, its parents?

EDUCATION REFORM AND SCHOOL FINANCE

ALLAN ODDEN

There is a difference between equal funding and adequate funding for effective education. As districts begin to look more closely at how they can implement effective systemwide reform, they should consider whether schools have adequate financial resources. In addition, they should consider whether schools and school districts are using those resources toward implementing proven strategies and structures. The author looks at three approaches to adequate school finance and offers suggestions for ensuring that schools receive the adequate funding they need.

School finance issues are shifting from equity to adequacy in districts throughout the United States. The question is no longer simply whether there are disparities in revenues per pupil across districts—whether one district has more or less than another—but whether each district and each of its schools has an adequate level of resources and uses those dollars to educate its students to state and district high standards.

This shift is fortuitous for several reasons. First, although the equity focus of school finance reform produced a more equitable distribution of dollars per pupil, it did not necessarily produce sufficient revenues for the goals of standards-based education reform (Ladd & Hansen, 2000). Second, school finance equity was focused on fair access to education resources whatever the goals, while school finance *adequacy* is focused on having students learn to high-proficiency standards. Third, as will be shown, school finance adequacy requires a conscious linking of effective educational strategy to both resource distribution and use. And all three combined determine whether students learn more, particularly in big-city education systems.

An Adequate School Finance System

Two questions are vital to determining whether the school finance system is adequate. The first question is whether the foundation expenditure level is high enough for the typical school district to teach the typical student to state proficiency standards. The second is whether the system is flexible enough to meet student needs and allow all districts to provide an adequate education program.

Three methods are used to determine the adequacy of the foundation expenditure level.

Expenditure and Performance Approach. This method identifies districts that have been successful in teaching their students to proficiency standards and sets the adequacy level at the weighted average of the expenditures of such districts (Guthrie & Rothstein, 1999). Unfortunately, this generally excludes all large urban districts as well as very wealthy and very poor districts. As a result, the districts identified in the analysis are usually nonmetropolitan districts of average size and of relatively homogeneous demographic characteristics that generally spend below the state average. The criticism of this approach, which has been used in Ohio as well as Illinois, is that the adequate expenditure level is not relevant to big-city districts, even with adjustments for pupil needs and geographic price differentials.

Cost Function Approach. This approach uses regression analysis with expenditure per pupil as the dependent variable and student and district characteristics, as well as desired performance levels, as the independent variables. The result produces an "average" adequate expenditure per pupil for the average district, and then adjusts that figure to account for differences in pupil need and educational prices as well as diseconomies of both large and small size. The expenditure level is higher as the performance level is higher.

Although both of these approaches link spending levels to performance levels, neither indicates what educational strategies produce those performance levels.

Evidence-Based Approach. The third approach involves identifying evidence-based educational strategies, costing them out, and then aggregating them to identify adequate site, district, and state expenditure levels. This approach more directly identifies educational strategies that produce desired results, so it also helps guide school sites in how to use dollars in the most effective ways (Odden & Busch, 1998; Odden & Picus, 2000).

The evidence-based approach uses both research findings and commonalities across several comprehensive school designs, which themselves are compilations of research and best practice knowledge, into cohesive schoolwide strategies (Northwest Regional Educational Laboratory, 1998; Stringfield, Ross, & Smith, 1996). This approach identifies a set of ingredients that are required to deliver a high-quality instructional program, and then determines an adequate expenditure level by placing a price on each ingredient and aggregating to a total cost.

What are some of these ingredients? Research shows that high-quality preschool, particularly for students from lower-income backgrounds, has significant long-term impacts on student academic achievement and other desired social and community outcomes (Barnett, 1995; Slavin, Karweit,

& Wasik, 1994). Thus, the state school finance system should allow each district to provide preschool for at least every child ages 3 to 4 from a family with an income below 1.5 times the poverty level.

Research further shows that full-day kindergarten, particularly for students from low-income backgrounds, has significant, positive impacts on student learning in the early elementary grades (Slavin et al., 1994). Thus, the state school finance system should allow each district to count each kindergarten student as a full 1.0 student in the formula in order to provide a full-day kindergarten program.

Research on school size is clearer than research on class size; the optimum size for elementary schools is 300–600, and the optimum size for secondary schools is 600–900 (Lee & Smith, 1997; Raywid, 1997–1998). Thus, no elementary school unit should be larger than 500 students, and no secondary school unit should be larger than 1,000 students. Given the current stock of large school buildings, this means creating several independent "schools" within these larger buildings, each with a separate student body, separate principal, and separate entrance. It also means a moratorium on construction of large school buildings in the future. All subsequent proposals should be for a school unit of 500 students.

Research on class size shows that small classes of *15* (not 18, not 20, and not a class of 30 with an instructional aide or two teachers) in kindergarten through grade 3 have significant, positive impacts on student achievement in mathematics and reading (Grissmer, 1999). The impact is larger for students from low-income and minority backgrounds. Thus, class sizes should be 15 in grades K–3. This policy might arguably be limited to schools with predominantly lower-income and minority students, but politically that would be problematic. Class sizes in other grades should be no larger than an average of 25, which is about the national average and the size on which most comprehensive school reform models are based.

Teachers need some time during the regular schoolday for collaborative planning and ongoing curriculum development and review. Schools also need to teach art, music, and physical education. This requires an additional 20% allocation of teachers, to those already required, to achieve the above class sizes.

Every school should have a powerful and effective strategy for struggling students—students who must work harder and need more time to achieve proficiency levels. Such students generally include those from lower-income backgrounds, those struggling to learn English, and those with learning and other mild disabilities. The most powerful and effective strategy is one-to-one tutoring provided by licensed teachers (Shanahan, 1998; Wasik & Slavin, 1993).

From the practice of many comprehensive school designs, a ratio of one fully licensed teacher tutor for every 20% of students in poverty, with a minimum of one for every school, is the standard. Thus, school units of 500 students should have from one to five teacher tutors. This allocation would cover the needs of students from low-income backgrounds, students whose native language is not English, and the learning disabled.

Schools should be free to use the resources for whatever strategy they select but should be held accountable for having these students learn to proficiency levels. Students with more severe disabilities would need to be funded on a program-and-service basis. The extra costs for all low-incidence, high-cost, severely disabled students should be fully borne by the state.

Schools also need a student-support, family-outreach strategy. In terms of ingredients, the needier the student body, the more comprehensive such a strategy needs to be. The general standard is one licensed professional for every 20–25% of students from a low-income background, with a minimum of one for each school.

All school personnel need ongoing professional development. According to research on the costs of effective professional development—professional development that produces change in classroom practice that leads to improved student achievement—and on the costs of professional development needed to implement comprehensive school designs, schools need about $4,000 per teacher per year for ongoing professional development (Odden, Archibald, Fermanich, & Gallagher, 2001). This would allow each school to have one full-time professional development coach on site and to provide for 100 to 200 hours of professional development per teacher each year.

Finally, schools need to embed technology in their instructional program and school management strategies. Based on the school designs that include such technology, the costs are about $250 per pupil or for a school of 500 students and $125,000 for purchase, updating, and maintenance of hardware and software, which for the next decade or so at least should be viewed as an annual operating cost (Odden, 1997).

In sum, school units of 500 students would need the resources indicated in Table 8.1. Secondary schools that serve 1,000 students should double the numbers. The figures would need to be prorated down for schools with fewer students, but schools should not have fewer than 300 students, except in sparsely populated, rural areas. The figures include full-day kindergarten. The resources are sufficient for schools to deploy any of a dozen or more comprehensive school reform strategies (Analt, Goertz, & Turnbull, 1999; Odden, 2000).

Preschool would need to be added for 3- and 4-year olds from lower-income backgrounds. The easiest way to do this would be to allow each

TABLE 8.1. School Resources

Elementary School Unit of 500 Students	Secondary School Unit of 500 Students
1 principal	1 principal
1 full-time instructional facilitator, coach	1 full-time instructional facilitator, coach
29 teachers; class size of 15 in K–3, otherwise 25	20 teachers; class sizes of 25
6 art, music, physical education, library, etc. teachers	4 art, music, physical education, library, etc. teachers
1–5 teacher tutors; 1 for each 20% of students from low-income background, with a minimum of 1	1–5 teacher tutors; 1 for each 20% of students from low-income background, with a minimum of 1
1–5 positions for student/family support; 1 for each 20–25% of students from low-income background, with a minimum of 1	1–5 positions for student/family support; 1 for each 20–25% of students from low-income background, with a minimum of 1
$70,000 for professional development	$70,000 for professional development
$125,000 for computer technologies	$125,000 for computer technologies
Secretarial support, lunch and food support, and operations and maintenance	Secretarial support, lunch and food support, and operations and maintenance

district to count each such student in determining the number of students in the district for state aid purposes. Preschool teachers would then need to be paid according to the district's salary structure. It would be wise, however, to allow many neighborhood institutions to provide preschool programs, including not only the public schools but also other community institutions, including perhaps churches, as is the case with Head Start.

Note that there are no instructional aides in this model. That's because no comprehensive school design includes instructional aides and research generally shows they do not add value (Achilles, 1999).

Paying Teachers Adequate Salaries

The final step in the state-of-the-art approach is setting teacher salaries. This step usually uses a statewide average teacher salary, which significantly understates what cities need to pay for quality teachers. Two approaches could be used to make the salary figure reflect what it takes to recruit and retain teaching talent.

The first approach is to use a cost-of-education index developed by the National Center for Education Statistics. This index generally shows that large cities need to spend 20–30% more for a given set of teacher qualities.

A second strategy is to determine salary benchmarks by labor-market regions in a state. This approach should identify not only the salary benchmark for beginning teachers but also benchmarks for mid-career and top-career teacher salaries.

The structure of teacher salary schedules should also shift from providing salary increases on the basis of years of experience and education units and degrees to more direct measures of teacher knowledge and skills (Odden, 2001; Odden & Kelley, 2002). Such a schedule, identified in Table 8.2, would link teacher pay levels to teacher performance and effectiveness in the classroom. The table also indicates where salary benchmark figures would be needed to identify the pay levels sufficient for a city such as Chicago to find and keep the level of teacher talent it needs. The state foundation expenditure level, then, would need to be high enough to allow all districts to pay their teachers at or above their appropriate salary benchmarks.

The type of new salary schedule identified in Table 8.2 has several additional advantages. This performance-pay structure is generally more attractive to younger teachers who are now being recruited into education. It allows for a faster track to the top of the schedule for teachers whose expertise can meet the performance standards more quickly than that of the average teacher. In addition, it can be augmented with a school-based incentive system that provides annual salary bonuses to teachers if the school as a whole meets preset targets for improved student achievement.

Implications for Superintendents

These new directions in school finance have several key implications for superintendents in large cities. The first is to work the political system to get the school finance adequacy issues onto the state's agenda and to shift away from the equity issue. Addressing adequacy will enhance equity, and adequacy—sufficient resources to teach urban students to high state performance standards—has both greater appeal to the policy community and will likely be fiscally more productive for big city school systems.

Second, redesign resourcing strategies. Whether by using a needs-based funding formula or a needs-based staffing formula, the goal is to provide

TABLE 8.2. Teacher Salary Schedules

Performance Category	Salary Benchmark	Knowledge and Skills Incentives (in addition to column 2)
Novice teacher, a teacher with a provisional license	Average beginning salary for all college graduates	Master's degree in content area
Apprentice teacher, a teacher who has just earned the standard license	Need a benchmark	15% additional for licensure in a shortage area such as math, science, special education
Career teacher, a teacher who is proficient in content specific pedagogy	Need a benchmark	Licensure in a second subject
Advanced teacher, a teacher who meets some advanced performance standard	Benchmark for top teaching talent	Small percentage or dollar increase for having expertise in a particular school-site design
National board-certified teacher	15% above that for advanced teacher	

each school with adequate resources for each of its students. So site resources may vary while the student performance goal remains the same—learning to state and district achievement standards.

Third, take resource reallocation seriously. Too many schools in too many urban districts use resources ineffectively. Resource reallocation at the district level in most large urban districts would likely produce large pots of dollars for strategically targeted professional development; conducting a professional development fiscal audit should be high on the agenda (Miles, Odden, Archibald, Fermanich, & Gallagher, 2003). Resource reallocation is also important at the school-site level to ensure that all dollars are used for educational strategies that produce large, positive impacts on student learning.

Finally, either have local researchers or district analysts conduct studies that identify the labor market the districts operate within for teaching talent. Most large districts have teacher shortages; economists would argue that shortages occur when individuals are not paid at a high enough level. Studies of the local labor market would provide the data district leaders and state policymakers need to identify the teacher salary levels that should be included in adequacy-driven school finance policies. Salary levels need to be set at levels that allow city districts to compete effectively for quality teachers.

REFERENCES

Achilles, C. (1999). *Let's put kids first, finally: Getting class size right.* Thousand Oaks, CA: Corwin.

Analt, B., Goertz, M., & Turnbull, B. (1999). *Implementing whole school reform in New Jersey: Year one in the first cohort schools.* New Brunswick, NJ: Rutgers University, Edward J. Bloustein School of Planning and Public Policy.

Barnett, W. S. (1995). Long-term effects of early childhood programs on cognitive and school outcomes. *The Future of Children: Long-Term Outcomes of Early Childhood Programs, 5*(3), 25–50.

Bensman, D. (2000). *Central Park East and its graduates: "Learning by heart."* New York: Teachers College Press.

Darling-Hammond, L. (1997). *Doing what matters most: Investing in quality teaching.* New York: National Commission on Teaching and America's Future, Teachers College, Columbia University.

Epstein, J. L. (2001). *School, family and community partnerships: Preparing educators and improving schools.* Boulder, CO: Westview Press.

Ferguson, R. A. (1991, Summer). Paying for public education: New Evidence of how and why money matters. *Harvard Journal on Legislation, 28,* 465–498.

Grissmer, D. (Ed.). (1999). Class size: Issues and new findings. *Educational Evaluation and Policy Analysis, 21*(2), [entire issue].

Guthrie, J. & Rothstein, R. (1999). Enabling "adequacy" to achieve reality: Translating adequacy into state school finance distribution arrangements. In J. Hansen & R. Chalk (Eds.), *Equity and adequacy in education finance: Issues and perspectives* (pp. 209–259). Washington, DC: National Academy Press.

Ladd, H. & Hansen, J. (2000). *Making money matter.* Washington, DC: National Academy Press.

Lee, V., & Smith, J. (1997). High school size: Which works best, and for whom? *Educational Evaluation and Policy Analysis, 19*(3), 205–228.

Meier, D. (1996). *The power of their ideas.* Boston: Beacon.

Miles, K., Odden, A., Archibald, S., Fermanich, M., & Gallagher, A. (2003). *Understanding and comparing district investment in professional development: Methods and lessons from four districts.* Madison: University of Wisconsin, Wisconsin Center for Education Research, Consortium for Policy Research in Education.

National Network of Partnership Schools: About NNPS [home page]. Available at www.partnershipschools.org

Northwest Regional Educational Laboratory. (1998). *Catalog of school reform models: First edition.* Portland, OR: Author.

Odden, A. (1997). Getting better by design: Vol. 3, *How to rethink school budgets to support school transformation.* Alexandria, VA: New American Schools.

Odden, A. (2000). Costs of sustaining educational change via comprehensive school reform. *Phi Delta Kappan, 81*(6), 433–438.

Odden, A. (2001). Rewarding expertise. *Education Matters, 1*(1), 16–24.

Odden, A., Archibald, S., Fermanich, M., & Gallagher, H. A. (2001). A cost framework for professional development. *Journal of Education Finance, 28*(1), 51–74.

Odden, A., & Busch, C. (1998). *Financing schools for high performance.* San Francisco: Jossey-Bass.

Odden, A., & Kelley, C. (2002). *Paying teachers for what they know and do* (2nd ed.). Thousand Oaks, CA: Corwin.

Odden, A., & Picus, L. (2000). *School finance: A policy perspective* (2nd ed.). New York: McGraw-Hill.

Raywid, M. (1997–1998). Synthesis of research: Small schools: A reform that works. *Educational Leadership, 55*(4), 34–39.

Riley, R. (2000, November). Message to the Family Involvement Network of Educators (FINE), Harvard University School of Education, Cambridge, MA. Available at www.gse.harvard.edu/hfrp/projects/fine/secretarymessage.html

Shanahan, T. (1998). On the effectiveness and limitations of tutoring in reading. *Review of Research in Education, 23,* 217–234.

Shirley, D. (1997a). Moving schools into the power arena. In *Community organizing for urban school reform* (Chapter 2). Austin: University of Texas Press.

Shirley, D. (1997b). Ysleta Elementary School. In *Community organizing for urban school reform* (Chapter 5). Austin: University of Texas Press.

Simmons, J. (2001). Voices of Chicago parents–parents united for responsible education. In J. Simmons et al., *School reform in Chicago: Lessons and opportunities* (pp. 495–500). Chicago: Chicago Community Trust.

Slavin, R., Karweit, N., & Wasik, B. (1994). *Preventing early school failure: Research policy and practice.* Boston: Allyn & Bacon.

Strategic Learning Initiatives. (2004). Unpublished Pilsen Education Network midyear report 2004–05. Chicago.

Stringfield, S., Ross, S., & Smith, L. (1996). *Bold plans for school restructuring: The new American schools designs.* Mahwah, NJ: Erlbaum.

Wasik, B, A., & Slavin, R. (1993). Preventing early reading failure with one-to-one tutoring: A review of five programs. *Reading Research Quarterly, 28,* 178–200.

PART THREE

LEADING CHANGE: HOW TO TRANSFORM A SYSTEM THAT RESISTS IMPROVEMENT

"We thought we were tops in quality only to learn that there were dramatically better ways."
—Robert W. Galvin, former Chairman, Motorola (1991, p. 18)

One of the hardest things to do is to change the system itself, and one of the most important jobs is leading that change: engaging people at all levels and continuously improving the way everyone works to meet the needs of the students, parents, and future employers. When Robert Galvin and the Motorola leadership did their homework, they discovered that there were "dramatically better ways" to improve their quality.

Effective tools do exist for transforming systems, however, and Part III describes principles that can guide change-makers, frameworks that can help everyone in the system to understand change, and a practical process that can be followed—and modified—as the organization moves from readiness to redesign to implementation and improvement. These tools have been used over the past 30 years by large firms, thousands of them successful in redesigning themselves and improving their results within 5 to 10 years. They often see improved results within a year. Smaller school districts have begun to use a similar process.

In his book *Change Forces with a Vengeance*, Michael Fullan (2003) described the process of district and school change as a journey, not a blueprint. When leaders of big city districts understand how to lead change through application of the principles of organizational change using a process that has been proven to be effective, the district will have the road map that will lead it through the journey of redesign. Schools should consider using the same process for their improvement.

REFERENCES

Fullan, M. (2003). *Change forces with a vengeance.* London: Routledge Farmer.
Galvin, R. W. (1991). *The idea of ideas.* Schaumburg, IL: Motorola University.

Chapter Nine

When "Best Practice" Is Not Enough: Three Studies

Educational reform, with several important exceptions, has yet to embrace the organizational development strategies that have resulted in improvement in many major companies.

Three recent studies provide a good review of how districts have faced their key challenges. The findings of these studies are consistent with other cross district studies (Cotton 1995; Hallett, 1995; North Carolina Department of Public Instruction, 2000; Sklar, Scheurich, & Johnson, 2002). The processes for leading change that the districts have used, while they contain important strategies and tools for reshaping district results, have resulted in only partial success.

Why? It appears that the school districts examined, while making individual reforms and changes, were not engaged in effective systemic change. Reviewing these studies will give us a good sense of what the current issues are—and will highlight the difficulties that any district will have unless it faces the fact that schools will not be substantially improved without change to the system itself.

1. FOUNDATIONS FOR SUCCESS

One comprehensive study, *Foundations for Success*, completed by the Council of Great City Schools in 2002, examined three districts—Houston, Sacramento, and Charlotte–Mecklenburg—that appeared to be closing the achievement gap between White and minority students and, generally, improving more rapidly than other districts in their state as measured by standardized tests. The authors note that while there has been much research on what makes an effective school, there is "relatively little on what makes an effective district" (Snipes, Doolittle, & Herlihy, 2002, p. xiii). Moreover, some of the "core problems" were identified more than a decade ago, but little has been done about them (Hill, 2003, p. 3).

We now know that Houston falsified its data and should not be included. The district got just average results ("A Miracle Revisited," 2005; "Questions on Data," 2003b). In addition, it is important to note that these districts were chosen on the basis of only 3 years of test results for Sacramento (1998–2000), 4 years for Houston (1998–2001), and 7 years for Charlotte–Mecklenberg (1995–2001). Given the variance in test results due to test design, not student performance, and the short time frame for two of the three districts—3 to 4 years—it is difficult to draw strong conclusions about the quality of the results and their sustainability.

Among the key findings were that these three improving districts were doing the following:

- Focusing on specific goals for student achievement, aligning curricula with state standards, and translating these standards into instructional practice
- Defining a role for the central office that included "guiding, supporting and improving instruction at the building level" (in contrast to top-down mandates) (Snipes, et al., 2000, xviii)
- Supporting data-driven decision making and instruction
- Beginning reforms in the elementary grades instead of trying to fix everything at once
- Providing intensive instruction in reading and math to middle and high school students even if it came at the expense of other subjects
- Focusing on the lowest-performing schools and providing them with more resources
- Holding district and building leadership personally responsible for producing results

Three districts selected for comparison, although they claimed to be doing similar things, were not. These districts lacked the following:

- A clear consensus among stakeholders about district strategy and priorities
- Specific, clear standards, achievement goals, timelines, and consequences
- A central office that took responsibility for improving instruction
- Central office policies connected to the intended changes in teaching and learning in the classrooms
- An ability to steer curricula and define instructional expectations so that schools weren't left to decipher them on their own

But even the model districts were not achieving outstanding results. In the time examined, these were their achievements:

- Progress at the elementary school level only "generally exceeded" state gains on standardized tests.
- There was no progress on test score improvement or closing the gap between Whites and minorities in high school (Snipes et al., 2000, p. xvii–xix).

The study concluded that "unless a district tries to reform their system as a whole, trying any one of these approaches may be a wasted effort" (Snipes et al., 2002, p. xxi).

2. AN IMPOSSIBLE JOB?

The leadership of the nation's 100 largest districts was the subject of *An Impossible Job? The View from the Urban Superintendent's Chair*, a study done by Howard Fuller, a former Milwaukee superintendent, and others in 2003. They considered such questions as the following:

- Is the failure of superintendents to overcome the challenges of improving results due to lack of personal skill, inadequate training, the inherent weakness of the office, or a combination of the three?
- What do superintendents think is needed to create more effective schools in large cities?

A major conclusion of the study was that the superintendents interviewed wanted authority that matched their responsibilities. To accomplish this, they requested that following reforms be instituted:

- Principals should select/hire new teachers.
- Superintendents should have the authority to close schools and reassign staff.
- The schools should control improvement/professional development funds.
- The school board should limit its jurisdiction to oversight on the budget, goals, and accountability.
- Board meetings should be limited to one a quarter (Fuller et al., 2003).

The reforms in Chicago suggest that these requests, while important, would not be enough to result in the change these superintendents seek. In the reforms of 1988 and 1995, Chicago principals were given authority to exercise the first two points on this list, and schools have had about 20% of the professional development funds under their control. While Chicago's progress is impressive at the elementary level, for 50% of its schools in low-income neighborhoods, at current rates of high school improvement, it will be 36 years before 90% of the students who finish elementary school graduate from high school.

Fuller's study concludes that the many conditions of the job have "set [the superintendents] up for failure," that "the job is undoable," and that, above all, they lack "the ability to close the achievement gap." Superintendents feel they need to be freed from the constraints they face, and they want "the authority they need to become true educational CEOs" (Fuller et al., 2003, pp. 1, 2). Fuller's critique gave no indication that he was aware of the experience of Brazosport, which occurred 6 years before his study was published (see Chapter 2).

The research on system change indicates that what is needed is other significant changes in the district culture, structure, and redesign strategies.

3. SCHOOL COMMUNITIES THAT WORK

In 2000, The Annenberg Institute for School Reform began an important project to research and plan how to scale-up and sustain districtwide educational improvement. The results would "help create, support and sustain urban education systems" in which all schools met high academic standards and would close the achievement gap for minority students. "One fact is clear: urban districts, as currently structured and operated, do not adequately provide [the necessary supports to close the gap]" (Annenberg Institute, 2003).

Researchers came up with key questions for designing a "smart district" that would provide the needed supports:

- What should districts do, and how should they work to achieve this goal?
- What knowledge, resources, and supports are required for school systems and urban communities to build the needed infrastructure?
- What is the best way to provide the necessary support for scaling-up best practice to schools, including the kind of organization or network of organizations, and how they might be managed? (Annenberg Institute, 2003).

One of the study's first results was the Annenberg Institute's publication of a portfolio of tools for district redesign. The seven tools include the following:

1. Identifying principles for effective teaching and learning
2. Assessing the central office for results and equity
3. Keeping the best teachers and school leaders
4. Developing effective partnerships to support local education
5. Introducing student-based budgeting
6. Assessing inequities in school funding within districts
7. Moving toward equity in school funding within districts

This toolkit, based on best practice, provides a strategic focus for district leaders who wish to create and sustain a high-performing school system. It begins to describe some of the support that schools in all but a few urban districts have been missing so that they can scale-up and continuously improve best practice within and across their buildings and school networks. As Marla Ucelli, the director of the project, explained, however, "The tools were not intended to add up to a model for systems transformation" (Ucelli, personal communication, September 2003).

WHAT THESE STUDIES LACK

While these studies provide important insight, what they lack is a proven process, a practical strategy with concrete tools for district leaders to use in transforming failing districts into high-performance districts. This includes understanding the steps needed to assure that the district leadership is ready to change and then the steps needed for redesign and implementation. These vital principles and practical steps for high-performance redesign are discussed in the next chapter.

REFERENCES

Annenberg Institute. (2003). *School communities that work*. Providence, RI: Author.

Cotton, K. (1995). *Effective schooling practices: A research synthesis, 1995 update*. Portland, OR: Northwest Regional Education Laboratory.

Fuller, H. J., Campbell, C., Celio, M. B., Harvey, J., Immerwahr, J., & Winger, A. (2003). *An impossible job? The view from the urban superintendent's chair*. Seattle, WA: Center on Reinventing Public Education.

Hallett, A. (Ed.). (1995). *Reinventing central office: A primer for successful schools.* Chicago: Cross City Campaign for Urban School Reform.

Hill, P. (2003). *School boards: Focus on school performance, not money or patronage.* Washington, DC: University of Washington Progressive Policy Institute.

A miracle revisited. (2003, December 3). *New York Times*, p. A1.

Questions on data cloud luster on Houston schools. (2003, July 11). *New York Times*, p. A1.

North Carolina Department of Public Instruction. (2000, March). *Improving student performance: The role of district level staff* [Evaluation brief, Vol. 2, No. 4]. Raleigh: Public Schools of North Carolina, Department of Public Instruction.

Skrla, L., Scheurich, J. S., & Johnson, J. F. (2002). *Equity/driven achievement-focused school districts.* Austin: Charles A. Dana Center, University of Texas at Austin.

Snipes, J., Doolittle, F., & Herlihy, C. (2002). *Foundations for success: Case studies of how urban school systems improve student achievement.* New York and Washington, DC: Manpower Development and Research Corporation and Council of the Great City Schools.

Chapter Ten

The High-Performance Paradigm Shift

To think differently about organizational design for high performance, we must look in business literature, not education literature, at the story of what happened in a Welsh coal mine over 50 years ago.

In 1950 Eric Trist of the Tavistock Institute in London got a call from the owner of a coal mine in Wales. Could Trist come see how his miners had reorganized their work and tell him if the reorganization was going to give him problems? Their tons of coal produced per day were up, morale was up, and costs were down.

At the mine, Trist learned that the miners, concerned about their safety when they started to work in a part of the mine where older timbers held up the mineshaft, had dealt with the problem by training everyone on their team in the safety skills that previously only one person—the supervisor—had. They had also provided cross-training in other important skills, taken on the supervisor's tasks (eliminating his position), and shared those tasks among the team members to help work proceed more effectively. The men had taken the initiative to reorganize their work and had become a self-managing team. Each had become engaged in developing a solution to their common problems and, through participation, had created a new solution. The solution the miners crafted with the owners' support was based on the core values of trust, teamwork, cooperation, participation, fairness, and integrity. As a consequence, they benefited from improved safety procedures and better pay, and the performance of the organization improved.

Trist was impressed. These men, working underground and in the dark, had created nothing less than a paradigm shift in organizational thinking, one where less supervision and more effective teamwork led to better results for both owner and workers.

The ideas spread to other parts of the coal industry by the end of the decade. Cross-training, self-managing teams, fewer levels of management, and the organizational leadership and culture needed to design and support these ideas became ubiquitous—because they worked. "Since then, no other method of organization development has proven as successful in improving bottom line organizational effectiveness while paying attention to human values" (Passmore, 1988, p. ix). By the 1970s, Royal Dutch Shell, Procter & Gamble, General Motors, W. L. Gore & Associates, Quad/Graphics, and others had begun to bring these concepts from Europe, Australia, and Japan to North America (Simmons & Mares, 1982).

The lessons are applicable to education. The mine owner did exactly what better principals do with their teachers and what classroom teachers do with their students. He had high expectations about what his workers could accomplish. He trusted them to work hard and expected them to take responsibility. He encouraged them to take the initiative to redesign their jobs. These values and the organizational culture he created are two characteristics of high-performing organizations.

In traditional organizations, managers often have low expectations of the people who report to them and think that employees don't want to take initiative or are lazy. As a result, traditional managers think that employees need more supervision, which increases costs and limits effective communication by adding layers of management. Low expectations also discourage employees from taking initiative and developing creative solutions to daily problems.

The beliefs that school superintendents or CEOs have about their employees help determine how they manage people and shape the organization's structure. This directly affects what the organization is capable of achieving (Galvin, 1991; McGregor, 1966). For example, when superintendents or CEOs feel that decisions need to be made primarily by employees at the top and middle of the organization, and people at the bottom are not expected to problem-solve or make decisions, the people at the bottom will stop thinking and stop contributing; that level of the organization will decline in productivity.

High-performance organizations focus on achieving a balance between two goals: meeting the needs of the customers for ever higher quality in their services and products, and meeting the needs of the employees for an ever higher quality of life at work. These organizations also seek to jointly optimize the interaction of their social system, including the organizational culture and recognition program, and the technical system, including mechanization levels, organizational structures and operating standards (Trist, 1981). Innovators such as Eric Trist, Richard Beckhard, William Passmore, Edward Lawler, and David Hanna helped develop processes for organizational design and redesign that then supported the quality improvement process (Beckhard & Harris, 1987; Hanna, 1988; Lawler; 1996; Trist, 1981).

Table 10.1 contrasts conditions and behavior in traditional design with those in high-performance organizations. The typical conditions that

TABLE 10.1. Designing High-Performance Organizations

Traditional Design	High-Performance Features	Broad Design Objectives
Oversimplified jobs	Whole, complex jobs	1. Development of commitment and energy in all employees
Overreliance on supervisor's control	Employee autonomy	
Overcentralization of authority	Delegated authority	2. Utilizing social and technical resources effectively
Overreliance on individual rewards	Group/system rewards	
Illogical breakdown of activities	Elimination of barriers	3. Maximizing cooperation
Overreliance on technical solutions	Human and technical solutions	4. Developing human abilities
Undervaluing human resources	Human resources valued	
Investment in maintaining status quo	Concern with innovation	5. Accelerating innovation
Underattention to environment (e.g., parents and employers)	Attention to environment	6. Awareness of external environment

Source: Passmore, 1988, p. 102

limit the effectiveness of traditional organizations are outlined in the left-hand column. In the center column, the key design features of a high-performance organization emerge. In traditional organizations, there is an "overcentralization of authority," which is "delegated" in high-performance organizations. Six broad design objectives help implement these goals, as shown in the right hand column of the table. At the beginning of a redesign process, William Passmore would recommend using an assessment survey to evaluate the existing strength of these six dimensions within the organization—if a school district, especially in the central office (Passmore, 1988; Walton, 1986).

CONTINUOUS IMPROVEMENT FOR SCHOOLS AND DISTRICTS

Other essential business concepts are applicable to the problem of improving educational systems. About the same time that Trist was observing and reflecting on the mine workers, W. Edwards Deming, a General Electric statistician, was in Japan with other quality experts Joseph Juran and Kaoru Ishikawa. These men helped to create Japan's approach to quality improvement, which transformed the performance of both the firms and the economy (Deming, 1982). From his experience, Deming formulated the "Fourteen Points" for continuous improvement (Deming, 1982, p. 3). When the quality improvement concepts began to be integrated with the process for organizational redesign, the way to create high-performance organizations took shape.

Data show that when private-sector firms combine the quality improvement and organizational development strategies, their financial results improve significantly. Typically, they cut two or more layers of management. When *Fortune* 1000 firms that were "high adopters" of these strategies were compared to *Fortune* 1000 firms that were "low adopters," their return on sales was 63% higher and their return on investment was 62% higher (Collins, 2001; Harry & Schroeder, 1999; Lawler, Mohrman, & Benson, 2001). The evidence above indicates that most CEOs of larger high-performance firms no longer see the "factory," or centralized management model, as either effective or efficient (Simmons & Mares, 1982).

Principles for quality improvement have also helped to improve educational systems. Deming's Fourteen Points were translated into action to continuously improve and transform schools and districts starting in the early 1980s, when David Langford integrated them into his business classes with at-risk students at Mt. Edgecumbe High School in Sitka, Alaska. When graduation rates improved, the principal and superintendent took notice. Myron Tribus, a former executive vice president of Xerox, visited the school and began to write about the application of Deming's quality principles to improving schools (Tribus, 1984, 1990a, 1990b, 1990c). Shortly thereafter, schools in New York City, Texas and Arizona started their own efforts (Schmoker, 1999; Schmoker & Wilson, 1993).

Currently, smaller pioneering districts—including Brazosport and Aldine, Texas; Edmonton, Canada; and St. Paul, Minnesota—are using some of the quality and organizational redesign principles with significant results. So are Pearl River, New York, and Chugach, Alaska, winners of the National Baldrige Award for Quality in 2001, and Palatine, Illinois, winner in 2003. Others have used them in the past including Johnson City, New York; Union City, New Jersey; and Pinellas County (St Petersburg), Florida (APQC, 2004; Baldridge website; Center for Children & Technology, 2000; Conyers & Ewy, 2004; Davenport & Anderson, 2002; Schmoker, 1999; Schmoker & Wilson, 1993).

The list below adapts Deming's Fourteen Points to school reform.

FOURTEEN POINTS FOR CONTINUOUS IMPROVEMENT IN EDUCATION

1. Focus on constantly improving teaching quality and serving the needs of students and parents. Do not waver from this commitment.
2. Be led by a shared vision of quality, values, beliefs, and mission in which negativism and mistakes are unacceptable.
3. Create a culture of mutual trust and caring among members of the community of learners. Drive out fear of asking questions and taking a position so that everyone can work effectively for the students, school, and district.
4. Reduce dependency on standardized tests and grades to measure learning and develop new methods to measure and evaluate student progress.
5. Improve constantly and forever every process for planning, teaching, and serving students and parents in order to improve quality and productivity and to decrease costs.
6. Institute on-the-job training. Most people have not been properly trained because no one has told them how.
7. Deepen and broaden leadership. The role of supervisors is not to tell people what to do but to help them do a better job.
8. Transform school district performance by encouraging and recognizing teamwork across departments and classrooms, leadership at every level, and the results.
9. Break down isolation and barriers among teachers, parents, students, principals, and central office staff.
10. Make decisions based on data; regularly collect and analyze data from stakeholders on student, employer, and community needs and school results.
11. Focus all members of the school and district on just two or three

measurable objectives at a time in order to improve the quality of their daily work.

12. Institute for everyone a vigorous program of education and re-training in these new methods, including teamwork and data analysis. It should mainly take place on the job and be led by peers who have been trained as trainers.

13. Take action to accomplish the transformation of the district and each school. A special top-management team (district) and leadership team (school) with an action plan are essential to implement the management philosophy and these 14 points. A critical mass of people in the organization need to understand and implement the basic concepts.

14. Celebrate the success of individuals, teams, schools, and the district often (Simmons, 1993).

Table 10.2 provides an overview of how the principles would affect a traditional central office in a large urban system. The changes in perception and expectation discussed below demonstrate just how radical the changes are—a paradigm shift in thinking and behavior. What does a school or district look like before and after the redesign is implemented? Who's responsible for success? How is the good work recognized? Everyone takes responsibility for the success of the organization, not just the superintendent or top manager. The culture of the organization encourages people to be innovative and redesign the rules, not use them as excuses for mediocre quality.

In 1970, Johnson City School District was the lowest-achieving among 14 districts in Broome County, New York, and had the lowest per-capita income. Using many of the concepts of the Fourteen Points and the Z Process, according to John Champlin, the superintendent, "It takes two weeks to change the climate in the pilot school and one year to see gains of achievement. In three years the entire district (of nineteen schools) was showing improved achievement, and it just kept climbing" (Schmoker & Wilson, 1993, p.38).

By 1977, 70% of its students were reading at grade level, and by 1984 the number ranged between 80% and 90%. By 1986, 77% of Johnson City students were getting New York State's Regents Diploma. The state average was 43%. It was among the top three districts in the county.

Then, about 20 years later, Brazosport, Texas, Palatine, Illinois, and Pinellas County (St. Petersburg) Florida began a similar journey (Schmoker & Wilson, 1993). In the Chugach, Alaska, School District, "results on the California Achievement Test dramatically improved in reading, from the 28th percentile in 1995 to the 71st in 1999; in math from 54th to 78th;

TABLE 10.2. Key Factors in Central Office and School Transformation

Key Factors	Traditional Organization	High-Performance District and School
Responsibility for success	The principal and superintendent	Everyone
Improvement	The boss, senior managers, and technical experts	Everyone continuously learning and problem-solving
Leadership	Authority at top	Everyone shares the vision and is empowered to achieve it
Principals/superintendents	Watchdogs	Coaches/teachers
Managing people	Boss's control	Their own commitment to vision, mission, core values, beliefs, and teamwork
Culture	Follow the rules	Redesign the rules
Quality	Inspected-in by others	Built-in by each employee and team
Customers	Who cares about them?	Reason for being
Coaching and training	Limited	Continual
Job design	Single task	Whole job/multitasking
Organizational structure	A pyramid of layers of management	Fewer layers of management and semiautonomous work teams
Recognition for results	Infrequent	Often
Decision making	Mainly at the top	All levels
Employment security	People expendable	Minimal job loss
Incentives	Wage/salary	Pay individuals and teams for results
Relationships within and across stakeholders	Do not care	Central to success; People practice the seven habits of highly effective people
Labor relations	Conflict/resistance to change	Mutual gains bargaining

Source: Simmons, 1993, p. 239.

and in language arts from 26th to 72nd." Pearl River, New York, has achieved 92% student satisfaction, 96% parent satisfaction, and 98% teacher satisfaction ratings (Baldrige National Quality Program, website).

Among big-city districts, Houston has used some of the methods to improve some district management processes, winning the Broad Foundation Award for Outstanding School District in 2002. (Boston has been a runner-up for the award for 3 years.) Unfortunately, Houston administrators falsified reports on graduation rates and other data. The accurate data show that Houston is only an average or slightly below average districts in terms of results ("A Miracle Revisited," 2003).

Starting in about 2000, more than 10 districts with up to 70 schools started using the Brazosport model, and most of them got impressive results their first year. They include St. Paul, Minnesota; Roswell, New Mexico; Penn-Harris-Madison County, Indiana; and Horry County, South Carolina (APQC, 2004).

In the next chapter we will next explore how to apply high-performance principles, including a step-by-step guide on how to do the hard work of transforming an organization's processes and results.

REFERENCES

American Productivity and Quality Center (APQC). (2004). *Educators in action: Examining strategic improvement efforts.* Houston: Author.

Baldrige National Quality Program website, www.quality.nist.gov

Beckhard, R., & Harris, R. (1987). *Organizational transitions: Managing complex change* (2nd ed.). New York: Addison-Wesley.

Center for Children and Technology. (2000). *The transformation of Union City: 1989 to present.* Newton, MA: Education Development Center.

Collins, J. (2001). *Good to great: Why some companies make the leap and others don't.* New York: HarperCollins.

Conyers, J. G., & Ewy, R. (2004). *Charting your course: Lessons learned during the journey toward performance excellence.* Milwaukee, WI: American Society for Quality.

Davenport, P., & Anderson, G. (2002). *Closing the achievement gap: No excuses.* Houston: American Productivity and Quality Center.

Deming, W. E. (1982). *Out of the crisis.* Cambridge, MA: MIT Center for Advanced Engineering Study.

Galvin, R. W. (1991). *The idea of ideas.* Schaumburg, IL: Motorola University.

Hanna, D. (1988). *Designing organizations for high performance.* Reading, MA: Addison-Wesley.

Harry, M., & Schroeder, R. (1999). *Six sigma: The breakthrough management strategy revolutionizing the world's top corporations.* New York: Doubleday.

Lawler, E. E. (1996). *From the ground up: Six principles for building the new logic corporation.* San Francisco: Jossey-Bass.

Lawler, E. E, Mohrman, S. A., & Benson, G. (2001). *Organizing for high performance: The CEO report.* San Francisco: Jossey-Bass.

McGregor, D. (1966). The human side of enterprise. In W. G. Bennis & E. H. Schein (Eds.), *Leadership & motivation: Essays of Douglas McGregor* (pp. 5–6). Cambridge, MA: MIT Press.

A miracle revisited. (2003, December 3). *New York Times,* p. A1.

Passmore, W. (1988). *Designing effective organizations.* New York: Wiley.

Schmoker, M. (1999). *Results: The key to continuous improvement* (2nd ed.). Alexandria, VA: Association for Supervision and Curriculum Development.

Schmoker, M. J., & Wilson, R. (1993). *Total quality education: Profiles of schools that demonstrate the power of Deming's management principles.* Bloomington, IN: Phi Delta Kappa.

Simmons, J. (1993). *Fourteen Points for continuous school improvement in education.* Unpublished manuscript.

Simmons, J., & Mares, W. (1982). *Working together: Employee participation in action.* New York: Knopf.

Tribus, M. (1984). *The Mt. Edgecumbe High School story.* Retrieved June 21, 2003 from http://deming.eng.clemson.edu/pub/den

Tribus, M. (1990a). *The contributions of W. Edwards Deming to the improvement of education.* Retrieved June 21, 2003 from http://deming.eng.clemson.edu/pub/den

Tribus, M. (1990b). *TQM in education: The theory and how to put it to work.* Retrieved June 21, 2003 from http://deming.eng.clemson.edu/pub/den

Tribus, M. (1990c). *When quality goes to school, what do leaders do to put it to work?* Retrieved June 21, 2003 from http://deming.eng.clemson.edu/pub/den

Trist, E. (1981). *The evolution of socio-technical systems.* Toronto: Quality of Working Life Center.

Walton, M. (1986). *The Deming management method.* New York: Perigee.

Chapter Eleven

The Z Process for Leading Change: How You Do It Is Even More Important Than What You Do

The design objectives and the Fourteen Points clarify what districts need to do to both create and sustain the transformation. When it comes to organizational improvement, however, how you make change is even more important than the change you make. If the stakeholders do not participate adequately in the process, they will not develop the understanding and ownership that they need to make the changes work. If the change process is flawed, then the desired change will not be implemented.

In the past 40 years three redesign phases have emerged that best capture the process for transforming organizations that has been used by organizations around the world. The three phases, as shown in Figure 11.1, are preparing the leadership of an organization for change (readiness); developing action plans within and across departments in the organization (redesign); and then implementing the redesign and continuously improving it.

The results of this process have been documented in more than 100 studies, and they are reflected in the improved growth in the productivity of the American economy and the daily performance of the world's strongest firms as well as smaller ones (Collins, 2001; Harry & Schroder, 1999; Lawler, Mohrman & Benson, 2001; Lawler, Mohrman & Ledford, 1995; Peters, 1987; Simmons & Mares, 1982).

Unfortunately, the examples of public school districts embracing these strategies are few, and we have mentioned them in earlier chapters. Districts make excuses, saying "we're not a business" or "schools and districts are monopolies and not subject to market pressures which would force a competitive response." Florida Light & Power is also a monopoly, however, but nonetheless won the international Deming Prize for its improvement in quality and performance (Hudiberg, 1991).

FIGURE 11.1. The Z Process for District and School Improvement

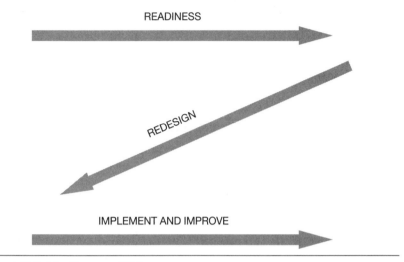

Other excuses include the frequent turnover of school leaders and the lack of political support to protect superintendents as they focus on this strategic priority. If district leaders are concerned about losing additional generations of students, however, they cannot afford not to take some of the steps that other organizations have used over the past three decades to successfully meet high pressures to perform.

Following is an overview of the three phases of the Z Process: readiness, redesign, and implementation and improvement. Some specific tasks or principles in each phase are discussed below.

READINESS

Just as school district officials are quick to point out that they are not wholly responsible for student outcomes, change in a district must include the other stakeholders who play a role in a student's success. Preparing the district and the school community for the hard work of change includes studying and seeing what others have done and learning how they have done it. Readiness for change is itself a process for which leaders need to plan and allocate time. All too often readiness is either just assumed ("I'm ready to change, so everyone else must be ready too") or overlooked. When people are in a rush to start the work of redesign before they are ready, effective district change will fail. This stage is also an opportunity for the district to actively and clearly hear the community's interests and goals for its children. Designing and implementing this phase requires a well-tested process for involving stakeholders and experienced coaching for the leadership team (Axelrod, 2000; Axelrod, Axelrod, Beedon, & Jacobs, 2004; and Dolan, 1994).

REDESIGN

Working in departmental and cross-functional groups, the staff of districts and schools should study best practice, starting in their own schools and districts, and create plans for their own classrooms, grade levels, and school teams. Their work should be aligned with the district's vision, mission, and management philosophy. School leaders visit exemplary schools in their district and the nation, regardless of the size, as well as classrooms in their own schools, to observe the best practice for school improvement that they think will transform the quality of teaching and learning. This process of learning builds on the skills that Chicago schools have in developing annual school improvement plans. After observing exemplary school systems, district teams develop a draft of their redesign. They share it with their colleagues in other departments. Finally, the design team gets the approval of the superintendent-appointed steering committee before implementation.

IMPLEMENTATION AND IMPROVEMENT

Each team or department implements the redesign plan it has created. The results of implementation are studied to create a process of continuous improvement. This phase requires systematic follow-up through a process of feedback from customers and other stakeholders. The design and work teams evaluate using information from the feedback process and other research. Teams develop corrective action plans to help define and resolve priority problems. Sustaining success also requires continuous learning, training, coaching, and support for all employees in the district to apply the basic tools of continuous improvement in their daily work.

Many of these concepts have been used in districts and schools across the country, including Illinois, Texas, Florida, California, and Alaska. They have provided impressive results in companies around the world. They provide an easy-to-use roadmap for managing change. With the proper leadership and sustained support, the results will transform the structure, culture, and work processes. The results will accelerate student performance and improve the quality of work life for the employees.

The 15 steps to implement the Z are described by Figure 11.2.

APPLYING THE Z PROCESS: HOW BRAZOSPORT CLOSED THE GAP

When Joe Bowman from Dow Chemical asked Jerry Anderson, the Brazosport superintendent, "Why aren't the students in the south side schools doing as well as the students on the north side?" the change process began for Brazosport. The process that Jerry, Patricia Davenport, and their team followed looks very much like the Z Process, although they didn't call it that.

The district's leadership team went through each of the five "readiness steps." When Jerry decided to accept Bowman's invitation for him to attend the 5-day workshop on quality improvement at Dow, he committed to deepening his own understanding of new strategies and tools for leading change. A month later he brought the rest of the team to go through it (Davenport & Anderson, 2002). They made site visits, developed a vision of what the district could become, and developed an agreement on how they would proceed (Davenport & Anderson, 2002).

The team together learned that to improve quality, "you don't fix blame, you fix the system" (Davenport & Anderson, 2002, p. 22). They learned Edward Deming's Fourteen Points and the four-part improvement cycle, "Plan–Do–Check–Act," used in process analysis, planning, problem solving, and decision making. They learned the importance of benchmarking their practices against the best in the country. They learned to be "process-oriented and data-driven" in order to use the "money and time we had more effectively and efficiently" (Davenport & Anderson, 2002, p. 35). They learned from their reading, discussions and reflecting on their own experience that "there are no excuses for low student performance. All students can learn. All teachers can teach." (Davenport & Anderson, 2002, p. 10).

These readiness steps of the Z Process, taken over 4 months or so, helped them deepen their understanding of what they needed to do and raised their confidence in their ability to do it. When the Z Process "fails," it is usually because leaders omitted steps in the readiness phase or rushed through them so that the leadership team was not ready to lead their organization through the next two phases of the Z.

The steps for the redesign phase at Brazosport focused on improving

FIGURE 11.2. The Z Process: Fifteen Steps for the Successful Launching of Continuous Improvement in District Offices and Schools

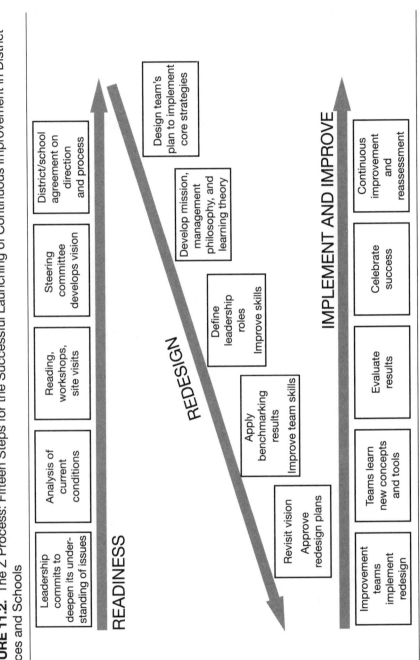

the quality of classroom instruction. The district leadership looked at their data to identify best practice and found a teacher who was getting some of the best results with students from low-income families. They then found it was similar to what other teachers who were getting good results with at-risk students were doing. They developed the Eight-Step Process, which follows the Plan–Do–Check–Act cycle for continuous improvement. (While Brazosport used data from test scores, the data could just as well have come from other sources, including classroom assessments looking at student work.) Their system emphasizes mastery of the material before moving on in a process of assessment, reteaching, and tutoring (Barksdale & Davenport, 2003). The model is closely aligned with the Mastery Teaching model of Benjamin Bloom.

During the implementation and improvement phase, people began to visit Mary Barksdale's classroom to observe. Teams of teachers, first at Velasco and then at other schools, began to look at their data and created priority areas where students were weak. In the summer, they then developed an instructional calendar dividing up the year: when they would work on what. Teachers began to develop a "lesson bank" of effective teaching strategies. When they tried the lessons out, they got good results. Then the teams worked to continuously improve their results.

Soon principals from other buildings came see how the Velasco teachers were getting their results. By 1997, 5 years after the Dow workshops, all the Brazosport schools had adopted the Eight-Step Process. And by 1998, the district was evaluated as "exemplary" (Davenport & Anderson, 2002).

A key lesson from the Brazosport success is that the superintendent's team had an external coach, consultant, and critical friend through their partnership with Joe Bowman and his colleagues at Dow Chemical's headquarters. The work required for effectively applying the Z cannot be done without such support. The members of the Dow team were experts in designing and implementing continuous improvement. The Palatine, Illinois, district had support from Ed Bales and his team from Motorola University for the training and coaching. Both of these firms had had over 20 years of experience applying the concepts. The other districts that have begun using the Brazosport model are using external assistance as well (APQC, 2004). Here are some additional ideas to help implement the Z Process.

MORE IDEAS FOR USING THE Z

For the "readiness" leg, the activities for each step usually include study, reflection, discussion, and next steps on the topics. This leg concludes with agreement among the superintendent, union president, and steering committee on the objectives for the redesign and guidelines for the redesign teams to follow in the second and third legs of the Z. Most of the steps on the second and third legs have activities similar to those on the first leg plus planning and consensus among and across the design teams, and approval of the plans by the district steering committee. The first two legs may require up to 12 to 18 months, depending on what is happening in the organization at the time. The third leg, focused on implementation and continuous improvement, is an ongoing activity, which could take 2 years or more for the implementation of the initial action plan and the first cycle of continuous improvement activities.

In Brazosport it took 5 years for all the schools to voluntarily adapt the Eight-Step Process for improved teaching. While 5 years may seem like a long time, compare that to the top-down initiatives of urban districts across the country that have been started with fanfare and funding only to disappear without a trace in less than 1 year.

Each of the 15 steps of the Z Process may represent a major activity lasting 2 weeks to 2 months or longer. Some of the steps within a leg can overlap. Each step is put into operation by the design team of people collected from across the organization to assure cross-departmental learning, assisted by organizational development specialists.

Since people own what they help create, people who will be asked to implement the redesign need to be involved in shaping it. In addition, they need to communicate their preliminary plans to others and get their buy-in before seeking approval of the district steering committee.

A redesign team might work like this. The director of human resources sets up a redesign team for the selection and training of principals. From their reading and site visits during the readiness phase of the Z Process, the HR director would have learned that the team should begin by creating a "process map" describing each activity of the existing selection and training process, including the days needed to do each activity. They then need to benchmark their process against best practice in other districts and organizations, including the private sector and the military. (There are websites for benchmarking data.) The HR director's team would be responsible for implementing and communicating the recommendations for redesign after they are reviewed by other departments that would be affected and then approved by the district steering committee.

Some districts may wish to undertake additional tasks.

In phase 1, specific tasks could include the district leadership doing the following:

- Using the conference model to assess stakeholder needs and get them engaged in discussing old and new approaches (Axelrod, 2000; Axelrod et al., 2004).
- Developing a shared vision, mission, management philosophy, and message. Members of the school board and site-based councils can use the adopted vision as the basis to articulate the reasons for change to an anxious public; administrators can rely on the mission and district data to make the case for change to parents; and teacher leaders can use the vision to work with hesitant colleagues.
- Identifying a specialist in organization redesign to provide facilitation, coaching, and strategy during the design and implementation of the Z process.
- Launching an outside audit of the district's professional development and HR programs.

In phase 2 the optional tasks could include the following:

- Convening a redesign team, including all stakeholders, co-chaired by the superintendent and union president, to analyze underperforming schools and the barriers to their progress. Recommend a process for their redesign. Designate exemplary schools as demonstration sites to assist teachers, parents, and principals in deepening their understanding of best practices. Involving all stakeholders affected by the upcoming changes is key.
- Taking central office and union leaders to see districts—such as Boston; Edmonton, Canada; Brazosport, Texas; and St. Paul, Minnesota—that have reinvented their central office as well as businesses—such as the GM Saturn plant, Harley Davidson, Motorola, Southwest Airlines, and Ford Motors—that have all become world-class through putting a high-performance strategy into place.
- Commissioning a blue ribbon panel of community and district leaders to study and recommend best practice for classroom-based student assessment (For a model, Chicago Public Schools, 2003).
- Establishing a policy-planning department in the central office to provide research-based policy papers needed to help the leadership weigh the merits of various policies, such as student retention, probation, and opening and closing schools to improve achievement. The superintendent could oversee an advisory council of system stakeholders to identify problems and support implementation.
- Fostering labor–management collaboration by sponsoring a workshop and site-visit process to study high-performance organizations

with unions. Review the benefits of mutual-gains bargaining, tapping the experience of labor and management leaders from both education and the private sector who have worked together to craft such agreements.

- Mobilizing the necessary financial support to support the change process, including federal and philanthropic funding.
- Taking advantage of corporate expertise and support for deep, large-scale change to transform quality.

In phase 3, special tasks could include the following:

- Developing incentives to create networks of neighborhood schools to implement the best strategic improvement models for schools. Multiple school networks can accelerate the impact of new skills and policies by reducing isolation, lowering the cost, and accelerating the sharing of best practice among teachers, principals, parents, and students.
- Fostering political will, ensuring that a city's political leadership is willing to help move solutions from the boardroom to the classroom and from the classroom to the boardroom.

The Z Process plus the design principles discussed in Part One have enabled thousands of large organizations in the private sector—and some smaller school districts—to successfully redesign their operations (Senge et al., 2000; Schmoker, 2001). That's because the combination of the high-performance concepts, including the four strategies and the Z Process, tap into and enhance the ideas and energy of all stakeholders. They involve people as partners who participate in defining and solving problems, not just employees taking orders. Most important, this approach helps focus all employees on meeting and exceeding the needs of the people they are serving: parents, students, employers, and the community.

THE LEADERSHIP NEEDED

What kind of leadership is needed to apply the high-performing design objectives, the Fourteen Points, and the Z Process? It is the kind of leadership demonstrated by Gerry Anderson and Patricia Davenport leading the transformation in Brazosport and by John Conyers and Bob Ewy leading it in Palatine—and can be summarized in these seven lessons of leadership:

1. At all levels, leaders across the district become learners about high-performance systems.

2. Leaders model the process of study, reflection, and open discussion that they expect their own staff and everyone in the system to use.
3. The district's redesign objective should focus on better meeting both the needs of students to improve their performance and the needs of the district employees for a better-quality work life.
4. The leadership practices and expects from all employees the daily application of the core values of high-performance teams and organizations: trust, fairness, cooperation, participation, honesty, and open communication.
5. The people closest to the problems—teachers, parents, principals, and students—are the experts and need to be empowered and trained to find and implement solutions.
6. The results of the redesign contribute to building a culture in the school and central office based on the core values.
7. The desired outcome is growing learning organizations where adults practice in their daily work those habits of learning and respect for one another that they want students to learn and practice. As a consequence, the results continuously improve.

These lessons of leadership, when applied to traditional organizations, can create paradigm shifts and can produce high-performance organizations.

PULLING IT ALL TOGETHER

The key principles and strategies to help school systems prepare for systemic change developed in Part One of this book and the essays of the experts in Part Two point the way toward achieving high levels of performance in school systems that are so complex that they seem, at times, to defy understanding and improvement. Because school systems are made up of ever smaller units that replicate the whole, it stands to reason that implementing these strategies within smaller units—such as the 25,000 individual classrooms or 600 schools in Chicago—will facilitate building them into the overall district infrastructure. Likewise, building them into the school system infrastructure will enable their adoption on each level. The Z Process is designed to help this happen by providing a way to adapt and implement the four core strategies. This would simultaneously generate the ideas, energy, skills, and commitment plus develop a synergy to raise the whole system to a higher level of both efficiency and effectiveness.

We hope that this book has provided a practical roadmap for taking

FIGURE 11.3. To Close the Gap in Student Performance

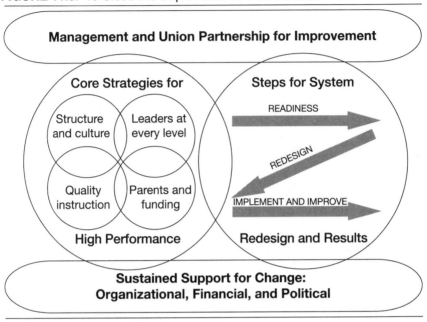

the challenging steps urban school systems need to take to make deep, lasting change. The Z Process shows how the four core strategies can be implemented with concrete steps the district leadership needs to take to assure results; Figure 11.3 integrates the four core strategies and the Z Process. It adds a labor–management partnership that is essential for achieving results (See Adam Urbanski's essay in Chapter 6). No matter how good the strategies are, without a powerful process for designing and implementing change like the Z, and the sustained support for change that includes political will plus organizational and financial resources, the gap in student performance will not be closed.

If the leadership of America's urban school districts can study best practice for creating high-performance organizations from education, the military, and the private sector—and look in the mirror and assess their own readiness for change—they will have taken two important steps toward realizing their vision for the district.

REFERENCES

American Productivity and Quality Center (APQC). (2004). *Educators in action: Examining strategic improvement efforts.* Houston: Author.

Axelrod, R. H. (2000). *Terms of engagement: Changing the way we change organizations.* San Francisco: Berrett-Koehler.

Axelrod, R. H., Axelrod, E., Beedon, J., & Jacobs, R. W. (2004). *You don't have to do it alone: How to involve others to get things done.* San Francisco: Berrett-Koehler.

Barksdale, M. L., & Davenport, P. W. (2003). *8 steps to student success: An educator's guide to implementing continuous improvement.* Retrieved October 31, 2004 from www.8stepstostudentssuccess.com

Chicago Public Schools. (2003, January). *Report of the Chicago Commission on curriculum-based assessment.* Chicago: Office of the CEO, Chicago Public Schools.

Collins, J. (2001). *Good to great: Why some companies make the leap and others don't.* New York: HarperCollins.

Davenport, P., & Anderson, G. (2002). *Closing the achievement gap: No excuses.* Houston: American Productivity and Quality Center.

Dolan, W. P. (1994). *Restructuring our schools: A primer on systemic change.* Kansas City, MO: Systems and Organization.

Harry, M., & Schroeder, R. (1999). *Six sigma: The breakthrough management strategy revolutionizing the world's top corporations.* New York: Doubleday.

Hudiburg, J. J. (1991). *Winning with quality: The FPL story.* White Plains, NY: Quality Resources.

Lawler, E. E, Mohrman, S. A., & Benson, G. (2001). *Organizing for high performance: The CEO report.* San Francisco: Jossey-Bass.

Lawler, E. E, Mohrman, S. A., & Ledford, G. E. (1995). *Creating high performance organizations: Employee involvement and total quality management.* San Francisco: Jossey-Bass.

Peters, T. (1987). *Thriving on chaos: Handbook for a management revolution.* New York: Knopf.

Schmoker, M. (2001). *The results handbook: Practical strategies for dramatically improved schools.* Alexandria, VA: Association for Supervision and Curriculum Development.

Senge, P., Cambron McCabe, N. H., Lucas, T., Kleiner, A., Dutton, J., & Smith, B. (2000). *Schools that learn: A fifth discipline fieldbook for educators, parents, and everyone who cares about education.* New York: Doubleday.

Simmons, J., & Mares, W. (1982). *Working together: Employee participation in action.* New York: Knopf.

Chapter Twelve

Don't Let This Book Sit on a Shelf: A Call to Action

Since being labeled "worst in the nation" in 1987, many schools in Chicago have gone on to become a shining example of the positive possibilities of reform. And other big-city districts such as Boston and San Diego have wrought successes from embarking on systemwide reform in thoughtful, deliberate ways.

But reform cannot be considered entirely successful until it has achieved its fundamental goal: providing a high-quality education to *all* students. The next step for Chicago and the nation, then, is to continue to move from a system *with* successful schools to a system *of* successful schools. This, in fact, is a step that many urban districts are primed to take.

School boards, superintendents, union leaders, school principals, their teacher leaders and site-based councils, and school improvement partners—all of us—can do this when we acknowledge that what we are doing is not working for many of the students and society, by getting beyond excuses, and by committing the time needed to study and apply best practice for accelerating change in every classroom in these urban districts. Each of us needs to stand in front of the mirror and say, "Am I part of the problem, or part of the solution?" And then take a next step.

Chicago has parents, teachers, principals, community leaders, and school advocates who in 1987 made such a commitment to change their failing schools, and their effort has yielded impressive results. Other cities have made similar efforts. It is time in Chicago to remember why we were successful before and to make an even stronger effort now.

The lessons and strategies outlined in this book—along with the commentary and issues raised by leading experts—are meant to encourage district leaders and all parties with a stake in school reform to begin looking through the lens of systemic organizational change, to start thinking about how to take that next step toward system overhaul, and, finally, to act.

As we noted earlier, pilot programs have their place. But simply mandating an entire system to scale-up along the pilot's lines is a recipe for failure. The system must take determined, proven steps to ready itself for change and create an infrastructure where wholesale reform will flourish, not founder.

And that is the argument that has underscored every major point made in this book: *We must change the entire system to get the positive results we are urgently seeking for all students.* School district leaders need to identify a proven strategy for deepening understanding and systems change—like the Z process discussed in Chapter 11—that can transform district results. The strategy must include an analysis of the readiness of the leadership team to lead the change process. It must include key system players in the redesign of the most highly leveraged components of the system: teacher professional development; principal leadership, selection, and support; and parental engagement. Finally, the strategy must include a process for effective implementation, feedback on what's working and what's not, and continuous improvement and alignment.

What we are calling for in this book is really no less than a cultural revolution of sorts in urban school districts across the nation. That revolution envisions a school system focused on teamwork rather than weekly mandates from on high; focused on results, not compliance; focused on gleaning best practice from the district's own classrooms, the business world, and the military; focused with laser-like precision on all the ingredients so essential to improving what happens in a classroom between a teacher and a student; and focused on creating effective leaders at all levels of the organization, from the superintendent and principals to teachers and parents.

What is now clear to a growing number of people in Chicago and other cities is that poor children can learn at levels that exceed the national averages. School leaders in low-income neighborhoods can learn how to improve the quality of the teaching and learning in their classrooms, and they can learn how to better engage parents in their children's learning. Since school reform in Chicago began in 1988, as the results clearly show, almost 50% of the teacher leaders, principals, and parent leaders have learned that they can make a difference by setting high expectations for themselves and their students; having the freedom, tied to accountability, to make decisions; and having the financial resources to carry out those decisions at their schools.

It is also clear that urban school systems around the country must collaborate with the many parties invested in their systems and aggressively reach out beyond the district confines to engage the broader community. We have seen in Chicago that learning how to collaborate is not easy and requires special leadership to achieve. But as Figure 11.3 shows, such moves are key to making any lesson, strategy, principle, idea, or practical agenda work. A readiness process for the leadership team of the district is the first step in shaping a district's priorities and turning them into realities. The study and discussion help capture and apply the energy and ideas of people "outside the box" to solving problems—as well as helping garner much-needed outside resources and building a citywide sense of urgency about school improvement.

Schools in Chicago and elsewhere have demonstrated that they can learn how to improve and sustain that improvement. Now, can the leadership in districts like Chicago learn what they need to know to be able to reinvent themselves so that they can effectively scale-up and speed-up the adoption of best practice? In reality, it's a rhetorical question. Because as a society we cannot afford for the answer to be "no."

Let's remember that, as Harvard Business School Professor Rosabeth Moss Kanter (1983) has said: "Change is disturbing when it is done *to* us, exhilarating when it is done *by* us" (p. 63). If we "do" the changes necessary to scale-up the successes already experienced in some urban classrooms and schools in every district, we certainly will reap the reward: improving the futures of millions of students each year with the highest-quality education possible. That's the goal.

REFERENCE

Kanter, R. M. (1983). *The change masters*. New York: Simon and Schuster.

About the Authors

Judy Codding is chief executive officer and president of America's Choice, Inc., as well as Vice President for Programs and chief operating officer for the National Center on Education and the Economy. Among the programs for which she is responsible are the America's Choice School Design Network, New Standards, America's Choice Curriculum, and America's Choice Leadership Program. Codding previously was a teacher, a principal, and an associate in education at the Harvard Graduate School of Education and has written several books.

Charlotte Danielson is a consultant on education. Formerly she was at the Educational Testing Service in Princeton, New Jersey, where she served on a design team for Praxis III and coordinated development of the Assessor-Training Program. She has taught at all levels of education, from kindergarten through college, and has worked as a consultant on curriculum planning, performance assessment, and professional development. She has written several professional publications for the Association for Supervision and Curriculum Development and for Eye on Education.

Linda Darling-Hammond is Professor of Teaching and Teacher Education at Stanford University, where she has launched the Stanford Educational Leadership Institute and the School Redesign Network. She is also executive director of the National Commission on Teaching and America's Future. Prior to her appointment at Stanford, Darling-Hammond was co-director of the National Center for Restructuring Education, Schools, and Teaching. Darling-Hammond is past president of the American Educational Research Association, a two-term member of the National Board for Professional Teaching Standards, and a member of the National Academy of Education. Her research, teaching, and policy work focus on issues of teaching quality, school reform, and educational equity.

W. Patrick Dolan built a consulting group that works on labor–management approaches to systemic change. The work has included long relationships with Ford and the United Auto Workers, Goodyear and the United Rubber Workers, the Federal Aviation Administration and its unions. Dolan and Associates works with more than 200 school districts and has state-wide efforts in Illinois, Wisconsin, Minnesota, Washington, and North Carolina. Dolan has written two books, taught both high school and college, was a dean at Georgetown University, and holds a doctorate in organizational behavior from the Harvard University Graduate School of Education.

Richard F. Elmore is Professor of Education at Harvard University and a senior research fellow with the Consortium for Policy Research in Education (CPRE). He is currently co-director of a CPRE research project on school accountability and is co-principal investigator of a multiyear study of instructional improvement and professional development in School District 2 in New York City. He has served as co-editor or co-author of several books.

Michael Fullan is dean of the Ontario Institute for Studies in Education of the University of Toronto. He has developed a number of partnerships designed to bring about major school improvement and educational reform. He participates as a researcher, consultant, trainer, and policy adviser on a wide range of educational change projects with school systems, teachers federations, research and development institutes, and government agencies, both in Canada and internationally, and has written extensively on the topic of change.

Gail Goldberger is a writer and editor specializing in nonprofit communications and policy-and-issues journalism. She has published feature articles in publications as diverse as *Travelers' Tales, Chicago Wilderness, Chicago Arts and Communications, JUF News,* and the Chicago Audubon Society's *COMPASS.* She was a fund-raising professional for vanguard social and health-related programs and is currently working with a multi-issue environmental organization on the Southeast Side of Chicago.

Kate Jamentz is Associate Superintendent of Teaching and Learning in the Fremont Union High School District and formerly Director of Programs in Professional and Organizational Learning at WestEd. She has been both a teacher and principal at the elementary and middle school levels. From 1991–1994 she headed up the California Assessment Collaborative, which supported districts and schools in implementing standards-based practice and in becoming increasingly accountable for improved student performance. She is the author of several books and articles about standards and assessment reform. Before joining WestEd, Jamentz served as director of a statewide project studying the development and use of performance assessments.

Susan Moore Johnson is Professor of Education in Learning and Teaching at the Harvard University Graduate School of Education. A former high school teacher and administrator, Johnson studies school organization, educational policy, leadership, and change in school systems. She is the author of several books and journal articles and is currently heading up a multiyear research project on the next generation of U.S. public school teachers.

Judy Karasik is a writer, editor, and consultant. Her work includes full-length studies on national service and youth service, and opinion pieces in the *New York Times* and the *Chronicle of Philanthropy*. She is also the co-author of *The Ride Together: A Brother and Sister's Memoir of Autism in the Family*, written with her brother, the cartoonist Paul Karasik.

Carolyn Kelley is Associate Professor of Educational Leadership and Policy Analysis at the University of Wisconsin–Madison. Her expertise is in educational policy, organizational theory, teacher compensation, and the preparation of school leaders. She has conducted extensive research on the effect of teacher compensation in schools. Her current research examines the structure and scope of human resources management and efforts to define, develop, and assess administrative mastery in education.

Valerie E. Lee began her career teaching math and science in a series of private and public schools, both in the United States and abroad. In addition to her faculty appointment in the School of Education at the University of Michigan, Lee also serves as a faculty associate at the University of Michigan's Institute for Social Research. Her research centers on issues of educational equity, quantitative methods, school effects, and cross-national studies of quality and equality. Her research has been published in numerous books, journals, and reports.

Allan Odden is Professor of Educational Leadership and Policy Analysis at the University of Wisconsin–Madison. He is the co-director of the Consortium for Policy Research in Education (CPRE), director of the CPRE Education Finance Research Program, and principal investigator for the CPRE Teacher Compensation project. Odden was a mathematics teacher and curriculum developer in East Harlem for 5 years and was Professor of Education Policy and Administration at the University of Southern California and Director of Policy Analysis for California Education. He served as research director for educational finance projects in seven states and has also worked on teacher-compensation changes at the state and district level. Currently Odden, who has written extensively, is directing research projects on school-finance redesign, resource reallocation in schools, the costs of instructional improvement, and teacher compensation.

Kent D. Peterson is a professor in the Department of Educational Administration at the University of Wisconsin–Madison and works with the Comprehensive Regional Assistance Center in Region VI. He was the founding director of the Vanderbilt Principals Institute and the co-director of the Wisconsin LEAD Academy. He was director of the National Center for Effective Schools Research and Development and was a researcher for the Center on Organization and Restructuring of Schools. He has published several books and articles and currently writes a monthly Internet column, "Reform Talk," for the Comprehensive Center for Region VI.

John Simmons is president of Strategic Learning Initiatives, a not-for-profit organization focused on creating learning communities, especially with public schools. He has worked in the education field for the past 30 years in the United States and abroad. Simmons has consulted for more than 300 private firms, public agencies, and unions in the United States and abroad. Since 1990 he has worked with Chicago Public Schools (CPS) including the former CEO of the CPS. He helped establish a national collaborative for Looking at Student Work and helped design the Chicago Academy for School Leadership. Previously, he was on the staff of the Policy Planning Division, World Bank, for 7 years, an Adjunct Professor of Management at the Kellogg School of Management, Northwestern University, lecturer in economics at Harvard, and visiting professor at Princeton and the University of Massachusetts–Amherst. He has written several books on education, organization, and economic development.

Marc Tucker is President of the National Center on Education and the Economy. Mr. Tucker authored the 1986 Carnegie Report, *A Nation Prepared: Teachers for the 21st Century*, which called for a restructuring of America's schools based on standards; created the National Board for Professional Teaching Standards; created the Commission on the Skills of the American Workforce and co-authored its report, *America's Choice: High Skills or Low Wages!*; was instrumental in creating the National Skill Standards Board and served as the chairman of its committee on standards and assessment policy; and, with Lauren Resnick, created the New Standards consotrium, which pioneered the development of performance standards in the United States and created a set of examinations matched to the standards. He has authored and co-authored many books on education and business.

Adam Urbanski is president of the Rochester (New York) Teachers Association and vice president of the American Federation of Teachers. He is the director of the Teacher Union Reform Network, aimed at creating a new vision of teachers unions that supports needed changes in education. He was a trustee of the National Center for Education and the Economy and a senior associate at the National Commission on Teaching and America's Future. Urbanski has served on the advisory board of Harvard University's National Center for Education Leadership, the National Board for Professional Teaching Standards, and the National Assessment Governing Board.

Margery Wallen has staffed Illinois Governor George Ryan's Task Force on Universal Access to Preschool since June 2001. She has worked since 1995 on early childhood care and education issues at the Ounce of Prevention Fund, a nonprofit public–private partnership that invests in the healthy development of babies, children, adolescents, and families. She has worked in coalitions, forming strong working relationships with state government officials, business leaders, and law enforcement personnel. Prior to her tenure at the Ounce of Prevention Fund, she worked in the Bureau of the Budget and state government human service agencies for 12 years.

Index

NAMES

Abramson, T., 160
Achilles, C., 202
Allensworth, E., 49, 87, 154–155
Alvarado, Anthony, 59, 86
Analt, B., 201
Anderman, E., 154
Anderson, Gerald, 25–28, 35, 219, 227, 229, 232–233
Andrias, Jane, 191–193
Archibald, S., 201, 204
Axelrod, E., 226, 231
Axelrod, R. H., 226, 231

Bales, Ed, 229
Barksdale, Mary L., 26–27, 229
Barnett, W. S., 199–200
Barton, P. E., 11, 33
Beckhard, Richard, 216
Beedon, J., 226, 231
Belzer, S., 154
Bennett, William, 2
Bennis, Warren, 65
Bensman, D., 43–44, 191
Benson, G., 218, 224
Berends, M., 115
Bernstein, H., 160–161, 164
Berry, B., 160–161
Bersin, Alan, 1, 44, 45, 55–62
Bloom, Benjamin, 27, 229
Bodilly, S., 115
Bowman, Joe, 7, 25, 227, 229
Bries, J., 25
Briggs, K., 40, 44–46, 91
Brookhart, L., 165
Browne, B., 160
Bryk, Anthony S., 14, 18, 21, 35–36, 40, 41, 87, 91
Bryk, B., 154–155

Burton-Sahara, Myrtle, 35
Busch, C., 199
Bush, George W., 55

Cambron McCabe, N. H., 232
Camburn, E., 87
Campbell, C., 211–212
Carter, K., 152
Celio, M. B., 211–212
Champlin, John, 35, 220
Chen, X., 158, 164
Chung, R., 158
Cipriano Peppel, J., 93, 95
Clinton, W. J., 55
Codding, Judy, 38, 67–68, 70–76
Cohen, David, 166
Cole, R. E., 4
Collins, A., 125
Collins, J., 218, 224
Conyers, John G., 35, 219, 232–233
Cook, Chauncey, 35
Cooper, E., 152
Cortés, Ernesto, Jr., 194–196
Costello, Joan, 122
Cotton, K., 209
Cuban, L., 41

Daley, Richard M., 15, 16
Danielson, Charlotte, 44, 49, 168–174
Darling-Hammond, Linda, 44, 49, 51, 150–167, 186, 189
Datnow, A., 115
Davenport, Patricia, 25–27, 219, 227, 229, 232–233
Deal, T. E., 78
Debolt, G., 165
Dell'Angela, T., 16

Deming, W. Edwards, 26, 218
Diamond, J. B., 86, 100
Dolan, W. Patrick, 44, 102–108, 226
Doolittle, F., 209–211
Doyle, W., 152
Duke, D. L., 78
Duncan, Arne, 16–17, 42, 55, 56, 60, 61–62
Dutton, J., 232

Easton, J. Q., 14, 18, 20–21, 154–155
Edge, K., 120
Edmonds, R., 154
Einstein, Albert, 24
Elkind, David, 33
Elmore, Richard, 7, 42, 44, 47, 66, 68, 86, 93–101, 96, 99
Epstein, Joyce L., 193, 194, 197
Ewy, R., 219, 232–233

Ferguson, Ronald, 51, 156, 186, 189
Fermanich, M., 41, 48, 50, 201, 204
Fetler, M., 150
Fine, M., 43
Finnegan, K., 20, 21, 28
Fletcher, S., 158
Fowler, C., 158
Frelow, F., 158
Fullan, Michael, 40, 65–66, 115–121, 207–208
Fuller, E., 150
Fuller, Howard J., 211–212

Gallagher, H. A., 201, 204
Galvin, Robert W., 35, 207, 216

SUBJECTS